# School Law

## Fifth Edition

## A California Perspective

Arthur J. Townley
*California State University*

June H. Schmieder-Ramirez
*Pepperdine University*

**Kendall Hunt**
publishing company

Cover image © Shutterstock.com

www.kendallhunt.com
*Send all inquiries to:*
4050 Westmark Drive
Dubuque, IA 52004-1840

Copyright © 2001, 2005, 2007, 2010, and 2016 by Kendall Hunt Publishing Company

ISBN 978-1-4652-8921-6

Printed in the United States of America

# Contents

# *Preface*

The authors are pleased to present the fifth edition of *School Law: A California Perspective,* a textbook designed for students who are completing an administrative credential or graduate degree in educational administration. It can also serve as a reference for those teachers and administrators who are currently serving in a school leadership role. The authors found a variety of law books written from a national perspective, but saw need for an education law book emphasizing those critical issues confronting California educators. The objective of this text is to fulfill that need.

Any author of a school law text faces the formidable task of selecting those topics, legislation, and court decisions that are most relevant in the current school setting. Drawing on our collective experience of more than 70 years as teachers and administrators in California public education, this text offers a practical and realistic perspective of school law for students and administrators.

The text discusses the relevant laws and court decisions that will assist administrators and teachers in making decisions about students, personnel issues, curriculum and instruction, fiscal and legal matters, and copyright. Given the dynamic nature of the law, no single text can serve to keep school personnel abreast of the most recent legislation and court decisions. However, familiarity with the underlying principles of legislation and court decisions will give school personnel more confidence in dealing with legal questions.

The information in this text will serve as a guide for teachers and administrators as they provide leadership to schools, but it is not intended to serve as a substitute for legal counsel. Educators confronting legal problems should always seek the advice of a competent attorney.

## Contents of Enclosed CD-ROM

- Slides
- Transparencies
- Student Workbook

## Purpose of the Workbook

School law management is built upon a distinct body of knowledge. The successful administrator must understand the general concepts and terms in education law to serve as an outstanding leader in a school or district. Moreover, an administrator needs to be skilled in researching legislation and court decisions as a basis for informed and wise conclusions in complex, sometimes urgent, circumstances. This text and workbook are designed to assist the educational leader in acquiring those insights and skills.

The purpose of the workbook is to assist the student in solidifying the information and concepts taught in the text and classroom. In addition, the student is provided with practical exercises designed to apply those skills and concepts.

## How to Use the Workbook

Each chapter of the workbook has five parts: a brief introduction to the chapter, a true/false pretest to assess prior knowledge of the information and concepts in the chapter, a list of key terms, a section calling for review of important court cases, and an application section. The student should complete each true/false quiz before reading the chapter in the textbook. The questions alert students to important points to note while reading.

After studying the chapter in the text, students define the key terms and respond to all or selected questions at the end of the chapter. For further reinforcement, the student should return to the workbook for further work with key terms and court cases. The application section provides the student an opportunity to apply the knowledge, skills, and concepts already learned. After studying the chapter, the student should re-take the pretest, then check his or her answers against the key to the pretests contained.

# CHAPTER 1

# Sources of School Law

*"We the People of the United States, in Order to form a more perfect Union, establish Justice, ensure domestic Tranquility, provide for the common defense, promote the general Welfare, and secure the Blessings of Liberty to ourselves and our Posterity, do ordain and establish this Constitution for the United States of America."*

— Preamble to the Constitution

## Introduction

The beginning school administrator soon finds that the laws governing education are complex and difficult to interpret—but extremely important. For example, a new assistant principal, during her first day on the job, is told by a student that another student has drugs in her locker. Can the assistant principal, based on this information, search the locker and look for the drugs? Should she call the police and ask them to search the locker? Or should she attempt to find other evidence of drugs before she takes direct action?

As she considers her decision, the assistant principal may try to remember whether, in her school law class, she learned where to find legal information about proper procedures in such a situation. Unfortunately, no single book is likely to offer a clear directive.

School law has many sources. *Black's Law Dictionary* (2008) defines the "law of the land" as "the aggregate of legislation, judicial precedents, and accepted legal principles; the body of authoritative grounds of judicial and administrative action." The California Civil Code (Section 22) defines law as "a solemn expression of the will of the supreme power of the State." This supreme power, or controlling authority, is derived from several sources: the federal Constitution, state constitutions, statutes passed by federal and state legislative bodies, and court decisions. This chapter reviews those sources.

## The U.S. Constitution and Education

The United States Constitution is the highest level of law in this country. It was completed in 1787 and is the oldest written national constitution in the world. A major objective of the founding fathers was limiting the power of the government and securing the liberty of citizens. The Constitution's separation of the executive, legislative, and judicial branches of government, the checks and balances, and the explicit guarantees of individual liberty were designed to accomplish this objective by striking a balance between authority and liberty.

The Constitution was written broadly so as to endure changing times and circumstances. While it can be changed by amendment, the process is difficult and seldom utilized. Although written more than 200 years ago, the Constitution has been amended only 27 times—and ten of those amendments came into effect shortly after the Constitution was ratified in 1789.

The authors of the Constitution deliberately made it difficult to amend by requiring approval of two-thirds of both houses of Congress. A second avenue was a convention to be called by Congress upon application by the legislatures of two-thirds of the states. Amendments proposed by Congress must be ratified by three-fourths of the state legislatures or conventions in the states.

What does the federal Constitution say about education? Nothing! Therefore, education is a function of the state. Why not a function of the local community or of the federal government? The answer lies in the Constitution itself. Nowhere is the word "education" mentioned. Therefore, the Tenth Amendment to the Constitution answers the question. This amendment states, "The powers not delegated to the United States by the Constitution, nor prohibited by it to the States, are reserved to the States respectively, or to the people."

Although provision for education is thus established as one of the powers reserved to the states, the Supremacy Clause of the Constitution (Article VI, Section 2) declares that the Constitution and the laws enacted by the U.S. Congress "in pursuance thereof" are the supreme law of the land. Thus, all statutes passed by Congress, state constitutions and statutes, and policies of local boards of education are subject to and may not violate the provisions of the federal Constitution. The portions of the Constitution that have had the greatest impact on the operation of public schools are Article 1, Sections 8 and 10, and Amendments 1, 4, 5, 8, 10, and 14. Nearly always, one or more of these constitutional provisions serve as the basis for education-related cases taken to federal courts.

On the other hand, one must keep in mind that although education is a function of the states, the federal government exerts considerable influence in educational issues. This influence on the part of the federal government has come primarily through the provisions of the Constitution just enumerated, decisions of the U.S. Supreme Court, and acts of Congress.

## The General Welfare Clause (Article 1, Section 8)

Article 1 of the U.S. Constitution grants Congress "power to lay and collect taxes . . . and provide for the common defense and general welfare of the United States." This provision is based on the assumption that a high level of education is essential for the civic and economic prosperity of a democratic nation—the general welfare. Congress relies on this article when it passes federal statutes and provides federal tax dollars for school programs. The courts have generally upheld the power of Congress to authorize taxes and expenditures related to the general welfare of the United States—including education. Courts have ruled that:

- Intelligence is commerce as defined in the Constitution, and Congress has a right to regulate it (*Gibbons v. Ogden*, 1824)
- Congress is not limited in the expenditure of public monies to the direct or express grants of legislative power found in the Constitution (*United States v. Butler*, 1936)
- Congress can tax and spend under the General Welfare Clause (*Helvering v. Davis*, 1937).

Congress, utilizing its authority under the General Welfare Clause, has enacted a body of legislation to promote and support education. Federal statutes have provided extensive education programs for pre-school-ers through adults in such areas as defense education, vocational programs, math, and science. Legislation has also been enacted to promote civil rights and prohibit sex discrimination. Statutes have authorized services for students whose primary language is not English and for those with special learning difficulties. In addition, Congress has approved legislation designed to protect the confidentiality of pupil records and to eliminate bias against pregnant students. Other funds from the federal government have been directed to such purposes as free and reduced-cost food programs, student transportation, Native American education, and establishment of the military academies.

These laws have generally been upheld by the U.S. Supreme Court, which has interpreted the General Welfare Clause as authorizing Congress to tax and to spend money for a variety of educational activities. However, the court has not given Congress authority to do anything it pleases to provide for the general welfare—only to tax for such purposes. Therefore, while Congress may levy taxes to provide support for education, it may not legislate control of education (Webb, Metha, & Jordan, 1996).

## Obligation of Contracts Clause (Article 1, Section 10)

The Obligation of Contracts Clause in the U.S. Constitution provides in part that no state may "pass any . . . law impairing the obligation of contracts." Court decisions have affirmed that contracts entered into by school districts are fully protected. Examples include personnel contracts and other contracted services. This provision of the Constitution prohibits a state legislature, for example, from passing a law detrimental to a teacher who has acquired contractual status under existing statutes. Specifically, the obligation provision comes into play if a state legislature seeks to alter a teacher tenure or retirement statute in which contractual status prevails under the law (*Ball v. Board of Trustees*, 1904). The clause also protects from arbitrary dismissal those school personnel who are employed under contract. A teacher who has a contract may be dismissed during the term of that contract only with showing of cause and due process. This article has been litigated in numerous public school cases.

## First Amendment

First Amendment implications for education are developed in greater detail in a later chapter in this text. Only a brief discussion is presented here. The

First Amendment addresses several basic personal freedoms. It provides that

> Congress shall make no law respecting an establishment of religion, or prohibiting the free exercise thereof; or abridging the freedom of speech, or of press; or the right of the people peaceably to assemble, and to petition the Government for a redress of grievances.

The Freedom of Religion Clause has become an honest—and sometimes dishonest—source of conflict in America's schools. Since the mid-20th century, schools have become the battleground for some of the most volatile disputes over the appropriate role of religion in public life (McCarthy, Cambron-McCabe, & Thomas, 1998). In addition, the first part of the amendment, the phrase regarding religious freedom, has led to litigation challenging government aid to parochial schools.

The freedom of speech clause has resulted in numerous court cases involving rights of students and teachers to freedom of expression. Over the past several decades, student rights under this amendment have been extended to total freedom of speech on school grounds (Odden, 1995). Students and their attorneys have addressed situations ranging from demonstrations against governmental action to censorship of writings in student newspapers.

Another constitutional issue is the degree to which students have fundamental rights as against the authority of school officials to restrict student behavior. The right of assembly section has precipitated litigation involving student organizations as well as employee rights to organize and bargain collectively.

Among the many court decisions based on the First Amendment are the following:

- Neither students nor teachers shed their constitutional rights to freedom of speech or expression at the schoolhouse gate (*Tinker v. Des Moines*, 1969)
- School districts may develop dress codes and regulate hair length (*Massie v. Henry*, 1972)
- Lewd and indecent speech by students is not protected by the First Amendment (*Bethel School District No. 403 v. Fraser*, 1986).
- The first amendment does not prevent educators from suppressing student speech, which promotes illegal drug use (*Morse v. Frederick*, 2007).

## Fourth Amendment

The Fourth Amendment provides that "the right of people to be secure in their persons, houses, papers, and effects, against unreasonable searches and seizures, shall not be violated, and no warrants shall issue, but upon probable cause." This amendment has been the subject of litigation involving searches of students' lockers and persons as well as teachers' rights to privacy.

The issues surrounding search and seizure of students have increased in complexity in recent years. Increasingly, school teachers and administrators are concerned with drug possession and use by students. This situation is not likely to abate in the next several years. The National Institute of Drug Abuse (2014) reports good news in that the use of alcohol, marijuana, cigarettes, and illicit drugs continues to decrease; however, the organization reports growing concern over the high rate of e-cigarette use by middle and high school students.

Weapons on campus have also greatly increased in the past decade. The Fourth Amendment, written to protect citizens against unreasonable search and seizure, has been interpreted as requiring law enforcement officials to have probable cause that a crime has been committed and to obtain a search warrant before conducting a search. Prior to 1985 some courts held school officials to the same standard. However, in *New Jersey v. T.L.O.* (1985), the U.S. Supreme Court ruled that school officials' interest in maintaining discipline in the schools was sufficient to justify a lesser standard than probable cause. Consequently, school officials may conduct searches based on a "reasonable suspicion" provided that:

- there is "individualized" reasonable cause or suspicion that the search will reveal evidence of a violation of the law or school rules, and
- the scope of the search is reasonably related to the objective of the search and is not "excessively intrusive" in light of the age and sex of the child and the nature of the alleged infraction.

In determining whether a particular search is reasonable, the courts have distinguished between school property, such as lockers, and personal property. The courts have decided that students may have exclusive use of a locker with regard to other students, but possession is not exclusive with regard to school officials, who retain control of the lockers. In fact, courts have said that it is the duty of school officials to search a locker if suspicion arises that something of an illegal nature may be concealed there (*People v. Overton*, 1969).

A topic of controversy at many school sites is use of drug-sniffing dogs to help eliminate the drug problem on campus. Courts disagree on this issue, too. In *Doe v. Renfrow* (1980) the Seventh Circuit Court viewed use of dogs as preliminary to the search itself and therefore legal, provided the dogs were used to detect a substance on particular students, not all students or random groups. An opposing conclusion was reached by the Fifth Circuit Court in *Horton v. Goose Creek Independent School District* (1982), which ruled that using drug-detecting dogs to sniff students is an unconstitutional invasion of student privacy. The Horton case did not preclude school officials from using dogs to search lockers and cars.

Alexander and Alexander (2001) concluded that with the real or perceived use of drugs by school-aged children, courts would give schools greater authority to strip search students. He wrote that in order to conduct a strip search the school official must have reasonable suspicion that a student has concealed drugs or a weapon. This reasonable "test" requires a school employee to have information that a student has concealed drugs or a weapon or notices bulges in clothing or other indications of concealment.

In 2009, the U.S. Supreme Court clarified, to some extent, when a strip search may be legal. This case was *Safford v. Redding*. In an 8-1 decision, the Court stated that such a search is justified only if a school official has strong reason to believe a student is hiding a dangerous drug or weapon in his or her underwear. This decision is discussed in greater detail in Chapter 5.

Turning to employees' right to privacy, we note that litigation has arisen with regard to health and physical requirements for school employees, especially where testing is required for AIDS infection or for use of alcohol or drugs. The courts have held that mandatory urine and blood tests, if neither part of a routine medical examination required by law nor agreed to by the employee, violate the Fourth Amendment prohibition against unreasonable searches. However, such testing may be required in case of an "individualized 'reasonable' suspicion" of a condition that imperils the proper functioning of the employee or the well-being of others coupled with unavailability of any less intrusive means of resolving the suspicion (Valente, 1998). Should an employee's history or job duties affect student safety, the employer may require relevant testing

without violating the Fourth Amendment. Bus drivers form the employee group that most commonly falls into this category.

## Fifth Amendment

For schools, the pertinent part of the Fifth Amendment guarantees that "no person . . . shall be compelled in any criminal case to be a witness against himself, nor be deprived of life, liberty, or property, without due process of law; nor shall private property be taken for public use, without just compensation." The first clause is relevant to cases in which teachers have been questioned by supervisors about alleged activities with subversive organizations. In education cases, this clause has been invoked by teachers who refused to answer questions about their affiliations and activities outside of school. The courts have granted school officials the right to require employees to answer questions about their activities outside the classroom, but only if the activities relate to the teacher's qualifications or fitness to teach (*Beilan v. Board of Public Education*, 1958).

The due process protection of the Fifth Amendment is not usually cited in education cases because it pertains specifically to acts of the federal government. Rather, the Due Process Clause of the Fourteenth Amendment is used because it applies directly to the states.

The last clause in the Fifth Amendment is important in those cases where a state or school system is seeking to obtain private property for school purposes. This right of the government to take private property for the common good is called the "right of eminent domain." The right is exercised by a state or school district when an owner refuses to sell property for such purposes as a government building or a school site. When the power of eminent domain is exercised, the owner of the property must be given just compensation.

## Eighth Amendment

The part of the Eighth Amendment that generally relates to schools is the section that provides protection against "cruel and unusual punishment." This amendment has been invoked to challenge corporal punishment in schools. The U.S. Supreme Court has decided that corporal punishment is not cruel and unusual punishment as anticipated by the Eighth Amendment (*Ingraham v. Wright*, 1977). However, this decision does not prohibit states or school districts from restricting such punishment. Thus, as discussed in another section of this text, corporal punishment is forbidden in California and 30 other states. The last state to abolish this type of discipline was New Mexico in 2011.

Our neighbor to the north, Canada, took similar action in January, 2004, to prohibit corporal punishment in schools of that nation. The decision allowed for coercive force, if necessary, to restrain unruly students. Later the same month, on the other hand, the court decided that parents and care-givers could use "reasonable force" with children, not to include infants or adolescents (Supreme Court, 2004b; Moore, 2004).

## Tenth Amendment

As noted earlier, the Tenth Amendment to the U.S. Constitution provides: "The powers not delegated to the United States by the Constitution nor prohibited by it to the States, are reserved to the States respectively, or to the people." This clause confers on states the authority to control education and to devise and implement their own system of taxation. This state power to control education was tested in an early Supreme Court case (*United States v. Butler*, 1936), when the court concluded that "all powers not expressly granted to the United States by the Constitution or reasonably implied therefrom were reserved to the states." This statement provided a case law basis for the power of a state to tax and to appropriate funds for public schools.

## Fourteenth Amendment

The Fourteenth Amendment, approved in 1868 in the wake of the Civil War, is the constitutional provision most often invoked in education-related cases because it pertains specifically to state actions. The Fourteenth Amendment provides that no state shall "deprive any person of life, liberty or property, without due process of law." Numerous education cases citing this provision have come to the courts. Liberty rights include interest in one's reputation and the right to personal privacy. Property rights include a tenured teacher's right to continued employment and a student's right, under compulsory school attendance laws, to attend school.

The Fourteenth Amendment also provides that no state shall "deny to any person within its jurisdiction the equal protection of the law." This Equal Protection Clause has been relied upon in a wide variety of education cases in recent years. Some cases have addressed alleged discrimination based on race, ethnic background, sex, age, or handicapping condition; others have dealt with inequity in state financing of public schools.

Bear in mind that the Fourteenth Amendment has been interpreted by the courts to require both substantive and procedural due process. The definition of substantive due process is vague, but is generally construed to involve the constitutionality of the content of the charges. Procedural due process is more definitively described and requires two conditions: notification and fair hearing. In numerous cases, the courts have made it clear that both types of due process must be present to suspend or expel a student (*Garcia by Garcia v. Miera*, 1987; *Goss v. Lopez*, 1975).

## State Constitutions

The United States is organized into two divisions of government activity: a federal legal system and fifty separate state legal systems. Each state has its own constitution to establish its basic laws. Like the U.S. Constitution, state constitutions provide a foundation for enactment of innumerable statutes that govern the activities of the state and its citizens. However, unlike the federal Constitution, every state constitution includes a provision for education. These provisions range from very specific to very general. They have in common the overall intent to ensure that schools and education are encouraged and that a uniform system of schools is established (Webb, Metha, & Jordan, 1996).

The education section in each state constitution is very important to the courts in determining whether particular legislative enactments are constitutionally required, permissible, or inappropriate. While state constitutions establish a framework for education, they do not give unlimited power to state legislatures in providing for the public schools. Rather, they set the boundaries within which each legislature may operate. Thus, a state legislature must act within the scope of both state and federal constitutions.

Collins (1969) reported that the constitutions of 45 states provided for the establishment of "common schools," and 35 states established specific methods for financial support. The constitutions of

30 states expressly prohibit use of public funds in religious schools, and the constitution of every state except Maine and North Carolina contains a provision prohibiting religious instruction in public schools.

# The Constitution of California

Contrary to the U.S. Constitution that, as we have seen, does not mention education, California's first constitution, adopted in 1849, established the office of State Superintendent of Public Instruction. Following this action, other laws were passed regarding education (Kunzi, 1978). In 1879, California replaced the 1849 constitution with a new document. The new constitution was more specific and detailed than the earlier version. Although it has been amended many times, its basic structure and pattern remain unchanged (Palmer, 1983).

The importance of education was acknowledged in the 1879 constitution. A philosophy of education was expressed in Article IX, Section 1, of that constitution. This section requires the legislature to encourage intellectual, scientific, moral, and agricultural improvement:

> A general diffusion of knowledge and intelligence being essential to the preservation of the rights and liberties of the people, the Legislature shall encourage by all suitable means the promotion of intellectual, scientific, moral and agricultural improvement. The distribution and sale of published material, including copyright material, has been declared by the Legislature to be a public purpose in furtherance of Article IX, Section 1.

Other sections of the 1879 constitution also address educational issues; it retained the State Superintendent of Public Instruction and included a state board of education, county superintendents of schools, and county boards of education. Included are sections dealing with financial aid to schools, a minimum salary for teachers, and adoption of textbooks. The 1879 constitution also provided that no public money might be appropriated to support sectarian or denominational schools and that no sectarian or denominational doctrine could be taught in the public schools.

Almost from the day when the 1879 constitution was approved, dissatisfaction with it surfaced. The 1897 legislature considered a new Constitutional Convention, but 60% of the electorate rejected the idea. No further proposal was submitted to the people until 1913, when the legislature again raised to the electorate the question of a Constitutional Convention. This proposal too, was soundly defeated.

Discussion of a complete revision of the 1879 California constitution has continued until the present. Over the years the constitution has become swollen with obsolete items and minutiae. By 1929 nearly 200 amendments had been approved. However, the next effort to revise the 1879 constitution did not occur until 1963. At that time the legislature created the California Constitution Revision Commission, a 60-member panel that included distinguished state leaders drawn from virtually every sector of the population. Some pruning of the constitution was clearly in order because the California constitution then contained more than 75,000 words; it was ten times the length of the U.S. Constitution and longer than any other state constitution except that of Louisiana.

The work of the 1963 commission was not completed until the election of June 1976. Suggested changes were submitted to the voters in 1966 and 1968. The 1966 election resulted in elimination of some 16,000 of the 22,000 words in selected sections. The 1968 proposals would have reduced the constitution from 14,000 words to 2,000, but this proposition was rejected by the voters. Not giving up, the commission placed five propositions on the ballot in June, 1970; only one passed. The subsequent November saw four small changes approved. Seven additional measures were approved by voters between then and 1974. Finally, in June, 1976, a clean-up proposal took care of rearranging and renumbering sections (Lee, 1991).

A new Constitution Revision Commission worked from 1994 to 1996; its recommendations never came to a vote. With the California budget crisis in 2008–2010, there again is a strong call for establishing another Commission to revise California's Constitution. Time will tell, if once the budget crisis is over, the call for the revision of California's Constitution will fade, as it has in the past.

# Initiatives and Referenda

It is probably safe to say that any citizen of the world who had access to the media in 2003 increased his or her knowledge of the initiative process when California's governor, Gray Davis, was recalled from office. The governor had served less than a year of his second four-year term when the recall was placed on the California ballot and approved by the citizens of California.

The initiative and referendum are products of a movement toward direct democracy that was led by the Progressive faction of the Republican Party around 1900. The federal government does not have a provision for initiative or referendum. However, 24 states have the initiative process and 49 states have some form of referendum (Initiative & Referendum Institute, 2014).

The initiative process enables voters to bypass the legislature and place an issue directly on the ballot for voter approval or rejection. By this means, citizens may adopt laws or amend the state constitution. Any measure on the ballot other than a slate of candidates for office is called a "ballot measure."

California is one of the few states in which the initiative process may be used to amend the constitution—and the only one in which a statutory amendment adopted by initiative cannot be modified by the legislature unless the initiative so provides. California is also one of only 18 states that permit recall of state-level officials by this means. Of the states that use the initiative process, California is by far the most active. The process has become increasingly popular with special interest groups for achieving the objectives of their organizations.

For a measure to be placed on the ballot, a petition must have been circulated to citizens of the state and the required number of signatures obtained. An initiative measure that obtains the required number of signatures may be submitted to the voters at a primary, general, or special election. Obtaining signatures on petitions has become big business; firms hired by proponents to solicit signatures charge as much as $2 for each signature.

There are two types of initiatives: The first is referred to as "statute revision," a proposal that requires signatures equal to 5% of the total votes cast for governor in the preceding gubernatorial election. The second type of initiative is referred to as a "constitutional amendment process." This ballot measure requires signatures equal to 8% of the total gubernatorial vote in the preceding election (Shelley, 2003). That number is lower than the requirement in any other state except Montana.

California's initiative process traces its history to 1911, when Governor Hiram Johnson led a crusade to give citizens the opportunity to directly approve, amend, or cancel legislation approved by the state legislature and governor. A special election was called in 1911, at which time the initiative process was approved as an amendment to the state constitution by a margin of 168,744 to 52,093 votes. Other states, including South Dakota, Utah, Oregon, Montana, Oklahoma, Missouri, Michigan, Arkansas, and Colorado, had approved this process prior to California's action (Shelley, 2003).

The California Secretary of State has compiled a list of all initiative proposals from the year 1912 to 2015. In all, 1,828 were titled and summarized for circulation. Of this number, 363 qualified for the ballot, and 123 were approved (Padilla, 2015).

These include an array of bond measures for various projects, the state lottery, and higher "sin taxes." Perhaps the best known issue among educators is Proposition 13, which set a limit on property taxes. Among the measures that failed was a ban on bull riding, steer roping, and prize fights.

The second type process that gives voters direct democracy is referred to as the referendum. The referendum gives citizens the power to reject laws or amendments proposed by the state legislature. Passage of a referendum measure does not necessarily result in adoption of a law, but it may prevent a statute adopted by the legislature from becoming legal. The initiative is used much more frequently than the referendum and is generally considered the most important and powerful of the two processes.

# Federal Statutes

Every legislature enacts, amends, and repeals laws. These laws, or statutes, constitute the second highest level of law, following constitutions. Whereas constitutions provide broad statements of policy, statutes establish the specifics of operation. Both the U.S. Congress and state legislatures have passed innumerable laws that affect education.

During each legislative session the U.S. Congress enacts or renews numerous statutes that impact public schools. Many of these statutes provide financial assistance for a variety of special instructional programs, research, and services for needy children. Examples at the national level include Title 1, Economic Impact Aid, the food services program, and Native American education. Other examples of federal legislation that impact education include civil rights legislation, funds for vocational education, and rules and regulations regarding special education.

Federal statutes are subject to review by the federal courts, which determine whether a law violates the federal constitution. If not, it is binding on all citizens and governmental agencies. As we shall see, a similar relationship exists between state statutes and state courts; that is, state statutes are subject to challenge in state courts. In addition, state legislation and state court decisions, in those areas of responsibility not delegated to the states, must conform to federal law and the U.S. Constitution and may be subject to review in federal courts.

## State Statutes

As previously discussed, although the Tenth Amendment grants to states the control of education, laws enacted by the states cannot override federal law or the state or federal constitution. Like Congress, successive state legislatures continually review and revise, supplement, repeal, and replace statutes.

Although delegating the actual operation of school districts to local boards, a state legislature also responds to societal needs and pressure groups by enacting new or revising old legislation. Some acts are general in nature and leave broad discretion to school boards, while other legislation mandates specific actions to local boards. In addition to providing direction to school districts for general operation of the schools, most state governments retain operation of certain types of specialized schools, such as those for the blind and deaf.

## California Education Code

Nearly all California laws regarding education are published in the Education Code, although some provisions are also found in other codes, such as the Government Code. The Education Code is not based on a prior code, but is a collection of rules and regulations for the organization and administration of California's public schools. As the state has increased in population, the laws affecting education

have increased in number and complexity. This collection of laws is contained in eleven volumes and is updated each year. It is also posted and searchable on the Internet at http://www.leginfo.ca.gov/calaw.html.

Administrators and attorneys who specialize in school law will verify that the statutes contained in the Education Code are complex, ambiguous, and often contradictory. Superintendents, often with a tone of humor and remorse, refer to the Education Code as "full employment for attorneys." To add credence to this view, California Supreme Court Justice Stanley Mosk made the following observation about the Education Code:

> Both parties agree that it is difficult to reconcile sections of the Education Code. Apparently the code as a whole is a crazy-quilt product of well-meaning legislative attempts to accommodate the divergent views of teachers, school boards, parents and the public. To one looking for an answer in many circumstances, the result is like trying to peer through opaque glass (dissenting opinion in *Taylor v. Board of Trustees*).

It was not very long after California joined the union in 1850 that the legislature began to pass laws. The first session of the legislature enacted a total of 146 chapters. These laws established the structure of local government, formalized a system of taxation, and regulated elections (Palmer, 1983). Over the next several decades numerous laws were enacted. Keeping track of the various enactments became a complex and difficult task. Therefore, in 1929, the legislature created the California Code Commission. The commission was given the task of codifying all of California's laws.

The commission reviewed all the laws passed in previous sessions of the legislature and recommended creation of the Education Code (Kunzi, 1978). The Education Code was subsequently revised in 1959 and in 1977. These revisions did not result in substantive changes in the statutes, but were attempts to collect and codify statutes that had been enacted over the years.

In 1972 the people of California, through the initiative process, made a major change in the Education Code. This initiative changed the philosophy of the Education Code from a *mandatory* to a *permissive code*. Prior to this change in the state constitution, school districts were seen as agencies of the state with limited authority. Responding to the initiative, the legislature enacted Education Code Sections 35160 (applicable to elementary and secondary districts) and 70902 (applicable to community colleges), which are virtually identical. Education Code Section 35160 states:

> On and after January 1, 1976, the governing board of any school district may initiate and carry on any program, activity, or may otherwise act in any manner which is not in conflict with or inconsistent with, or preempted by, any law and which is not in conflict with the purposes for which school districts are established.

In theory, the approval of this initiative by the citizens of California grants school districts greater latitude to make decisions at the school district level. In practice, many of the restrictions of the Education Code are still in place and require a district to seek legal advice prior to establishing a new regulation or procedure. Port (1998) states that the failure of the legislature to revise the code to accommodate its new permissiveness has resulted in confusion and, consequently, the permissive language is of little value.

Most school boards and superintendents still feel restricted by the mandates of the Education Code and lobby to have it abolished completely. Nevertheless, some—perhaps those who were bolder or more creative—state that they are no longer required to lobby legislators for approval of a new program and claim greater latitude in local decision-making.

## Title V—Administrative Code

In addition to confusion over the requirements of the Education Code, Title V of the California Code of Regulations, which contains the rules and regulations established by the California Department of Education to implement the Education Code, often interprets code sections in ways that are conflicting and difficult to understand. Also, as a result of the large number of education laws approved each year, Title V has not been kept up-to-date.

In lieu of keeping Title V current, the California Department of Education attempts to interpret legislation and provide direction by sending advisory letters to school districts. This advice is often frustrating to school administrators. For example, Assembly Bill 3482 was approved by the legislature and signed by the governor in 1996. This legislation established a program known as the "Teacher Reading Instruction Development Program." One section of the bill requires

> that each certificated teacher of pupils enrolled in kindergarten and grades 1 to 3, inclusive, possess the knowledge and skills to effectively teach pupils to read.

Sounds quite clear cut, right? However, the advisory letter from Ruth McKenna (1996), Chief Deputy Superintendent, addressed to all district and county superintendents, reads:

> The district agrees to provide certification to the California Department of Education on or before August 30, 1997, that not less than 90 percent of certificated employees who provide direct instructional services to pupils enrolled in kindergarten or any of the grades 1 to 3, inclusive, have received inservice training in the reading components.

The letter from McKenna included a place for the school superintendent to certify that the training had been accomplished. If you were a school superintendent, required to provide the training and certify that it had been accomplished, would you be clear as to who had to be trained? The law reads, "kindergarten and grades 1 to 3, inclusive." The Department of Education directive states, "kindergarten or any of the grades 1 to 3, inclusive." Must you train all kindergarten, first-, second-, and third-grade teachers? Or might you use the word "any" in the directive from McKenna and only train teachers in kindergarten and *either* grade one, two, *or* three? One school superintendent and her staff spent valuable time attempting to interpret the directive, called the county superintendent of schools, and were still uncertain about their obligations.

## Other California Codes

In addition to the Education Code, California has 27 other collections of statutes organized by topic, among them the Government Code, Welfare and Institutions Code, Penal Code, Public Contracts Code, Business and Professions Code, and the Health and Safety Code. Each of these codes contains sections that directly affect education.

For example, the Public Contracts Code contains regulations regarding the awarding of contracts for school construction. The Health and Safety Code gives direction to the school nutrition program. The Government Code describes procedures for conducting "closed sessions" at school board meetings. As one would expect, a number of statutes affecting school discipline are contained in the Penal Code, including a section (628.2) that requires each school principal, at specified intervals, to submit to the superintendent a complete report of crimes committed on school grounds.

# The Court System

The provisions of federal and state constitutions, statutes, and policies of local boards of education do not guarantee proper execution of the law. The founding fathers developed a three-prong system of government: the legislative branch to make the law, the executive branch to enforce the law, and the courts to interpret the law.

The court system provides a means through which individuals or groups who believe their constitutional rights have been violated may seek adjudication. It is important to remember that the courts do not take action on their own initiative. Rather, it is the role of the judiciary to resolve disputes by interpreting a law after its enactment and to review its constitutionality. Courts settle only those disputes referred to them for a decision (Reutter, 1994). In school-related matters, the courts have generally taken the position that they will not intervene in a dispute unless all internal appeals—that is, appeals within the district, county, and state education structure—have been reviewed and exhausted (Webb, Metha, & Jordan, 1996).

Nevertheless, despite their solely reactive mode, courts have limited the authority of government over public education at both federal and state levels as school operations have been challenged in the courts. Decisions on issues ranging from corporal punishment to racial desegregation of public schools have been made by the courts. On the other hand, courts have affirmed the authority of states to regulate such matters as certification, powers of school boards, curriculum requirements, the school calendar, accreditation, and numerous financial matters.

## Federal Judicial System

The federal judiciary was established as a separate and independent branch of the U.S. government. The federal system includes district courts, Courts of Appeals, and the U.S. Supreme Court. An action involving a federal issue may be filed in a federal district court. Issues that qualify for hearing at the federal level include civil rights, free speech, due process, and equal protection. Once a lawsuit is filed in a particular court system, that system retains jurisdiction until conclusion of the issue. For example, a case on appeal from a federal district court goes to the federal court of appeals for that circuit where that federal district court is located.

The backbone of the Federal Judicial System is the district courts. At the current time, there are 94 district courts. They are the court of original jurisdiction in the Federal Judicial System. Each state has at least one district court, and many states have between two and four courts.

The next level of the Federal Judicial System is the Court of Appeals. There are 13 U.S. Courts of Appeals, organized by geographic regions. The smallest is the 1st Circuit with responsibility for Maine, Massachusetts, New Hampshire, Rhode Island, and Puerto Rico. It has six judges with the largest, the 9th Circuit having 28 judges.

They decide appeals from the district courts within their jurisdiction. Circuit court decisions are binding throughout the circuit where they are rendered. If a plaintiff is dissatisfied with the decisions of the federal court of appeals, a further appeal may be made to the U.S. Supreme Court. Additional information is provided on the 9th Circuit, the largest of the 13 circuits.

### Ninth Circuit Court of Appeals

The 9th Circuit includes Alaska, Arizona, California, Hawaii, Idaho, Montana, Nevada, Oregon, and Washington. In addition, the Northern Mariana Islands and Guam are also included. The 9th Circuit was established during the California Gold Rush and has been resolving disputes for more than 150 years. In the early years, differences were occasionally resolved with pistols. A reminder of that past is a nick in a bench in the main courtroom left by a bullet fired in a 1917 conspiracy trial.

Cases brought in the federal courts in any of these states or territories may be appealed to the Federal Court of Appeals for the Ninth Circuit. Circuit court decisions are binding throughout the circuit in which they are rendered.

Today, the nation's largest and busiest federal appeals court resolves disputes without the intensity of gun battles, but the disputes between conservatives and liberals over civil rights, immigration, the death penalty, and criminal law have been equally intense. The court disposes of approximately 13,000 cases in a typical year while reviewing about 70 cases. Judges write dissents on a few dozen each year, and the U.S. Supreme Court hears just a small number that are appealed.

Williams (2009) quotes Jeffrey Fisher who teaches law at Stanford University, "A lot of important policy cases involving interesting and difficult questions come out of the 9th circuit." Most legal scholars dismiss statistics on reversals as of little significance in that only a small number of cases are reviewed for all circuits.

There is a long-standing belief that the 9th Circuit is the most liberal of the appellate courts and has more cases overturned by the U.S. Supreme Court than the other courts. There is a certain amount of truth in this perception. Keim (2014) reviewed the 2011-12 term and found that 86 percent of the 9th Circuit decisions were reversed at least in part and this number reveals a long-running trend of cases being disproportionately overturned.

# U.S. Supreme Court

The U.S. Supreme Court is the court of final appeal on federal law questions. There are nine members of the court. Five of the nine must approve a decision for it to stand. Once a decision is made, all other courts in the U.S. follow the precedent set by the decision. A ruling can be overturned only by an amendment to the Constitution or by a subsequent ruling by the court.

Supreme Court Justices, Court of Appeals Judges, and District Court Judges are nominated by the President and confirmed by the U.S. Senate. The members of the U.S. Supreme Court are appointed for life, and remain in office until they resign, die, or are removed from office. The Constitution does not establish specific requirements for the position. Senators or Members of the House of Representatives usually recommend candidates.

The candidates are nearly always members of the President's political party. Members of Congress and the Department of Justice have developed an informal criterion that is considered for the appointment. All Supreme Court Justices have been lawyers, and for the last 150 years have all been graduates of an accredited law school. For the last few decades, almost all Supreme Court nominees have been federal judges (Grabianowski, 2009).

Of the education-related questions that eventually reach the court, petitioners most frequently claim that a state's statutes or the policies of a local board of education have violated their constitutional rights or some provision of federal law. The Supreme Court is not required to consider an appeal, but must agree to hear the matter. This agreement is referred to as *certiorari,* abbreviated *cert.* A case is accepted for review only if four justices vote to grant *certiorari.* The Supreme Court uses this procedure as a discretionary device to choose the cases it wishes to hear.

Several thousand cases are appealed to the Supreme Court each year, with only a small number being heard. However, in recent years the number of education cases appealed and heard by the court has increased. This trend of parents and citizens to sue in the courts accelerated markedly after the *Brown v. Board of Education* decision in 1954. Once segregation had been declared unconstitutional, other education policies were challenged in the courts. Examples include: prayer in the school, government aid to parochial schools, compulsory school attendance, education of the handicapped, and student discipline (Wenkart, 1995).

As discussed in later sections of this text, the U.S. Supreme Court has made numerous decisions regarding education. In addition to the above examples, the court has considered corporal punishment, affirmative action, sex discrimination, compulsory attendance, and school-church issues.

# State Judicial System

There are two types of courts in California: trial courts and courts of appeal, the latter including the California Supreme Court. Formerly, municipal (urban) and justice (rural) courts constituted a level of trial court below the superior courts. However, since the approval of Proposition 220 in 1998, which provided for court unification, all 58 counties have unified their municipal and superior courts into a single superior court system (Judicial Council, 2004).

Most actions involving school districts originate in the superior court of the county in which the district is located. The most common action used by a plaintiff in an action against a school district is a petition for a writ of mandate (Port, 1998). This action is a request for a court order requiring a school district to take, or refrain from taking, a particular action.

Appeals from superior court decisions proceed to the courts of appeal in the judicial district in which the superior court is located. If the plaintiff appeals the decision of a California court of appeal, the matter goes to the California Supreme Court. Like the U.S. Supreme Court, the California Supreme Court is not required to hear a matter and may let the decision stand as decided by the court of appeal.

## California Court of Appeals

California has six Courts of Appeal and one California Supreme Court. The role of the Courts of Appeal is to review the Superior Court cases to decide if legal errors were made. Their job is not to conduct new trials.

In each Court of Appeal, a panel of three judges decides appeals from Superior Courts. The Courts of Appeal can agree with the decision of the Superior Court, agree in part and disagree in part, or disagree and reverse the lower court's decision. The Court's decisions are called "opinions." The opinions are public and are posted on the court's website.

The Governor appoints the judges for ten-year terms. New justices are subject to a retention vote by the public at the next general election after their appointment, and each ten years thereafter.

## California Supreme Court

The California Supreme Court has one Chief Justice and six Associate Justices who are appointed by the Governor for twelve-year terms. New justices are subject to a retention vote by the public at the next general election after their appointment, and each twelve years thereafter.

The requirements for appointment to the California Supreme Court include service as an attorney who is qualified to practice law in California, or service as a judge of a California court for ten years immediately preceding the appointment. The highest court in California supervises the lower courts through the Judicial Council of California, and also supervises California's legal profession through the State Bar of California. All lawyer admissions and disbarments are by recommendations of state bar associations. The California Bar Association is the largest in the United States with more than 250,000 members, and 180,000 actively practicing law in the state (California State Bar, 2015).

## Case Law

Case law differs from statutes, regulations, or other sources of law in that it consists of that body of law originating from historical usage and custom and from previous court decisions. When conflict occurs regarding the interpretation of a law, courts resolve these conflicts; such decisions become known as case law. Case law is based on the doctrine of *stare decisis,* which means "let the decision stand." The doctrine requires that once a court has laid down a principle of law as applicable to a certain set of facts, it will apply that principle to all future cases in which the facts are substantially the same. Other courts of equal or lesser rank will apply the principle similarly (*Black's,* 2004).

The doctrine of case law does not mean that previous decisions are never challenged or overturned. A higher or subsequent court may reject the reasoning of a lower or earlier court and overturn a previous decision. A court may even reverse its own prior decision. Perhaps the most notable example of the U.S. Supreme Court reversing itself on reconsideration is the case of *Brown v. Board of Education of Topeka* (1954). In *Plessy v. Ferguson* (1896) the Supreme Court had said "separate but equal" schools for blacks and whites were constitutionally permissible. The *Brown* decision reversed this position and ruled that separate schools for blacks and whites were inherently unequal, hence unconstitutional.

## Administrative Law

Administrative law consists of the formal regulations and decisions of state and federal agencies that govern public functions. These regulations carry the force of law. They are subject to judicial review and stand as law unless found to conflict with federal or state constitutional provisions, statutes, or applicable case law.

At the federal level, the U.S. Department of Education and the National Institute of Education are the agencies most directly concerned with education. The director of each of these departments is appointed by the President. Other federal agencies that establish regulations affecting education include the Department of Agriculture, the Department of the Interior, the Bureau of Indian Affairs, and the Department of Labor.

In California, the state agencies that have most control over education are the California Department of Education and Board of Education. The members of the California Board of Education are appointed by the governor, with the advice and consent of the state senate, while the State Superintendent of Instruction is elected by the people. Generally, after the legislature has enacted a law, the California Department of Education is responsible for issuing a regulation to guide local districts in implementing the law. These regulations can affect almost every aspect of school operations, including adoption of textbooks, bilingual education, and certification of teachers.

## Attorney General Opinions

Another source of education law is the official opinions of the state attorney general. The attorney general is the chief legal officer of the state and acts as legal advisor to state agencies. Often, the attorney general is requested to render an opinion regarding interpretation of a law. This request usually originates with the governor, a legislator, or a local official. While such opinions are advisory, they are helpful in clarifying and interpreting the law (LaMorte, 1999).

## Access to Legal Information

Many United States and California court cases, California Department of Education policies and guidelines, the Education Code, and associated information are available via the Internet. Access may be obtained through search engines such as

Google at http://www.google.com
and Ask Jeeves at http://www.ask.com

A comprehensive list of Internet search engines is maintained at the

All-in-One Search Page at
http://www.AllOneSearch.com.

Information, especially about legal resources, is also accessible through

FindLaw's LawCrawler at
lawcrawler.findlaw.com.

The California Constitution, all California codes, including the Education Code and the Government Code, and current bills may be accessed at

http://www.leginfo.ca.gov/

An extensive list of Internet resources on the law is provided in chapter 2, Table 1. Finally, California counties maintain law libraries that are open to the public.

## Summary

American public schools are governed by a complex body of directives derived from constitutional provisions, statutory enactments, agency regulations, and court decisions. The sources of law include many different agencies within both the state of California and the federal government. In addition, the courts, through their decisions on the multitude of cases they hear, provide direction in interpreting policies enacted by the California legislature and the Congress of the United States.

Education law cannot be interpreted on the basis of one agency or one policy. All policies and agencies must be considered in understanding and applying the sources of law. While educators are not required to have formal legal training, they must be aware of the many facets of laws that govern day-to-day management of schools. School personnel, like all citizens, cannot plead ignorance of the law as a defense for illegal actions. Educators must be knowledgeable of school board policies and keep current on changing legislation and court decisions that affect their school leadership.

## Key Terms

1. attorney general opinions
2. case law
3. Education Code
4. Eighth Amendment
5. federal judicial system
6. federal statutes
7. Fifth Amendment
8. First Amendment
9. Fourteenth Amendment
10. Fourth Amendment
11. General Welfare Clause
12. initiative
13. Obligation of Contracts Clause
14. permissive education code
15. referendum
16. right of eminent domain
17. *stare decisis*
18. state judicial system
19. state statutes
20. statute revision
21. Tenth Amendment
22. Title V—Administrative Code

## Discussion/Essay Questions

1. It may seem strange to modern Americans that the founding fathers did not mention education in the U.S. Constitution. Was this just an oversight, or was there a reason for its absence?

2. The courts have generally upheld the power of Congress to pass legislation to collect taxes and spend monies for education. What section of the federal constitution is cited to support this decision? What are the grounds for the decision?

3. *New Jersey v. T.L.O.* greatly clarified discipline on school campuses. Give a brief review of this decision. Discuss how it clarified the ability of school administrators to maintain discipline.

4. The California Constitution generally maintains the structure and pattern that were established when it was approved in 1879. What are the arguments pro and con for a complete revision of the 1879 constitution?

5. Most of California's laws affecting education are included in the Education Code. This code is referred to as "permissive." What does that term mean? Has the idea been useful to California educators?

# CHAPTER 2

# Conducting Legal Research

*A computer search would have given me a list of pertinent cases, but without that I had to read everything. That is harder by far, but you end up learning a lot more. I remembered cases because making copies of everything was too expensive. Keeping cases in your head is good, too, because cases are like puzzle pieces floating around in your mind, and sometimes, they fall into place and form a picture.*

—Shon Hopwood, *Law Man: My Story of Robbing Banks, Winning Supreme Court Cases, and Finding Redemption*

Most everyone will agree that research can be rewarding, but it is tedious work. The author quoted above had lots of time for tedious work after being sentenced to 10 years in prison for participating in five bank robberies. Hopwood spent much of his time in the prison law library and became an accomplished Supreme Court practitioner. His first work as a practitioner was preparing a request for a fellow prisoner, *Fellers v. United States*, for a Supreme Court hearing. The court received 7,209 petitions that year from prisoners and it heard just eight of them. Hopwood and Fellers won the case (9 to 1). After Hopwood's release from prison, he obtained a law degree and continues to work on Supreme Court petitions.

The above quote and story of a bank robber is not meant to serve as a role model for school administrators, but to encourage the school leader to spend a bit of time researching the law prior to contacting the $300-an-hour lawyer.

## Introduction

Legal research involves finding statutes, regulations, law cases, law reviews, and legal interpretations. These enable us to discuss intelligently the application of legal concepts to our job settings and everyday lives. Yell (1998) addresses this concept well:

By accessing the law through legal research, educators will have a better understanding of the principles of law, the facts giving rise to these principles, and the application of those facts to situations they may encounter.

Research on legal issues is conducted in either of two basic ways. In the first instance, research may be conducted in a law library maintained at a university or in one of the public law libraries maintained by each county. The second way, which is growing in popularity, is via the Internet. Whichever option is chosen, certain principles must be followed.

As a beginning, primary legal documents and law-related commentaries are plentiful in both the physical and virtual law libraries. United States federal statutes, pending legislation and regulations, current federal appellate cases, California court opinions, legal opinions, and other information may be found. However, to conduct a successful search, the researcher must ask such questions as:

- Where does all this wonderful information reside?
- How do researchers determine when to scout the Web for information and when to rely on traditional resources?
- Do conventional online searching methods work at popular Web search sites?
- What other strategies should researchers apply?
- What evaluation skills should Internet researchers possess?

Furthermore, after finding the answer to a particular question, researchers must consider whether they can trust the information they find. To this end, questions must be raised to evaluate the quality and accuracy of any legal information. These questions include:

- Who is responsible for providing the information?
- Is it accurate, authentic, and complete?
- Is it timely and up-to-date?
- Is it objective?

And to use legal materials professionally, one must observe the usual guidelines regarding acknowledgment of sources, including the appropriate citation format for legal documents, whether obtained in print or via the Internet.

## Information Access

West Group (2000) addresses the impact of information on those who conduct legal research when it states:

The legal and information industries are going through some dramatic changes. Anticipating these changes, and recognizing the issues they raise for legal and business professionals, West Online has set in motion plans for the future that will enable us to adapt to the customer's evolving needs.

Today, for example, there is an increased emphasis on specialization. Customers are demanding information tailored to their own specialties and jurisdictions. And, with the globalization of economies, the need for legal information internationally is critical for attorneys and business professionals alike. Complicating matters is the fact that traditional boundaries of information needs are changing. Law firms can no longer operate using only "legal" information, while businesses need access to more and more legal information in order to operate within the law and to maintain a diverse and changing labor force. These professionals may need business news and information one day; public records the next; and regulatory, tax, or topical information the next. The need to put all of that information into the context of their situation requires tools that will enable them to cut through the myriad of content types and zero in on pertinent information.

Finally, domestic and international law is becoming more voluminous and complex, driving professionals' demand for easier ways to find and apply the law to any given situation. The ideal research products will point users to the right information and allow them to filter and make sense out of vast legal and nonlegal content in the easiest, most cost- and time-efficient manners.

## Primary and Secondary Sources

### Primary Sources

Before addressing research using a law library and the Internet, it may be helpful to discuss how information related to legal issues is defined as either a primary or secondary source. Primary sources are listed in chronological order, rather than by subject area. Examples of primary sources include federal and state statutes and regulations, as well as judicial decisions. Annotated codes, West's digest system with KeyCite, and Shepard's *Citations for Cases* are used to locate this primary material.

It should be noted that names of plaintiff and defendant sometimes reverse on appeal. Thus, if Smith sues the school district, the trial court case is identified as *Smith* (plaintiff) *v. Somewhere School District* (defendant). If the school district loses and appeals, the new case may be named *Somewhere School District v. Smith*. In this situation, *Somewhere School District* becomes the appellant, and *Smith* is the respondent.

Federal statutes are organized by topic and published in a series of volumes called the United States Code (U.S.C.). There are 50 numbered titles in the U.S.C. The titles are divided into chapters and sections. Each title contains statutes covering a specific subject. The U.S.C. is considered the official version of federal statutes.

Annotated versions of the U.S.C. present information that is more useful than the text of the statute alone and are updated more frequently than the U.S.C. itself. There are two annotated versions—the United States Code Annotated (U.S.C.A.) and the United States Code Service (U.S.C.S.). These annotated editions contain information pertaining to each statute. The U.S.C.A. includes summaries of court cases that have interpreted each statute, notes and citations about the legislative history of the statute, cross-references to related statutes, and research guides to other relevant materials published by West. The U.S.C.S. reprints the statutes and, at the end of every section, examines relevant cases, provides citations to administrative materials, and lists other aids. It must be noted that the annotated codes contain updates in paper supplements that are filed in a pocket inside the back cover of each volume. A legal researcher must check these updates to determine whether a statute has recently been amended or even completely abolished.

One of the best ways to find a federal statute is through the citation that identifies its location. Citations are written in standard form—title, number, United States Code, section number followed by the subsection letter and number, and year. An alternative way to find a federal statute is to use the Popular Name Index found at the end of the annotated codes. The index lists the popular name, statute number, date of passage, title, and section number. A third way to find a federal statute is to use the annotated code index, located at the back of the last volume, that lists statutes by subject.

Regulations are issued by administrative agencies to implement legislation. Federal regulations are published in the *Federal Register* and the *Code of Federal Regulations* (C.F.R.). The C.F.R. is organized by subject and contains 50 titles, each covering a general subject area. The C.F.R. contains the text of the regulation, a reference to the statute that authorizes the regulation, and the date of publication in the *Federal Register*.

As with federal statutes, one of the best ways to find a federal regulation is through the citation that identifies its location. The form for the citation is the same as for federal statutes—title, number, abbreviation (C.F.R. or Fed. Reg.), section number followed by the subsection letter and number, and year. An alternative way to find a federal regulation is to use the subject index at the end of each title of the C.F.R.

Law cases are published in volumes that are organized for federal courts according to the level of the court in which the case was decided; and for state courts, by geographical region and the level of the court. These volumes, called "reporters," are available in all law libraries. Sometimes a case may be found at a judicial site on the Internet (see Table 1 later in this chapter).

The federal government does not publish the decisions of the federal district or appellate courts. The text of these decisions may be found in either of two ways—through Internet links or through the law reporters of the West Publishing Company. West publishes the decisions of the U.S. District Courts in the *Federal Supplement* (abbreviated F.Supp.). Decisions of the U.S. Courts of Appeals are published in the *Federal Reporter*.

The decisions of the U.S. Supreme Court are found in three different publications. *United States Supreme Court Reports* (abbreviated U.S.) is the official reporter because it is printed by the U.S. government. West publishes the *Supreme Court Reporter* (abbreviated S.Ct.). Bancroft-Whitney/Lawyers' Cooperative publishes the *Supreme Court Reports, Lawyers' Edition* (abbreviated L.Ed.). The latter two publications contain synopses, related cases, and historical information. Decisions of the California appellate courts, including the appeals and supreme courts, may be found in West's *California Reporter*.

State law cases are organized chronologically, rather than by subject. To help researchers find a state law case in any of the reporters, each published case includes a citation that follows a standard format. The format contains, in sequence, the name of the case, the volume number of the reporter, the title of the reporter, the page number followed by the court hearing the case, and the year in which the decision was rendered.

It is often important to locate, in addition to a specific case, the cases cited by, and especially those that subsequently referred to, a case in hand. Equally important is knowing whether a judgement has been set aside or modified in subsequent decisions. All this information is found in a tool called a *citator*. For many years Shepard's *Citations for Cases* had a monopoly on this service; printed volumes filled many shelves in a law library. More recently, Shepard's has become an online tool with added features. Westlaw now offers a competitor, KeyCite, which is available only electronically (Giangrande, 2004). As of 2001, a third product, GlobalCite, did not approach either Shepard's or KeyCite in scope, according to one reviewer (Liebert, 2001). All three citators are subscription services, and all have advanced features that one must master to use them to best advantage.

## Secondary Sources

Secondary sources analyze or discuss legal doctrines and principles, but are not official because they are not actual statements of the law, merely interpretations of or opinions about the law. Nevertheless, they do tend to carry persuasive authority. Examples of secondary sources include legal journals such as West's *Education Law Reporter*, the *Journal of Law and Education*, and the Education Law Association's *Legal Notes* and *School Law Reporter*.

In addition, most law schools publish, either quarterly or annually, a law review that contains information on legal issues, historical research, and empirical studies. Typically, the law reviews contain articles written by legal scholars, commentary on legal issues, and book reviews.

Finally, there are newsletters published on a regular basis to address current issues in the legal field. Discussion of a legal issue in these newsletters is usually brief, but amplified with citations that direct the reader to more detailed information.

Bear in mind that there is always a sizeable time delay between the court decision and appearance of that decision in hard copy. Thus, Internet links provide the fastest access to the text of a recent court decision.

## Using a Law Library

A law library contains actual statutes, regulations, court decisions, and the resources necessary to locate them. In California, every county maintains a law library for use by the public. For instance, in San Bernardino County, there are law libraries in San Bernardino and

Rancho Cucamonga. In Riverside County, there are law libraries in Riverside and Indio.

Upon entering these law libraries, individuals may search the law volumes on their own or contact the librarian at the reference desk. One explains simply and briefly just what he or she is seeking, and the librarian will help find the necessary information. It has been the experience of both students and the authors that librarians' willingness to help makes a law library a comfortable place. Even those who generally use the Internet will find a visit to a law library an enriching educational experience.

Since most material cannot be checked out, patrons of a law library must be prepared to write the information they find on a legal pad or to photocopy it. A single copy of a limited quantity of material for nonprofit or scholarly purposes is generally considered fair use (see chapter 11). One may check with a librarian in case of concern about possible violation of copyright law.

## Using the Internet

The Internet and the World Wide Web (commonly abbreviated WWW) are not the same thing; rather, the WWW is but one way to access material on the Internet. Nevertheless, the Web has nearly monopolized the practice of online research since it came into widespread use in 1995. Actually, the WWW is a collection of servers, all linked together via the Internet and all "speaking" a common computer language called "hypertext transmission protocol" (HTTP). These servers are accessible to client computers running browser software such as Netscape Navigator or Internet Explorer. Browser software communicates with the server using HTTP and receives and formats documents encoded in "hypertext mark-up language" (HTML) or other formats.

Thus, the Internet is a network of networks, the physical collective of computers and wiring. The Internet can exist without the Web; however, the Web cannot exist without the Internet. HTTP, the protocol that allows Web servers and clients to talk to one another, is only one of several message protocols used on the Internet. Others include e-mail (SMTP), newsgroups (NNTP), terminal emulation (Telnet), and file transfer protocol (FTP) (Chapman, 2000).

Generally, to use the World Wide Web one must have a computer with a Macintosh or Windows platform. Individual users access the Internet with a modem and telephone line (56K recommended), a cable modem from a cable television company, or other cable or wireless connection. Such services are available for a relatively low monthly subscription rate. Once connected to the Internet, the searcher enters the address (URL) of the desired server location, or "Website." (See Table 1 for a list of useful URLs.) Depending upon your browser's idiosyncrasies, http:// may or may not be needed in front of the Internet address.

Once connected to a useful Website, one sorts through the menus much as one might search a library catalog. If a searcher does not have a particular Website in mind, any one of several WWW search engines or lists of sources, sometimes called "Webliographies," will help locate information.

Two well-known sources for legal research on the Internet are LEXIS/NEXIS and Westlaw. Both require a subscription to use their services. Their addresses are:

LEXIS/NEXIS:   www.lexis.com

Westlaw:         www.westlaw.com

At least one of these may be available in a law or university library. A school district or county office of education may also subscribe.

Numerous free Websites for research are also available. It must be noted that these Websites are only valuable and useful if the site is consistently and frequently maintained by someone with legal experience. It is important to note that Websites sometimes change their addresses. Therefore, additional searches may be needed.

A useful browser tool called "bookmarks" or "favorites" allows a searcher to keep a record of useful Internet locations. The bookmark can be recorded by the browser while the client computer is connected to the Website. The list of bookmarks is essentially an address book or directory of Internet sites to which one can return merely by selecting the bookmark. The popular browsers keep a list of sites recently visited. Unfortunately, when the session ends, the list is erased. It is, therefore, important to use the bookmark feature as the search is conducted.

## Tips for Conducting an Online Law Search

The Virtual Chase Website (maintained by Ballard Spahr Andrews & Ingersoll at http://www.virtual chase.com/) provides many tips for finding legal information on the Internet. Genie Tyburski (2004), Web Manager, tells us:

Unlike traditional law-related online tools such as LexisNexis and WestLaw, the Web is not a database. It is not an orderly means for storing definable data and related information. It better resembles the research environment of another era, before the advent of online information: Researchers began their task with a known source or by using a finding aid like a library card catalog or a case digest. Accordingly, you will improve your chances of success if you first identify a source—whether by title (United States Code) or by type of document (federal statutes). Then consider whether, and where, it exists on the Web.

Tyburski goes on to advise against entering a few keywords. Rather,

attempt a broader search that seeks one or two useful starting points. Look for government Web sites, professional associations, or advocacy groups. Also try the more traditional finding tools such as subject directors and database finding aids.

The Ballard firm (1999) warns not to rely on information until its source, accuracy, authenticity, timeliness, and objectivity have been ascertained. Skepticism is a virtue on the Web. A checklist available on the firm's Virtual Chase Website enables a searcher to evaluate the quality of information. Then, when a reliable source is found, the best advice is: "Don't let it go!" Reliable resources should be recorded with bookmarks, bookmark utilities, contact lists, card files, or one's own hyperlinked Web page.

Of the resources in Table 1, note particularly Find-Law.com and THOMAS. The former provides free access to numerous statutes, law cases, and other resources. Also a free service, this time from the Library of Congress, is THOMAS (named for Thomas Jefferson), a database of federal legislation, the Congressional Record, information about legislative committees, and other documents reaching back in some cases to the 90th Congress.

| Table 1 | Selected Law Websites on the Internet |
| --- | --- |
| American Civil Liberties Union | www.aclu.org/ |
| California Administrative Code | ccr.oal.ca.gov/ |
| California Codes | www.leginfo.ca.gov/calaw.html |
| California Courts | www.courtinfo.ca.gov/ |
| California Department of Education | www.cde.ca.gov/ |
| California Secretary of State | www.ss.ca.gov/ |
| Cecil Greek's Law Sites | www.criminology.fsu.edu/cjlinks/ |
| Chief State School Officers Council | www.ccsso.org/ |
| Cornell University Library | www.law.cornell.edu/ |
| FindLaw California | california.lp.findlaw.com/ca00_casecode/ |
| FindLaw's Law Crawler | lawcrawler.findlaw.com/ |
| Hastings Law College | www.uchastings.edu |
| Internet Law Library | www.lawguru.com/ilawlib/ |
| LawLinks: Internet Legal Resource Center | www.lawlinks.com/ |
| Legal Search Engines and Tools | www.lawguru.com/ |
| Library of Congress | www.loc.gov/ |
| LOIS Law Library | www.pita.com/ |
| National Archives & Records Administration | www.gpoaccess.gov/cfr/index.html |
| National Conference of State Legislatures | www.ncsl.org |
| The National Law Journal | www. law.com/jsp/nlj/index.jsp |
| Orange County Public Law Library | www.oc.ca.gov/lawlib/ |
| Supreme Court Decisions: | |
| 1990–present | supct.law.cornell.edu/supct/ |
| 1937–1975 | www.fedworld.gov/supcourt/index.htm |
| 1893–present | www.findlaw.com/casecode/supreme.html |
| 1000 most cited since 1793 | www.ii.georgetown.cdu/guides/supremecourt.cfm. |
| THOMAS, Library of Congress | thomas.loc.gov |
| U.S. Court of Appeals, 9th Circuit*: 1995–date | www.ca9.uscourts.gov/ |
| U.S. Department of Education | www.ed.gov/index.jhtml |
| U.S. Code | www.gpoaccess.gov/uscode/ |
| U.S. Tax Code | www.fourmilab.ch/ustax/ |

*Each circuit court can be accessed by putting a 1, 2, etc. instead of the 9.

Maximum benefit from the Internet is gained by focusing on those sites that are beneficial, not merely interesting. Wise use of time means knowing when to stop viewing because a site is no longer helpful. As Yell (1998) states, "It is important to realize that the Internet is not a panacea, nor is it a substitute for the law library. It is, however, an extremely valuable tool for the legal researcher."

## Recording the Information

After locating a relevant case, the researcher must record its essential elements so that the case is clearly understandable. An excellent template for recording information has been developed by Alexander and Alexander (1998) and is presented in the instructor's guide that accompanies their book. This template enables a researcher to record the important parts of a case and then write it in a brief form as follows:

### Parts of a Case

**Citation:** The names of the plaintiffs and defendants and the location of the case itself are set forth in a standard, much abbreviated, form. The following case was decided by the Supreme Court of Washington on April 6, 1967. It may be found in volume 426 of the *Pacific Reporter, Second Series,* beginning on page 471. If a case has been appealed, each court decision will be listed.

*Chappel v. Franklin Pierce Sch. Dist.,* 426 P.2d 471 (Wash. 1967)

**Résumé of the Case:** A brief statement summarizes the cause of action, relief sought, lower court findings, holding of the present court, and final action.

**Headnotes:** The publisher places from one to several headnotes at the beginning of each case. Each headnote states a point of law from the case as interpreted by the publisher. Key numbers beside each headnote indicate the subject or issue dealt with; for example, Civil Rights Key Note 3; Constitutional Law, 211; Constitutional Law 224 (sex discrimination cases); Schools 172.

**Counsel:** Attorneys of record for each party are then listed.

**Facts:** Next comes the court's summary of the facts of the case. In a court of appeal, the facts are not usually disputed. Rather, the issue on appeal is whether the lower court made an error *in law*—whether the appellant had a fair trial.

**Name of Judge:** If there is more than one opinion, the name of the judge who wrote the majority opinion appears at the beginning of the facts.

**Numbers in Text:** Portions of the text of the decision show numbers that match the headnotes. In addition, footnotes provide explanatory material and references to other cases.

**Body of the Decision:** The reasoning and decision of the court may extend from one or two pages to as many as 130. This is the majority opinion. A researcher's challenge is to identify the basis for the decision on each issue.

**Concurring Opinions:** A judge who agrees with the majority opinion may nevertheless have slightly different reasons for his or her position. His or her individual points are set forth in a concurring opinion.

**Dissenting Opinions:** If one or more judges disagree with the majority opinion, a dissenting opinion may be filed to set forth that judge's conclusion and explain his or her reasoning. Sometimes the dissents exceed the majority opinions in length, as occurred in the *Rodriguez* case. Of course, only the majority opinion carries the weight of law.

**Finding of the Court:** The action of a court of appeal may be to affirm the lower court's action, reverse, affirm in part, reverse in part, or reverse and remand for a new trial on the merits of the case.

### Sample Brief

Following is a sample legal brief summarizing a school law case that was decided by the Supreme Court of California in 1984.

**Citation:**   *Hartzell v. Connell*
Supreme Court of California,
In Bank, 1984
35 Cal.3d 899, 201 Cal.Rptr. 601,
679 P.2d 35

**Issue:** Imposition of fees for educational extracurricular activities violates the free school guarantee in the California constitution.

**Facts:** The Santa Barbara High School District offered a wide range of extracurricular activities, including 38 athletic teams. Prior to the 1980–81 school year, students could participate in these activities free of charge. In 1981 the school board cut its budget by $1.1 million, part of which was a reduction in financial support for extracurricular activities. To make the budget work, the ninth-grade athletic program was cut, and students were charged fees ($25) for participation in each dramatic production, musical performance, or athletic competition. The students did not receive credit toward graduation for participation in any of these extracurricular activities. Also, upon showing financial need, a student could have the fees waived. Barbara Hartzell, a taxpayer with two children in the public schools, together with the Coalition Opposing Student Fees, a group of community organizations, filed a lawsuit against the district, various school officials, and members of the school board.

**Finding of the Court:** The state constitutional provision for free public education prohibits charging fees for either regular or extracurricular programs.

**Reasoning:** The courts have emphasized the vital importance of student participation in extracurricular activities as part of their educational experience. Group activities encourage participation in community affairs, promote development of leadership qualities, and instill a spirit of collective endeavor. Students should not have the stigma of being needy recorded on public records.

## Summary

Legal research involves finding statutes, regulations, law cases, law reviews, and legal interpretations. This chapter has defined the difference between primary and secondary sources of information. The chapter also included information on using a law library and the Internet to research the law.

Knowing how to conduct legal research and where to go for information—whether that be the law library or Internet sources—gives teachers and administrators an immense advantage. They can quickly find current information to address immediate issues in the educational setting. This skill is of tremendous value in providing leadership to faculty, students, and community. A well-known admonition states, "Knowledge is Power!" One should never underestimate the value of knowledge!

## Key Terms

1. bookmark
2. California Reporter
3. citations
4. citator
5. Federal Reporter
6. KeyCite
7. LEXIS/NEXIS
8. primary sources
9. secondary sources
10. Shepard's Citations
11. THOMAS
12. United States Code (U.S.C.)
13. West's digest system

## Discussion/Essay Questions

1. What are the advantages of utilizing secondary sources when researching legal documents? The disadvantages?

2. Which of the Internet databases of U.S. Supreme Court decisions is easiest to search?

3. What are bookmarks and how are they useful?

4. Go to the Internet site at www.courtinfo.ca.gov. Select a topic of interest to you and write a brief summary of what you find.

5. Conduct a search of California Supreme Court cases involving student attendance. Write a brief of one case.

# CHAPTER 3

# School Governance and the Law

*There never is a good time for tough decisions. There will always be an election or something else. Governance is about taking tough, even unpopular, decisions.*

—Jairam Ramesh, member of Indian Parliament

## Introduction

One only has to follow the lack of decision making by the U.S. Congress to understand the difficulty of decision making. A newly elected school board member is almost immediately faced with financial and political dilemmas: Should teachers get a pay increase, and how much? Should an elementary school be closed in a declining enrollment school district? Should expenditures be decreased for science classes or athletics?

This chapter is about governance, or managing the school district. *Black's* (2004) defines "government" as "an organization through which a body of people exercises political authority; the machinery by which sovereign power is expressed." If one could compare the governance of a local school district with the federal or state government, the school board fills the role of the legislative branch. It is the board's job to establish policy, or make the law. The superintendent of schools has the role of a president or governor in that it is his or her job to abide by the policies of the board and to manage the district.

A student of government quickly learns that the roles of Congress, the President, and the federal courts are not clearly defined. The three branches of government often find themselves in conflict, charging one another with infringement of responsibility. This same situation often occurs with the governor, legislature and courts at the state level.

Similarly, the lines for governance of schools are not always clear. Misunderstanding, confusion, and conflict may exist between the local school district board and its superintendent. Their roles may blend or overlap. Often, a superintendent assumes the role of establishing policies or regulations that govern the district. Occasionally, a school board assumes, or largely assumes, the management role of the superintendent. By keeping this reality in mind, the reader will appreciate that the governmental agencies with prime responsibility for implementing the law occasionally appear to create law as well. This chapter focuses on the bodies that most influence the governance of a school district: the California State Board of Education and State Superintendent of Public Instruction, the county boards of education and county superintendents of schools, and the local boards of education and school district superintendents.

## California State Board of Education

The 1879 California Constitution established a state board of education, which consists of ten members appointed by the governor for a term of four years. A student member, appointed for a term of one year, also sits on the board. California Board of Education appointments must be made with the advice and consent of two-thirds of the state senate. The executive officer of the state board of education is required to keep a record of its proceedings and take charge of its correspondence. Education Code Sections 33000–33080 specify the composition and requirements of the state board. Section 33032 provides direction to the state board:

> The board shall study the educational conditions and needs of the state. It shall make plans for the improvement of the administration and efficiency of the public schools of the state.

An additional function of the state board is to grant waivers of Education Code sections to California school districts. A waiver is defined as "an exemption from a requirement of the Education Code." For example, California requires 175 days of student school attendance each year (E.C. 41420). However, a district that experiences an earthquake, a flood, or some other natural disaster may request the state board of education to waive the 175-day requirement. The state board has considered an array of waiver requests, from changing the days required to celebrate a national holiday to housing students in non-Field Act (non-earthquake-compliant) buildings.

Occasionally, the state board and State Superintendent of Public Instruction have clashed over the philosophy and direction of education. Since the State Superintendent of Public Instruction is elected, he or she has a certain degree of independence from the state board. In recent times, the most publicized clash between the state board and the State Superintendent of Public Instruction occurred when Bill Honig served as state superintendent.

## State Superintendent of Public Instruction

The 1849 California constitution provided for a popularly elected Superintendent of Public Instruction. The original term of office of three years was changed to four years in 1862. In 1990, the office was limited to two consecutive terms as part of Proposition 140, a general term-limit measure.

Education Code Sections 33100 through 33193 establish the powers and duties of the position. As noted above, the state superintendent serves as secretary to the state board of education. In addition, he or she is *ex officio* Director of Education. In this role, the superintendent is responsible for carrying out the policies of the state board. He or she is to provide leadership to county and district school superintendents and has financial responsibility for estimating the amount of state school funds to be apportioned to each county. The superintendent is also the chief state spokesperson in relation to the U.S. Department of Education.

In 1988 California citizens added duties to the job description of the state superintendent. Proposition 98—which was supported by a coalition of teachers, administrators, school board members, and members of the Parent Teacher Association—established the School Accountability Report Card. Each California district was required to develop this report card each year for review by parents and citizens of the district. The superintendent was responsible for overseeing implementation of this requirement.

Proposition 98 also gave the superintendent additional fiscal oversight of school districts. In consequence of more than 30 California school districts becoming insolvent, the state superintendent was given responsibility for working with county superintendents to monitor and review local school district budgets. Should a school district become insolvent, the state superintendent appoints an administrator to manage the local district. This administrator reports directly to the State Superintendent of Public Instruction. While the district is under state control, the appointed administrator assumes the authority normally assigned to the local district board of education.

The prime example of an insolvent district is Compton Unified School District, which was under state control for several years. Coachella Unified School District, in Riverside County, is another example of a district that was placed under state control due to financial insolvency.

## County Boards of Education

The county board of education is another entity involved in the governance of school districts. This body was established by the state legislature in 1879. The organizational procedures and duties of the county board are included in Education Code Sections 1000 through 1097. A county board may have either five or seven members, as determined by the County Committee on School District Organization. Board members are elected by trustee area. The duties of the board are contained in Education Code Section 1040:

1. adopt rules and regulations, not inconsistent with the laws of this state, for their own government
2. keep a record of their proceedings
3. approve the annual budget of the county superintendent of schools before its submission to the county board of supervisors
4. approve the annual county school service fund budget of the county superintendent of schools before its submission to the State Superintendent of Public Instruction
5. review at a regularly scheduled public meeting the annual audit provided for by the county superintendent of schools, including an audit of each district in the county.

The county office plays a major role in providing assistance to local districts. Its support is particularly needed in smaller districts. Some of its services include business and personnel management; special education, library, audiovisual, and health services; and assistance in developing and implementing instructional programs.

A major function of the county office is to provide credential services for teachers in local school districts. Prior to issuing a warrant for services, each county office is required to certify that teachers have met credential requirements in that county. In recent years an expanding role of the county has been to provide financial assistance and advice to school districts and to serve as a "watch dog" over their fiscal solvency.

## County Superintendents of Schools

County superintendents play a significant role in governing and regulating local school districts. This office has become particularly important in fiscal monitoring and control. The position of county superintendent was established by the 1849 California constitution. The superintendent may either be elected by the people or appointed by the county board of education.

There are 58 counties in California and 58 county superintendents of schools: 53 are elected and five are appointed. Four of the superintendents are appointed by the County Board of Education and the Board of Supervisors appoints the Los Angeles County Superintendent. The five counties that appoint the superintendent include Los Angeles, Sacramento, San Diego, San Francisco, and Santa Clara.

The state legislature establishes the qualifications for the position; these vary with the size of the county. The qualifications for county superintendent, along with the duties and responsibilities of the office, are contained in Education Code Sections 1200 through 1281.

Parallel to the duties of the State Superintendent of Public Instruction are the responsibilities of the county superintendent of schools as *ex officio* secretary and executive officer of the county board of education. General duties of the county superintendent are contained in Section 1240 of the Education Code:

1. supervise the schools of his or her county
2. visit each school at reasonable intervals to observe its operation and learn of its problems and, if desired, present an annual report to the county board of education and the county board of supervisors
3. enforce the course of study with state-adopted elementary textbooks and high school textbooks regularly adopted by the proper authority
4. verify accuracy of data on the school accountability report card as to sufficiency of instruc-

tional materials and the safety, cleanliness, and adequacy of school facilities
5. take one of several actions to provide instructional materials where they are lacking
6. review within the first four weeks of each school year any school in the first through third deciles on the Academic Performance Index that is not already under review through a federal or state intervention program
7. submit two financial reports per year to the county board of education certifying that his or her office can meet its financial obligations for the current and subsequent fiscal year
8. for any district whose budget or audit had been in question, report to the governing board of that district and to the State Superintendent of Public Instruction as to the district's current fiscal solvency
9. report to the California Commission on Teacher Credentialing the identity of any certificated person who knowingly and willingly reports false fiscal expenditure data
10. distribute all laws, reports, circulars, instruction, and forms that he or she may receive for the use of school officers
11. deliver to his or her successor all documents belonging to the office.

The county superintendent was assigned significantly greater responsibility for school district budgets in 1991 with the passage of Assembly Bill 1200. This legislation gave the county superintendent authority to audit the expenditures and financial affairs of school districts in the county, as noted above.

## Local Boards of Education

In all states except Hawaii, state legislatures have delegated the day-to-day supervision and operation of schools to local boards of education. These boards have the authority granted to them by the state constitution and legislative action. Their responsibilities usually include developing and enforcing policies, employing personnel, and managing the financial affairs of the district. Actions of a local board must fall within the legal boundaries established by federal and state constitutions, statutes, and court decisions.

California's Education Code Section 35010 establishes control of school districts by a local governing board: "Every school district shall be under the control of a board of school trustees or a board of education." The general public typically uses the phrase "school boards" (Wenkart, 1995).

A school district's governing board may exercise its powers and must take all actions authorized or required only at properly noticed meetings open to the public (E.C. 35140, 35144, and 35145). Minutes shall be taken at each meeting of the board, and all actions taken by the governing board must be recorded in the minutes and made available to the public (E.C. 35145). Extensive statutory rules and regulations, enumerated in sections in the 35000 series of the Education Code, must be followed. The reader interested in this voluminous set of regulations is advised to review the relevant sections.

Education Code Section 35107 establishes eligibility for election or appointment as a member of a local school board. The requirements are as follows:

- eighteen years of age or older
- a citizen of California
- a resident of the district
- a registered voter
- not disqualified by the constitution or laws of the state from holding civil office.

School board elections are scheduled every two years, and board members are elected for a four-year term. Generally, the governing board of a school district has five members elected at large by the voters of the district. However, in certain instances a board may consist of three members or seven. For details regarding the number of members of the local board, see Education Code Section 35012.

Generally, school board elections are held the first Tuesday after the first Monday in November in odd-numbered years (E.C. 5000). Board members may be compensated for service. The key word in Section 35120 of the Education Code is "may." The board "may" approve a resolution establishing board compensation. Once compensation has been established, its amount is set by the Education Code, based on the size of the district. Compensation may range from $2,000 per month in Los Angeles Unified School District (average daily attendance of 400,000 or greater) to $60 per month in a district with less than 150 average daily attendance.

## School District Superintendents

The governing board of any school district that employs at least eight teachers may also employ a district superintendent, delegating specified duties to him or her (E.C. 35026). One of a board's most important responsibilities is to appoint a competent superintendent of schools. The superintendent is the executive officer of the school system, whereas the board is the legislative, policymaking body. Because the board consists of laypersons who are not experts in school management, it is the responsibility of the board to see that management of the district is properly performed by professional personnel.

The primary duties of a district superintendent are spelled out in Education Code Section 35035:

1. serve as chief executive officer of the governing board of the district
2. prepare and submit the district's budget to the governing board
3. make appropriate assignment of all district certificated employees
4. implement district policy regarding transfer of teachers from one site to another
5. ensure that employees in certificated positions hold the required credentials
6. enter into contracts for and on behalf of the district, subject to ratification of the governing board
7. submit required financial and budget reports.

A major function of the superintendent is to gather and present information so that school board members can make intelligent policy decisions. In addition, the superintendent is responsible for the day-to-day operation of the schools within the district and serves as the major public spokesperson for the schools. The superintendent advises the board and keeps members informed of the status of new legislation, student achievement, and fiscal and personnel matters. The larger the school district, the greater the reliance of a board on its superintendent.

The superintendent's powers are broad, and the duties many and diverse. The power and influence of the school superintendent vary greatly from district to district, depending upon several elements. These include the management style and personality of the individual who holds the position, the make-up of the local school board, the history and traditions of the district, the length of time the superintendent has held the position, the number of years remaining on his or her contract, and a variety of other factors. In some districts the relationship between the superintendent and board is tenuous. When there is continued disagreement or a major conflict over policy between the board and the superintendent, the superintendent is usually replaced.

As the above description suggests, the scope and style of superintendent leadership differ from district to district. Some individuals who hold the position are referred to as "strong superintendents." This phrase usually means that the superintendent makes managerial decisions in fiscal, personnel, and curriculum areas, fully expecting board support and approval. This type of superintendent is usually proactive, a take-charge individual who may not always wait for board approval prior to action. The strong superintendent may even present some decisions to the board for ratification or approval after the fact.

Other superintendents are referred to as "weak." This adjective usually means that the superintendent sees his or her role as simply to implement the directions of the board. With this leadership style, most significant decisions are made with prior board approval. Obviously, the contrast of strong with weak superintendents is just one means of demonstrating the great variance that exists in this leadership role. Most school superintendents probably fall near the middle of the continuum, being perceived as strong on some issues and less strong on others.

## Principals

Principals are often compared to middle managers in private industry. The man or woman who holds this position is responsible for the day-to-day management of the school. The scope of the leadership role of the principal is broad. In addition to daily management of the myriad activities of students, teachers, and staff, a principal is expected to provide leadership in curriculum, personnel, and school finance. On any given day, the activities of a principal may range from supervising bus duty in the morning to attending a town meeting in the evening in hopes of influencing the fate of a bond election.

Basic leadership research confirms that if the policies established by the state legislature, State Superintendent of Public Instruction, and the local board and superintendent are to be successfully implemented, it is the leadership ability of the principal that will make it happen.

## Summary

This chapter has described the governance of education from the state level to school district management. Discussion of the several governmental entities clarifies their roles and responsibilities in school governance. For example, the state legislature, state board of education, county boards of education, and local school district governing boards are all legislative bodies that set policy.

However, responsibility for managing schools and school districts resides with the executive branch of the government, which is to say the State Superintendent of Public Instruction, the several county superintendents, and superintendents and principals in local districts. All these entities have responsibility for implementing the statutes and court decisions affecting schools. However, just as the lines of authority and responsibility are not always clear among the Congress, federal courts, and the President, the lines for governance of schools are sometimes unclear as well.

## *Key Terms*

1. Assembly Bill 1200
2. board minutes
3. California Board of Education
4. county board of education
5. county superintendent of schools
6. governing board
7. school principal
8. school superintendent
9. State Superintendent of Public Instruction
10. waiver

## Discussion/Essay Questions

1. A county superintendent of schools has a major role in providing services to local school districts. What do you consider to be the most important service provided by the county superintendent? Why?

2. What are the qualifications for election or appointment to a school board? Do you think any qualifications should be changed or added? If so, please discuss your suggested changes.

3. School board members may be compensated for services as a board member. Do you agree or disagree with this concept? State your rationale for this answer.

4. The State Superintendent of Public Instruction in California is an elected position. Do you believe that an elected state superintendent provides the best service for students, or would services improve if the position were appointed by the state board of education? Give the rationale for your answer.

5. There is a high rate of turnover in the office of school district superintendent. Discuss at least three reasons for this phenomenon.

# CHAPTER 4

# Student Citizenship and Discipline

*Collaborative rule-making promotes mutual respect, cooperation, self-discipline and personal responsibility.*

—David Schimmel, Collaborative Rule-Making and Citizenship Education

## Introduction

Since 1969, Phi Delta Kappan has conducted a yearly poll of the public's attitudes toward public schools. Student discipline was at the top of the list of problems facing the schools for 16 of the first 17 years of the polls. In 2004, student discipline dropped to second place and has stayed in second place through the 2014 polling. Financing public education has had the number one spot since 2004 (Bushaw & McNee, 2014).

If you ask 10 parents and 10 students to define student citizenship and discipline, you are likely to receive 10 very different answers. This chapter includes a discussion of the rights of students and the actions of elected officials, school administrators, and teachers to ensure good student citizenship and safety for all students.

All students have the right to a free public education. At first this statement seems straightforward and unambiguous. As one imagines an array of students representing various learning needs and personal goals, however, that simple principle becomes challenging, complex, and open to a variety of interpretations. Federal and state legislative bodies have produced voluminous laws in an attempt to clarify the meaning of "free public education." At one time in the nation's history, females and various ethnic groups were excluded from such education. Currently, the nature of free appropriate public education for bilingual students and immigrants is strongly debated. The amount of education has also been subject to interpretation: Does the concept extend to preschool and kindergarten? Should public education end only after eighth grade, twelfth grade, two years of college,

a bachelor's or master's degree, or even the doctorate?

Curriculum content has also been the subject of much debate. Should free public education be limited to basic skills of reading, writing, and arithmetic? What about the study of religion, sex education, the arts, etc.? This debate has not been resolved. These issues are often of major concern to parents, citizens, school boards, educators, legislators, and the courts. However important they may be, in recent years these concerns have been overshadowed by a frightening and urgent worry: how to ensure a student's right to attend a school that is safe and free of violence.

Among Webster's definitions of "discipline" are two opposing views of student discipline. One category includes teaching to develop self-control, character, orderliness, and efficiency. Another definition includes the acceptance or submission to authority. A final part of the definition associated with school discipline is the consequence of a student not reaching the standards of the first two. That definition is simply stated as "to punish" (Guralnik, 1968).

Surely, student discipline has been of concern to parents, citizens, and teachers since the first teacher began to teach. Books about the "Little Red School House" contain references to student bullying, fighting, and the boy who dipped the girl's pigtail into the ink well.

While a few schools had the reputation of being a "violent place," the U.S. and the world were exposed to unprecedented school violence on April 20, 1999. On that date, millions of viewers watched in horror the massacre at Columbine High School, Littleton, Colorado. Two teenage students carried out a shooting rampage by killing 12 fellow students, a teacher, and wounded 24 others, prior to taking their own lives.

Politicians, educators, and the general public were horrified and searched for answers as to why this tragedy occurred. Gun control, violent movies, video games, school cliques, and tougher discipline measures were debated. Some suggested that Columbine was an anomaly and was not likely to happen again. That illusion was discredited when in 2001, 14-year-old Andy Williams shot and killed two classmates and wounded 13 others. This event took place at Santana High School in Santee, California. Williams is now serving a 50-year prison term. The next shooting was in 2005 at Red Lake High School in Minnesota. A student shot a teacher and security guard and wounded seven others.

The violence reflected by the three massacres is not necessarily a predictor of future violent crime at schools. The National Center for Education Statistics (NCES, 2006) reports that the school violent crime rate declined from 48 violent crimes per 1,000 students in 1992 to 28 in 2003.

The NCES reports that in 2003, 12–18-year-old students were victims of about 740,000 violent crimes and 1.2 million crimes of theft. Seven percent of students, ages 12–18, said they had been bullied while 29% reported that drugs were offered to them on school grounds. Nine percent said they were threatened or injured with a weapon while on school property. Less than one percent reported rape, sexual assault, or robbery.

Teachers, too, are victims of violence at school. Between 1999 and 2003, teachers were the victims of 183,000 crimes at school. There were 119,000 thefts and 64,000 crimes of rape, sexual assault, and robbery. On average, these numbers translate into an annual rate of 39 crimes per 1,000 teachers (NCES, 2005).

Contributing to this situation, of course, are such factors as alcohol and drug use and gang activity. Among urban students, 29% reported that gang activity extended into their schools; 29% reported they had been offered, purchased, or were given an illegal drug while on campus; and 5% of high schoolers had imbibed alcohol at school within the month prior to the survey (DeVoe, Peter, Kaufman, et al., 2003).

Reports continue to state that one-fifth of teachers leave the profession within three years. A study published by the Center for the Study of Teaching and Policy at the University of Washington (Ingersoll, 2001) indicates that student discipline is one of four major factors that contribute to this turnover.

## America's Response to School Citizenship Problems

Americans are sharply divided on how students, both in and out of school, should be disciplined and controlled. Parents, citizens, legislative bodies, and the courts have responded to the concern over student citizenship in a variety of ways. On the one hand, the U.S.

Supreme Court appears to give schools great latitude in disciplining students, while at the same time asserting, as in *Tinker v. Des Moines Independent Community School District* (1969), that children in school are persons who do not shed their constitutional rights at the schoolhouse door. In this landmark case, the Supreme Court ruled in a seven-to-two decision that the district could not ban black armbands worn by students in protest against the Vietnam War.

## The Principle of Substantial Disruption

*Tinker* specifically held that schools cannot suppress speech "because of an undifferentiated fear or apprehension of disturbance." To justify suppression of a student's right to free speech, the court ruled that a school must prove that the student's First Amendment exercise would "materially and substantially" disrupt the school program. This case is discussed in greater detail in chapter 5.

The Supreme Court further clarified the material and substantial disruption standard in *Bethel School District No. 403 v. Fraser* (1986). In that case, a high school student gave a speech before the student body that was full of graphic and sexually explicit language. The student had been warned regarding the inappropriateness of the speech. Fraser, the high school student, received a three-day suspension for violating a school rule prohibiting the use of obscene language. The court found a marked distinction between the student's speech in Fraser and the students' armbands in Tinker. Fraser's speech, the court determined, did not merit First Amendment protection. Therefore, school administrators had the authority to suppress his free speech rights. The court concluded, "It is a highly appropriate function of a public school education to prohibit the use of vulgar and offensive terms in public discourse."

In 1994 a California court decided that schools can discipline students for inappropriate behavior that could lead to further disruption (*Lovell v. Poway Unified School District*, 1994). Lovell, a high school student, allegedly threatened to shoot a counselor. The court decided that in order to support an expulsion or suspension, the statement must indicate that the student possesses an intent to harm or assault. In the Lovell case, the court could find no such intent. Nontheless, the court stated that a school board could impose boundaries on a student's free speech rights by prohibiting threats of physical injury.

A 1995 Supreme Court ruling, *Vernonia School District v. Acton,* affirmed the constitutionality of giving schools the right to search students. Judge Scalia wrote that "the expectation of privacy of minors is not as great as that of adults." He cited mandatory physical examinations and vaccinations by public schools as "legitimate intrusions." He further added, "A 'reasonable' search does not have to be the least intrusive search in order to pass muster under the Fourth Amendment."

The question facing policy leaders in this country is how to achieve safe schools and at what cost to the nation's taxpayers. Educators have proposed a multitude of solutions to the problem. A highly favored proposal made by teachers is reduction of class size so they can devote greater attention to correcting student misbehavior. Other stakeholders have advocated funding for both preschool and parent education and an increased number of counselors and psychologists at school sites. A strong plea has been made for resources to support development of new programs to cope with misconduct by younger students at elementary schools.

## Zero Tolerance

The campus aide escorted ninth-grade student Mary Jane to the office of Ms. Jones, assistant principal. Ms. Jones said, "Mary Jane (MJ), what happened?" MJ, "Nothing." Ms. Jones, "Nothing?" "Sarah called me a slut." Ms. Jones, "What did you do?" "I hit her." Jones, "Do you know what happens when you get in a fight on campus?" "I don't know." Jones, "Did you get a copy of the school rules?" MJ, "Don't know." Jones, "Did your counselor tell you the penalty for fighting?" MJ, "She said something." Jones, "The penalty for fighting is three days suspension from school; do you know what that is?"

MJ's suspension is an example of zero tolerance in a California school. MJ got in a fight at school and was automatically suspended. Student suspensions happen every day in California and in schools all across the United States. Zero tolerance initially was defined as "consistently enforced suspension and expulsion policies in response to weapons, drugs, and violent acts at school." Over time, zero tolerance has come to refer to school or district-wide policies that mandate predetermined punishment for a wide variety of rule violations.

Zero tolerance in schools became popular as early as the 1970s, and was largely confined to major infractions such as bringing guns or drugs on campus. Over time, however, it expanded to less egregious offenses such as school uniform violations, bringing cigarettes on campus, or talking back to a teacher.

Supporters of zero tolerance argued that swift discipline measures keep students safe and ensure a productive school and classroom environment. Administrators see zero tolerance as fast-acting intervention that sends a clear, consistent message that certain behavior is not acceptable.

In 1982, Joe Clark, principal of Eastside High School in New Jersey, became famous for suspending students for disrespect, fighting, and vulgarity. His toughness landed him on the cover of *Time Magazine* and he became the subject of a movie starring Morgan Freeman. Clark was only a little ahead of his time. Pressure became strong for schools to adopt what became known as zero tolerance, a term associated with President Reagan's antidrug effort.

In 1994, the U.S. Congress approved the Gun-Free Schools Act, which required all schools that receive federal money to expel all students who bring a gun to school. The law is believed to be the catalyst for what became the practice for schools to expel students for much lower level misbehavior.

In 1999, the Columbine High School shootings resulted in greater fear by the public and the expansion of student misconduct punishment under the preview of zero tolerance with a greater number of students suspended or expelled from school.

In 2012, authors from the Civil Rights Project at the University of California reported that 3.5 million public school students were suspended at least once in 2011-12. That is more than one student suspended for every public school teacher in America. To put this number in perspective, the number of students suspended in just one school year could fill all of the stadium seats for all the Super Bowls ever played (Losen, 2015).

After millions of "get tough" suspensions and expulsions, educators, school boards, and state legislatures started looking for an alternative method of ensuring school safety and keeping students in school. At the same time, research and public positions by psychologists, physicians, and teacher unions denounced zero tolerance as harmful to students academically and socially. The U.S. Department of Education also reported that this type of discipline disproportionately affects student who are black, Latino, or male. To reduce the number of suspensions and expulsions, the California Department of Education hosted workshops and posted behavioral intervention strategies on its website.

This push by the state and other interest groups began to show results in California. Statewide, suspensions decreased by 14 percent in 2012-13, and another 20 percent in 2013-14 from 329,370 to 279,383. Districts throughout the state experienced a drop in expulsions and suspensions. The Santa Maria School District's expulsion rates dropped 33 percent, and 11 percent fewer students were suspended in 2013-14. The district's assistant superintendent said, "Sending students home is not the first option, as it was for many years" (Lanham, 2014).

In 2014, the tide turned against zero tolerance in California with passage of Assembly Bill 420, which eliminates willful defiance or disruption of school activities as a reason to expel students. This bill also prevents administrators from using "willful defiance" to suspend K-3 students. California is now the first state in the nation to curtail suspension and expulsions for minor misbehavior. Assemblyman Roger Dickinson, who introduced the bill, said, "Kids who have been suspended or expelled are two times more likely to drop out and five times more likely to turn to crime" (Frey, 2014).

In 2013, all California school districts were encouraged to improve school climate as part of the state's Local Control Accountability Plan (LCAP). Schools were required to develop specific goals, actions, and expenditures to address suspension and expulsion rates. A state organization, Fight Crime: Invest in Kids (FCIK) evaluated the LCAPs for the 50 largest districts in the state. The organization found that 92 percent of the districts included goals to decrease suspension rates; however, FCIK (2015) found that many districts did not provide specific details of how the goal would be accomplished.

The remainder of this chapter focuses on student behavior and discipline measures to ensure a safe and orderly campus. Such measures are employed by teachers, administrators, and school boards to ensure well-managed classrooms where students can study and learn without peer misconduct distractions.

## Student Discipline

"Student discipline starts at home." Although there is little disagreement with this statement among most Americans, parents and educators are engaged in a great debate about expectations for student citizenship.

Student fighting is a good example. Every principal is confronted at one time or another by a parent who, when his or her child has been in a fight, proclaims that the student has always been told to "punch out" a student who calls him a name or pushes him while in the lunch line. Both teachers and administrators have heard the parent of a perennially tardy student exclaim, "I just can't get her to school on time!"

More students than ever enter school suffering from emotional and physical neglect. In many cases, little citizenship education has been provided in the home. Respect for privacy or property and the general rules of civility seem virtually unknown to many children and their parents. Children who enter school from such environments are a challenge to the teacher and the school system. Their disregard for school rules makes it difficult for a teacher to teach and for other students to learn.

Those who attribute increasing student misbehavior to lack of supervision have many statistics to cite. For example, as noted in an article in the *Los Angeles Times*, the proportion of single-parent families nearly doubled between 1970 and 1995, from 13% to 24%. U.S. census data show that the number continued a slow rise to 27.8% in 2002. This represented four out of every ten children. In just one generation the number of children born out of wedlock increased five times. Finally, "a leading social scientist says American parents spend about 40% less time with their children than did parents of a generation ago" (Marshall, 1995).

## Rules and Procedures

Clear, consistently enforced expectations and rules are necessary for effective classroom management and instruction. Teachers have always established classroom rules, but as society has become more complex, schools and local school boards have written policies to regulate student behavior. State legislatures, too, have become more prescriptive in setting expectations for student conduct. For example, the California Education Code, Section 233.5(a), provides general guidance regarding the teaching of morals, manners, and citizenship.

Each teacher shall endeavor to impress upon the minds of the pupils the principles of morality, truth, justice, patriotism, and a true comprehension of the rights, duties, and dignity of American citizenship, and the meaning of equality and human dignity, including the promotion of harmonious relations, kindness toward domestic pets and the humane treatment of living creatures, to teach them to avoid idleness, profanity, and falsehood, and to instruct them in manners and morals and the principles of a free government.

This code section was amended in 1994 when the legislature added the following:

Each teacher is also encouraged to create and foster an environment that encourages pupils to realize their full potential and that is free from discriminatory attitudes, practices, events, or activities, in order to prevent acts of hate violence.

To assist teachers in achieving this lofty objective, Section 48908 requires all pupils to submit to the authority of teachers.

The California legislature calls upon each school, "at its discretion," to adopt rules and procedures for student discipline once every four years, (E.C. 35291.5). This code section requires input from a representative chosen by each of the following: parents, teachers, administrators, and school security personnel. At junior and senior high schools, student input is also required. The rules must be consistent with state law and district policy. The final set of rules is to be approved by the principal or designee and a representative selected by classroom teachers. After the rules are adopted, the principal is required to provide parents with a copy of them at the beginning of each school year.

The California Administrative Code (Title V) also provides direction for student conduct:

Every pupil shall attend school punctually and regularly; conform to the regulations of the school; obey promptly all the directions of his teacher and others in authority; observe good order and propriety of deportment; be diligent in study, respectful to his teacher and others in authority, kind and courteous to schoolmates; and refrain entirely from the use of profane and vulgar language.

Title V regulations also address such issues as student cleanliness, dress, and care of property:

A pupil who goes to school without proper attention to personal cleanliness or neatness of dress may be sent home to be properly prepared for school, or shall be required to prepare himself for the schoolroom before entering.

A pupil who defaces, damages, or destroys any school property or willfully or negligently injures another pupil or school employee is liable to suspension or expulsion, according to the nature of the offense.

## In Loco Parentis

Teachers and school districts are granted wide discretion in disciplining students by the courts. The legal doctrine that defines the relationship of a teacher to a pupil is *in loco parentis* (Latin for "in place of parent").

The California legislature elaborated the principle of *in loco parentis* in Section 44807 of the Education Code:

Every teacher in the public schools shall hold pupils to a strict account for their conduct on the way to and from school, on the playgrounds, or during recess. A teacher, vice principal, principal, or any other certificated employee of a school district, shall not be subject to criminal prosecution or criminal penalties for the exercise, during the performance of his duties, of the same degree of physical control over a pupil that a parent would be legally privileged to exercise but which in no event shall exceed the amount of physical control reasonably necessary to maintain order, protect property, or protect the health and safety of pupils, or to maintain proper and appropriate conditions conducive to learning.

This section concludes with reference to Section 49000, which forbids corporal punishment.

## Parent Support

"If you get in trouble at school, you will be in bigger trouble at home." Most adults over age 40 are familiar with this admonition from parents. For many decades, this warning assisted teachers and principals in maintaining proper citizenship in classrooms and schools. However, at some point in the nation's history, the partnership between parents and teachers began to diminish.

Scholars who study children and their performance in schools attribute the decrease in parental support for teachers and schools to a variety of factors. Sociologists may charge this lack of cooperation between schools and parents to an increased number of mothers who are members of the labor force, thus no longer available to supervise their children. Fathers who still live in the two-parent home also seem to have less time for the child. A recent study found that more than half the fathers questioned were spending less than five minutes with their children on a typical workday (Marshall, 1995).

Psychologists may cite the increase in drug use among parents and students as a cause of increased student misbehavior. They may also identify an increase in the number of students who are living in one-parent homes as a cause of reduced supervision of students. Political scientists attribute an increase in student misbehavior to loss of respect for schools along with loss of respect for all governmental agencies.

While scholars will long debate the reasons for the decrease in student and parent respect for teachers, seasoned teachers testify that it has occurred. They also confirm that it is more difficult to gain the cooperation of parents when disciplining a misbehaving child than it once was. They verify that it is more difficult to motivate many parents to attend conferences and to respond to telephone calls or written notices.

Many teachers feel that attempting to contact parents about student misbehavior is non-productive. One reason is that, with the increase in one-parent families and mothers employed outside the home, teachers find they cannot readily reach a parent by phone. Arranging parent conferences to discuss student academic achievement or student behavior is also difficult. Secondly, a note sent home with the student, or even through the mail, often does not reach the parent's hand. Finally, if contact is achieved, many parents are unable to provide much assistance in coping with an unruly student. Due to their personal or professional situation, many parents are unable to supervise the student consistently or to offer incentives for improved citizenship.

## Corrective Behavior and/or Punishment

If a student breaks the rules, misbehaves, or disrupts the educational program, what action can a teacher, principal, or the school board utilize for correction or punishment? Even with the legal doctrine of *in loco parentis*, the school's authority is limited. In fact, in most states, the classroom teacher is limited to verbal admonitions and reprimands, detention, contacting parents of the child, corporal punishment, and referral to the principal. Moreover, a California teacher is prohibited from corporal punishment as a means of correcting student misconduct (E.C. 49000). The California teacher also has limited ability to suspend a student when misconduct occurs (E.C. 48910).

There is general recognition that the principal is a key figure in maintaining an orderly and safe school. Therefore, the principal has been given greater authority than a teacher to suspend or recommend expulsion of a student as a disciplinary measure.

A superintendent of schools has additional authority, beyond that of a principal, for dealing with disruptive students. He or she may transfer such students, age sixteen or older, to a continuation school. The superintendent also has the power to recommend expulsion of a student (E.C. 48432.5). Finally, the board of education has the authority to expel a student from the jurisdiction of the school district (E.C. 48900). Students and parents must be granted due process in each of these procedures.

## Detention

Detention is defined as keeping a child in the classroom or another designated place before school, at recess, during lunch, or after school. The courts have routinely upheld the right of teachers and principals to impose detention on unruly and nonattending students. The teacher is usually responsible for supervising the student during the detention period. However, it has become a common practice in many middle and secondary schools to have a separate room, with a separate staff member, for this purpose.

The teacher's right to assign detention varies from state to state. In California, teachers are prohibited from utilizing detention during recess or the lunch hour. An exception to this limitation is possible if a governing board has adopted rules and regulations authorizing the teacher to restrict for disciplinary purposes the time a student is allowed for recess (E.C. 44807.5). Some schools require students who have misbehaved to stay in the principal's office or another designated area during a portion of the recess period.

In many school districts, teachers are required to give the parent at least one day's notice prior to the student staying for after-school detention. After-school detention is limited to one hour, and a student may not be detained if he or she would miss regular bus transportation.

## Corporal Punishment

Corporal punishment is prohibited in most of the industrial world, but it is allowed in the United States. It is interesting to note that it is not allowed in the military, prisons, or mental institutions, but 19 states do allow this type of student punishment. While the greatest proportion of the states that allow it are southern states, others are in the western and middle states (Strauss, 2014).

In the landmark Supreme Court decision *Ingraham v. Wright* (1977), the court held that corporal punishment of students violates neither the Eighth Amendment nor the due process guarantees of the Fourteenth Amendment. The court said the Eighth Amendment's prohibition of cruel and unusual punishment applies to criminals only and is not applicable to disciplining students in public schools.

While the merit of utilizing corporal punishment to promote proper student citizenship and correct misbehavior will continue to be debated, this method of discipline is not available to California teachers and administrators. In 1986 Section 49001 was added to the California Education Code to prohibit physical punishment: "No person employed by or engaged in a public school shall inflict, or cause to be inflicted corporal punishment upon a pupil." Section 49000 presents the rationale of the legislature for prohibiting corporal punishment:

> The Legislature finds and declares that the protection against corporal punishment, which extends to other citizens in other walks of life, should include children while they are under the control of the public schools. Children of school age are at the most vulnerable and impressionable period of their lives and it is wholly reasonable that the safeguards to the integrity and sanctity of their bodies should be, at this tender age, at least equal to that afforded to other citizens.

The legislature clarified that prohibition of corporal punishment did not preclude teachers and school administrators from utilizing reasonable force to quell a disturbance. Reasonable force can be used when a student is threatening physical injury to another student or a teacher. Reasonable force may also be used when there is a threat to school property. A student's voluntary participation in athletics that results in physical pain was also excluded from the definition of corporal punishment (E.C. 49001).

## California's Suspension Laws

The California legislature has been more prescriptive than many other states in specifying types of misbehav-

ior or misconduct for which suspension or expulsion of students is allowed. In 1983 the legislature specified twelve acts for which a student may be suspended from school by a teacher, principal or superintendent. These have subsequently been expanded, the most recent additions involving sexual harassment and sexual assault and battery; hate violence; "terroristic" threats; harassing a student complainant or witness in a disciplinary procedure; harassment, threats, or intimidation with the intent of disrupting the school or invading the rights of another pupil; and carrying an imitation firearm that looks like the real thing (E.C. 48900 through 48900.7).

The reader needs to keep in mind that Education Code 48900 was amended in 2014 by Assembly Bill 420 (discussed previously). The amendment eliminates willful defiance or disruption of school activities as a reason to expel students. The administrator may not suspend K-3 students for those offenses.

Although either suspension or expulsion may result from the same misconduct, only a school board has authority to expel a student. Expulsion procedures will be discussed in a later section of this chapter. As the reader would expect, the grounds for suspension and expulsion were written by attorneys and are legal in nature. For purposes of this text, the grounds for suspension and expulsion are simplified and rearranged into groups according to the nature of the offense. As an administrator charged with the responsibility for suspending a student or recommending expulsion, one should review the actual Education Code sections. Students may be suspended or expelled if—on school grounds, going to or from school or a school-sponsored activity, or during the lunch hour, whether on campus or off—they have been involved with

- personal violence
  - attempting, threatening, or causing physical injury or willfully using force against another person, except in self-defense
  - attempting, threatening, causing, or participating in hate violence
  - attempting or committing sexual assault or committing sexual battery

- extortion or harassment
  - attempting or committing extortion
  - making terrorist-like threats against school officials or school property
  - harassing, threatening, or intimidating a pupil who is a complainant or witness in a school disciplinary proceeding

- intentionally engaging in harassment, threats, or intimidation with the actual and reasonably expected effect of materially disrupting class-work, creating substantial disorder, or invading the rights of other pupils
  - engaging in sexual harassment
  - engaging in hazing
- dangerous objects
  - possessing, selling, or otherwise furnishing any firearm, knife, explosive, or other dangerous object
  - possessing an imitation, but realistic, firearm
- drugs, alcohol, or tobacco
  - unlawfully possessing, using, selling, or otherwise furnishing, or being under the influence of a controlled substance, an alcoholic beverage, or an intoxicant of any kind
  - unlawfully offering, arranging, or negotiating to sell and then selling, delivering, or furnishing any controlled substance, alcoholic beverage, intoxicant, or material represented as such a substance
  - unlawfully offering, arranging, negotiating to sell, or selling any prescription drug.
  - unlawfully possessing, offering, arranging, or negotiating to sell drug paraphernalia
  - possessing or using tobacco or products containing tobacco or nicotine
- damage to or theft of property
  - attempting or committing robbery
  - stealing or attempting to steal school or private property
  - knowingly receiving stolen school or private property
  - damaging or attempting to damage school or private property
- disruptive or vulgar behavior
  - committing an obscene act or engaging in habitual profanity or vulgarity
  - disrupting school activities or otherwise willfully defying the valid authority of supervisors, teachers, administrators, school officials, or other school personnel engaged in the performance of their duties.

It is interesting to note that despite the careful attention devoted to the language in the suspension and expulsion laws, parents and attorneys continue to seek loopholes. For example, the Superintendent of the Vista Unified School District asked the assemblyman of that district to plug a potential loophole by drafting a bill that would add bomb threats to the list of expellable offenses. Superintendent Jack Gyves made this request after the district had received a number of bomb threats, and a parent made an issue of the fact that there was no specific language in the Education Code forbidding such threats. Gyves said, "95% of the time they're pranks, but when you're emptying a high school of 2,600 students, there are all kinds of opportunity for injury, panic, whatever" (de Vise, 1996).

## Suspension from School

Suspension from school is defined as removal of a student from ongoing instruction for adjustment purposes (E.C. 48925). Suspension is one of the most widely used measures of disciplining students, especially at the secondary level. The length of time for suspensions ranges from state to state, usually not exceeding ten days. California limits the maximum length of a single suspension to five days (E.C. 48911), although there are some exceptions. For example, a student who is being recommended to the school board for expulsion may be suspended while the expulsion is being considered. A longer suspension is also possible when the presence of the pupil constitutes a danger to persons or property or threatens to disrupt the instructional process or if a student is truly dangerous.

In contrast to detailed procedures for the expulsion of a student, state statutes are less specific regarding the procedures that should be followed when suspending students from school. Prior to 1975, procedural due process accorded to suspended students was poorly defined. Lower courts differed widely in their interpretation of Fourteenth Amendment guarantees in suspension cases. In 1975, however, the U.S. Supreme Court prescribed the minimum constitutional requirements in cases involving student suspension of ten days or less (*Goss v. Lopez*, 1975).

The court concluded that a student should be given an oral or written notice of the charge and, if he or she denies the charge, an opportunity to provide an explanation of the evidence. Compliance with these requirements would meet the due process requirement for a brief suspension. For suspensions, the court specifically rejected the usual trial-type format that would include involvement of attorneys and presentation and cross-examination of adverse witnesses, as is typical in criminal cases.

The courts give school districts considerable latitude in use of suspensions to maintain discipline. For example, *Abella v. Riverside Unified School District* (1976) established the following authority for California school districts:

> A school district has the authority to maintain discipline in the schools and to that end, may suspend or expel a pupil who refuses or neglects to obey any rules prescribed pursuant to the Education Code as long as the authority is exercised in a manner that will satisfy the statutory and constitutional standards for disciplinary proceedings.

## Legislative Guidelines and Limitations for Suspensions and Expulsions

Even with the wide latitude granted by the courts to use suspensions to correct student misbehavior, some limitations are placed on a principal or superintendent when suspending or expelling students. Authority with regard to the location of the offense is broad: A student may be suspended or expelled for misbehavior related to school activity or attendance while on school grounds; while going to or coming from school; during the lunch period whether on or off the campus; and during, or while going to or coming from, a school-sponsored activity. However, the act states that application of suspension or expulsion is not limited to these four situations.

On the other hand, the legislature placed a limitation on school boards and administrators by declaring its intent that alternatives to suspension and expulsion should be imposed for students who are truant, tardy, or absent from school activities (E.C. 48900). When E.C. 48900.6 was added in 1993, principals and superintendents were presented with one such alternative—authority to require a student to perform community service on school grounds during non-school hours in lieu of suspension. Community service could include work in the areas of outdoor beautification, campus betterment, and teacher or peer assistance programs.

With a few exceptions, districts may not suspend a student for more than twenty school days in any school year. Exceptions may occur if a student enrolls in or is transferred to another regular school, an opportunity school or class, or a continuation education school or class. In these cases, the maximum number of days a student may be suspended is increased to thirty within a school year (E.C. 48903). A governing board may also suspend a student enrolled in a continuation school or class for the remainder of the semester. Depending

upon when the offense occurred, this time limit may exceed twenty days (E.C. 48912.5).

The legislature provided direction to school officials by stating that suspensions and expulsions are not to be used as the primary means of student discipline. In this regard, Education Code Section 48900.5 contains the following guideline: "Suspension shall be imposed only when other means of correction fail to bring about proper conduct." However, a student may be suspended for any of the reasons enumerated in subsections (a) through (e) of Section 48900 (items 1, 4, 10, 12, 13, and 17 in our list on page 35), even upon a first offense, if the principal or superintendent determines that the student's presence on campus causes a danger to persons or property or threatens to disrupt the instructional process.

## Suspension by a Teacher

A teacher may suspend any student from his or her class when a student commits any of the acts set out in Section 48900 (see above). A teacher's suspension is limited to the day of the suspension and the following day. The teacher is required to report the suspension immediately and send the pupil to the principal for appropriate action. In addition, the teacher is required to ask the parent or guardian of the student for a conference regarding the suspension (E.C. 48910).

If suspension by the teacher requires a student to remain at the school site, the school district is responsible for providing appropriate supervision. A student suspended from a class shall not be placed in another regular class during the period of suspension. However, if the pupil is assigned to more than one class per day, the student may be permitted to attend other classes.

In the case of suspension by a teacher, the student may not return to that class during the period of the suspension without concurrence of the teacher and principal. A teacher may require a suspended student to complete any assignments and tests missed during the suspension (E.C. 48913).

## Suspension Procedures

Prior to student suspension the principal is required to complete the following procedures:

1. A principal or superintendent is required to conduct a conference. Whenever practicable, the teacher, supervisor, or school employee who referred the student should be present. At the

conference, the pupil is to be informed of the reason for disciplinary action and the evidence against him or her. The student must also be given the opportunity to present his or her version and evidence in his or her defense (E.C. 48911). An exception to this requirement is possible when the principal determines that an emergency situation exists. An emergency situation is defined in Section 48911 of the Education Code as "a clear and present danger to the life, safety, or health of pupils or school personnel."

2. At the time of the suspension, a school employee shall make a reasonable effort to contact the student's parent or guardian in person or by telephone. Whenever a student is suspended from school, the parent or guardian must be notified in writing of the suspension.

3. The suspension and its cause must be reported to the superintendent or the school board.

4. If the principal requests a parent conference, the parent or guardian shall respond to that request without delay. However, no penalties may be imposed on a student for failure of the student's parent or guardian to attend the conference.

5. In a case where expulsion of a student is being recommended, and the student's presence on campus constitutes a danger to persons or property or threatens disruption of the instructional process, the district may extend the suspension until the governing board has rendered a decision on the action. The parent must be notified in writing of the extended suspension.

# California's Expulsion Laws

## Expulsions

Suspensions are of a limited nature; the student is still under the supervision of the parent and the school district. An expulsion, however, is defined as the separation of the student from the supervision of the school district. Expulsion is an action vested exclusively in the board of education. Unless authorized by state statute, school superintendents and principals do not have authority to expel a student.

Courts have held that expulsion of students from school jeopardizes a student's property interest in an education. Therefore, students who are considered for expulsion are guaranteed at least minimum due process under the Fourteenth Amendment.

## Expellable Offenses

As discussed earlier, the specific acts for which students may be suspended from school are also violations that may result in expulsion from the district. The school board may expel students upon the first offense for causing physical injury to another person, possessing or selling weapons, possessing or selling illegal drugs, or committing robbery or extortion. However, the administrator must first determine that the pupil's presence on campus causes a danger to persons or property or threatens to disrupt the instructional process (E.C. 48900.5).

The board may also expel a student who has damaged or stolen school property, possessed or used tobacco, committed an obscene act, had possession of drug paraphernalia, disrupted school activities, or received school property if the board finds that other means of correction are not feasible, or have repeatedly failed to bring about proper conduct, and that due to the nature of the violation, the presence of the pupil causes a continuing danger to the physical safety of the student or others (E.C. 48915).

## Mandatory Recommendation for Expulsion

For some offenses a recommendation for expulsion by the principal or superintendent is mandatory. These offenses include:

1. causing serious physical injury to another person, except in self-defense
2. possession of any knife, explosive, or other dangerous object of no reasonable use to the pupil
3. unlawful possession of any controlled substance (except for a first offense involving sale of not more than one avoirdupois ounce of marijuana, other than concentrated cannabis)
4. robbery or extortion
5. assault or battery.

These offenses are listed in E.C. 48915. For these acts, the only possible exception to a mandatory recommendation for expulsion occurs if the principal or superintendent finds and reports in writing to the governing board that expulsion is inappropriate due to the circumstances.

A superintendent or principal must immediately suspend and then recommend expulsion when a student

1. possesses or furnishes a firearm (except in case of prior written permission)
2. brandishes a knife

3. unlawfully sells a controlled substance
4. attempts sexual assault or commits sexual assault or battery
5. possesses an explosive.

The student may not continue enrollment at a comprehensive secondary school or on the site where the offense took place, but is to be referred to an appropriate educational program (E.C. 48915).

## Expulsion of Students with Exceptional Needs

In the case of a student enrolled in a special education program, the Education Code places several conditions on a governing board. These conditions, which must be satisfied prior to consideration of expulsion of a student enrolled in a special education program, are as follows:

1. The school or district is required to conduct an individualized education program (IEP) team meeting.
2. The IEP team must determine that the misconduct was neither caused by nor was a direct manifestation of the pupil's identified disability.
3. The team must determine that the pupil had been appropriately placed at the time the misconduct occurred (E.C. 48915.5).

Provisions regarding students enrolled in special education are contained in Education Code Sections 48915.5, which references applicable federal law and regulations.

The reauthorization of the Individuals with Disabilities Education Act, signed into law in December 2004, allows schools to consider unique circumstances that might justify placing the student in an alternative setting. The time period for such a placement has been extended from 45 calendar to 45 school days. A student may be removed immediately for inflicting serious bodily injury while at school or a school function (Council, 2004). Special education students may also be suspended up to 45 days for bringing a weapon or drugs to school (California School Boards, 2004).

## The Expulsion Hearing

Education Code Section 48918 specifies the procedures for conducting expulsion hearings. The basic steps are enumerated below.

1. A hearing is required within thirty school days of the date the principal or superintendent determines that the pupil has committed any of the acts enumerated in Section 48900. A student and his parents are entitled, upon written request, to at least one postponement of the hearing for not more than thirty calendar days.
2. The pupil shall be entitled to a hearing to determine whether he or she shall be expelled. Written notice of the hearing shall be forwarded to the parent or guardian at least ten calendar days prior to the date of the hearing. The written notice shall contain the following information:
   a. the date and place of the hearing
   b. a statement of the specific facts and charges upon which the proposed expulsion is based
   c. a copy of the disciplinary rules of the district that relate to the alleged violation
   d. a notice to the student or the student's parent or guardian informing them of the right to appear in person or to be represented by counsel or a non-attorney advisor
   e. the right to inspect and obtain copies of all documents to be used at the hearing
   f. the right to confront and question all evidence presented

With respect to provision (f), the board, hearing officer, or administrative panel may, upon good cause, determine that the disclosure of the identity of a witness and the testimony of that witness would subject the witness to an unreasonable risk of harm. Upon this determination, the testimony of the witness may be presented at the hearing in the form of sworn declarations, which shall be examined only by the governing board, hearing officer, or administrative panel. Copies of these sworn declarations, edited to delete the name and identity of the witness, shall be made available to the offender.

   g. the right to present oral and documentary evidence, including witnesses, on the student's behalf.

3. The school board shall conduct the expulsion hearing in a session closed to the public, unless the pupil requests a public meeting.
4. An expulsion hearing may be conducted in any one of three ways: by the board, by a hearing officer, or by an administrative panel.

5. Within three school days after the hearing, the hearing officer or administrative panel shall determine whether to recommend expulsion of the pupil. If the hearing officer or panel decides not to recommend expulsion, the student is reinstated and immediately permitted to return to school. If the hearing officer or panel recommends expulsion, findings of fact in support of the recommendation shall be prepared and submitted to the governing board.

6. The decision of the board to expel a student shall be based upon substantial evidence relevant to the charges presented at the expulsion hearing. Findings shall not be based solely upon hearsay evidence. Technical rules of evidence do not apply at an expulsion hearing. However, relevant evidence with probative effect is required.

7. A decision of the school board as to whether to expel a student shall be made within ten school days after the conclusion of the hearing. Under certain circumstances and for good cause the school board may extend the time period.

8. A record of the hearing shall be made. The record may be maintained by any means, including electronic recording, so long as a reasonably accurate and complete written transcription of the proceedings can be made.

9. Final action to expel a student can only be taken by the governing board, and this action must be taken in public session, although without stating the pupil's name. A decision of the governing board to expel shall be supported by substantial evidence showing that the pupil committed any of the acts enumerated in Education Code Section 48900.

10. Written notice of the decision to expel or to suspend the enforcement of an expulsion order shall be sent by the superintendent to the pupil or the pupil's parent or guardian. The written notice shall notify the parent or guardian of the right to appeal the expulsion to the county board of education. The letter shall also notify the parent or guardian of his or her responsibility to inform a new school district of the expulsion.

The expulsion order and the causes shall be recorded in the pupil's mandatory interim record and shall be forwarded to any school in which the pupil subsequently enrolls upon receipt of a request from the admitting school for the pupil's school records. Provisions regarding an expelled student's eligibility to enroll in another program or district are contained in Education Code Sections 48915.1 and 48915.2.

## Summary

One can argue that public schools in America are in peril, and that survival in their present form is in serious jeopardy. Critics point out serious deficiencies in student academic achievement and the spiraling cost to the taxpayer of a free public education. However, the most serious threat to the schools is fear on the part of citizens, parents, and students that the neighborhood school is not a safe place for students.

State legislatures, school boards, and the courts have reacted to this concern for the safety of students in a variety of ways. On the one hand, greater constitutional protection has been extended to students. For example, corporal punishment has been restricted in many states, and students have gained greater due process protection when school administrators consider suspension or expulsion.

However, at the same time, there has been a trend toward less tolerance on campus of students who are unruly, disruptive, or dangerous. The move toward "zero tolerance" has been a response to students bringing knives, guns, and other dangerous weapons onto campus. Many states, including California, now mandate expulsion of students who bring weapons to school.

While unruly, disruptive students who actively present a threat to the general safety of students seem to be on the increase, the number of alternatives for dealing with these students remains essentially unchanged. A teacher has some options for controlling a difficult student: counseling, detention, working with a parent or guardian to improve citizenship, and limited power to suspend. A principal's authority is only slightly increased from that of a teacher: authority to suspend a student from school for a longer period of time or to recommend expulsion. The governing board has the ultimate power of expelling a student who has seriously defied school rules. The societal challenge of providing safe schools threatens to continue for some time.

## Key Terms

1. California Administrative Code (Title 5)
2. California Education Code
3. corporal punishment
4. due process
5. expellable offenses
6. expulsion
7. expulsion hearing
8. expulsion of students with exceptional needs
9. *in loco parentis*
10. mandatory expulsion
11. property rights
12. suspendable offenses
13. suspension
14. zero tolerance

## Discussion/Essay Questions

1. Within the past several years, student misconduct and violence have increased on school campuses. Discuss the major reasons for this increase.

2. The courts have granted teachers and principals power to control student conduct by the principle of *in loco parentis*. Define this principle and give examples of its use in public schools.

3. A teacher may suspend a student from his or her classroom. Discuss the procedures for and restrictions on suspension of a student by a teacher.

4. Suspensions and expulsions are becoming widely used by school districts to control student misconduct and violence on campus. What are the advantages and disadvantages of this means of attempting to control student behavior?

5. Seasoned teachers state that it is more difficult to gain cooperation in disciplining an unruly student than it once was. Do you agree or disagree with this statement? Support your conclusion with specific examples.

# CHAPTER 5

# Student Expression, Student Privacy, and the Constitution

*Neither students nor teachers shed their constitutional rights to freedom of speech or expression at the school-house gate.*

—*Tinker v. Des Moines*, 1969 - Justice Abe Fortas

## Introduction

High school students in a large high school in urban California pass through a metal detector each morning as they enter the school campus. When the local school board decided to install metal detectors, board members had received both support and resistance from the community. Speakers who lined up at school board meetings in support of the policy spoke about student safety. Those in opposition argued for student privacy. Support and opposition were about equally divided. However, as a result of an incident in 1999, support for metal detectors and other safety measures may be more strongly supported and student privacy a less persuasive argument in many American communities.

The incident referred to occurred on a June morning in 1999 at Columbine High School in Colorado. Two students, each dressed in a long black trench coat, opened rifle fire on their classmates and killed twelve fellow students. The "trenchcoat students," as they were referred to by the media, ran through the library and halls seeking to kill "athletic jocks" and black students. Columbine High School did not have a metal detector, but did employ a security officer who was aware of the background of these two students. Had the school installed metal detectors, would this tragedy have been avoided?

Columbine shooting dramatically demonstrated the tension between student rights and the responsibility of school administrators and teachers to maintain a safe campus. Few issues have stirred as much passion among parents, state legislatures, and the courts. Over the past several decades, courts have faced the challenge of drawing boundaries between the constitutional rights of individual students and the protection of the rights of the group. The guiding principle for establishing this balance has been the principle of *in loco parentis*. This concept is defined as the assumption of a parental role by teachers and administrators while children are under their jurisdiction.

What is the appropriate balance between students' freedom of expression and the rights of others in the education environment? If a teenage girl attends school with pink hair, jangly large nose rings, or a cropped shirt—or a male student comes in with a pierced tongue and green hair—do school personnel have the right to consider this appearance and attire inappropriate for a classroom setting? If a school official suspects that students are coming to school while under the influence of drugs, does that official have the right to require all students to submit to a drug test? Can the official search a student's backpack, locker, automobile, or pockets? May an administrator perform a strip search of a student?

School officials, state legislatures, and the courts have attempted to answer these questions. For example, the Supreme Court in *Vernonia School District vs. Acton* (1995) decreed that random urinalysis tests for drugs were legal.

Most cases of free expression involve student speech, student publications, or dress codes. Issues of student privacy include confidential student files and drug searches. This chapter addresses these issues, beginning with a brief historical discussion. Major court decisions are described. These issues remain controversial, so that continued societal discussion and new court cases may be expected.

## Student Expression

Before the late 1960s, whenever a disagreement arose between school authorities and students, the courts usually sided with the school authorities. The primary criterion considered by the courts was whether the actions of a teacher or administrator had been reasonable. In the early 1970s, however, several federal statutes were enacted that expanded the scope of student rights. A major concern of state legislatures was to give school officials sufficient authority to maintain safe campuses, while at the same time protecting student rights. Within the boundaries set by legislation, school administrators, too, struggle to maintain a proper balance between their obligation to maintain order and the rights of students to express themselves freely. Differences of opinion regarding application of the law frequently lead to court cases.

The past 40 years have seen the courts, as they interpret and apply the law, attempt to maintain the delicate balance between the constitutionally guaranteed rights of individual students and the obligation of society to ensure a safe learning environment for young people. Whether the courts have succeeded depends upon the political viewpoint of the observer.

Throughout our history, the courts and schools have established a bond based upon the mutual obligations of teacher and student. The courts have long recognized that if schools are to function, the teacher must be able to exercise authority. To this end, the courts attempted to accord authority to a teacher much like that of a parent. The concept is referred to as *in loco parentis*, which means "in the place of the parent." This principle emanated from English law. Although courts have expanded the allowable extent of student expression, and concomitantly narrowed school authority, they have not deleted the notion of *in loco parentis*.

## Constitutional Basis

The two constitutional amendments that are most often cited in student expression cases are the First Amendment and the Fourth. Of all the freedoms guaranteed in this country, none is more protected than freedom of speech and the press and the right to peaceable assembly as established in the First Amendment, which states:

> Congress shall make no law respecting an establishment of religion, or prohibiting the free exercise thereof; or abridging the freedom of speech, or of the press, or the right of the people peaceably to assemble, and to petition the Government for a redress of grievances.

The Fourth Amendment reads:

The right of the people to be secure in their persons, houses, papers, and effects, against unreasonable searches and seizures, shall not be violated, and no Warrants shall issue, but upon probable cause, supported by oath or affirmation, and particularly describing the place to be searched, and the persons or things to be seized.

In addition to these two amendments, several landmark cases provide boundaries and guidelines for student expression. A major issue addressed by the courts in these cases is "reasonableness." This term is not limited to constitutional issues. Indeed, whenever judges are confronted with sticky issues of tort law, the meaning of "reasonableness" comes into play. Its legal definition calls for behavior that is proper, rational, and fair, while rejecting behavior that is excessive or inappropriate.

## Tinker v. Des Moines—1969

The pros and cons of free speech were hotly debated during the 1960s. At that time, the daily news revolved around the Vietnam War and free speech on college campuses. Many riots occurred, with university students storming administrative offices and remaining for days. Many students were injured and some were killed during these confrontations. Soon, issues of free speech were no longer confined to colleges, but filtered down the grades in schools throughout the country.

During this period of national turmoil, the Supreme Court attempted to resolve the issue of student free expression. The key case was *Tinker v. Des Moines Independent Community School District* (1969).

Petitioner John F. Tinker, 15 years old, and petitioner Christopher Eckhardt, 16, attended high schools in Des Moines, Iowa. Petitioner Mary Beth Tinker, John's sister, was a 13-year-old student in junior high school. The incident that gave rise to the suit was triggered by a meeting of adults and young people in December of 1965 at the Eckhardt home. The participants discussed how to publicize their objections to the Vietnam War. It was decided they would wear black armbands during the holiday season.

After hearing of the plan, the principals of the Des Moines schools met and developed a policy that any student wearing an armband to school would be asked to remove it. A student who refused would be suspended until he or she returned without the armband. It is interesting to note that only a few of the 18,000 district students wore armbands. Some students made angry remarks to those who were wearing armbands, but there were no fights or threats of violence.

On December 16, 1965, Mary Beth and Christopher decided to wear the armbands to school. The next day, John Tinker wore his armband. The three students were suspended from school and sent home until they would come back without the armbands.

A complaint was filed in the United States District Court by the fathers of the students under Section 1983 of Title 42 of the United States Code. The key issue was whether wearing of insignia or other markings in school was a constitutionally protected right. After hearing the evidence, the court invalidated the rule prohibiting students from wearing black armbands as a protest against the war. The court stated that "undifferentiated fear or apprehension of disturbance is not enough to overcome the right to freedom of expression." The court declared that the administration could prohibit the wearing of symbols only if such activity would "materially and substantially disrupt the work and discipline of the school." The Supreme Court emphasized that educators have the authority and duty to maintain discipline in schools, but that, as they exert control, they must also consider students' constitutional rights.

Justice Fortas presented the opinion of the court. The court majority decided there was no evidence that the wearing of armbands would substantially interfere with the work of the school or impinge upon the rights of other students. Often quoted from the decision is the sentence, "It can hardly be argued that either students or teachers shed their constitutional rights to freedom of speech or expression at the schoolhouse gate."

The court was not unanimous in its decision. The minority opinion was written by Justice Black, who demurred from the majority decision because he did not want the schools to serve as a platform for the exercise of free speech. Justice Black pointed out that the armbands did cause comment in the schools. He felt that the display had taken the minds of students off their schoolwork and diverted it to thoughts about the Vietnam War. He felt that this decision could harbor a new revolutionary period in the nation's history.

Justice Black's comments are of interest because they demonstrate that the *Tinker* decision was debatable. It conveyed the view that courts should not be involved in running a school. In keeping with that position, subsequent cases have provided school administrators with seemingly broad authority to regulate student speech. A 1986 decision of the Supreme Court illustrates how the court views a student's lewd speech in a school assembly.

## Bethel School District No. 403 v. Fraser—1986

As summarized by U.S. Supreme Court Chief Justice Burger, the case arose from a speech by Matthew Fraser, a student at Bethel High School in Bethel, Washington, on April 26, 1983. In his speech, nominating another student for student government, Matthew "referred to his candidate in terms of an elaborate, graphic, and explicit sexual metaphor." The comments may seem mild by current standards; for example, Matthew remarked, "I know a man who is firm—he's firm in his pants, he's firm in his shirt, his character is firm—but most . . . of all, his belief in you, the students of Bethel, is firm." At the time, some students were embarrassed by the speech, while others applauded.

The Assistant Principal called Matthew into her office the next morning and informed him that the school considered his speech a violation of policy and that he would be suspended and removed as a graduation speaker. Matthew's father brought action in the courts and alleged that the speech was indistinguishable from the armband protest in the *Tinker* case.

The U.S. District Court held that the school's actions violated Matthew's right to freedom of speech, that the school's discipline rules were unconstitutionally vague, and that the student's removal from the graduation speaker's list violated the due process clause. The court awarded Matthew $278 in damages and $12,750 in litigation costs and attorney fees.

In the meantime, Matthew had been elected graduation speaker by a write-in vote of his classmates and gave the graduation speech. In 1985 the Ninth Circuit Court of Appeals affirmed the judgment of the district court.

Then, in 1986, the U.S. Supreme Court reversed the decision of the Ninth Circuit Court and found in favor of the school district. The Supreme Court held that the discipline imposed upon Matthew did not violate his First Amendment rights. The court differentiated the *Bethel* case from *Tinker* on two grounds: first, the plaintiff in *Bethel* did not espouse a particular political point of view, as did those in *Tinker;* second, *Bethel* did involve a substantial disruption of the school environment in that this particular speech was damaging, especially to a less mature audience.

The court considered the fundamental values of "habits and manners of civility." The sensibilities of fellow students were considered. The language of the speech, while acceptable in a gathering of adults, was not acceptable or permitted in front of children in a public school. Matthew's remarks were also considered offensive to female students because his comments glorified male sexuality and were acutely insulting to teenage girls.

Many courts followed the *Bethel* decision in granting more rights to school administrators. Thus, *Bethel* came to allow school authorities considerable latitude in censoring lewd and vulgar student expression. The court held that it is a responsibility of a school to protect its captive student audience from exposure to lewd, vulgar, and offensive speech. In cases where students belittled school administrators, the courts also found for the administrators, stating that a certain amount of decorum is necessary in schools to maintain the educational process. *Bethel* stands as a major case in determining the appropriate balance between students' constitutional rights and the duty of public school officials to maintain an appropriate and safe environment for learning.

## Morse v. Frederick—2007

Educators view *Morse v. Frederick* as an important victory in that the U.S. Supreme Court ruled that the First Amendment does not prevent teachers and administrators from suppressing student speech, which promotes illegal drug use. This decision was in 2007. The Court stated that schools have the right to discipline students for promoting illegal activities.

The incident occurred in 2002 when, for the first time in history, the Olympic Torch came to Juneau, Alaska. The torch was carried on a ten-mile route through the city and past the high school where Joseph Frederick attended. On that day, students were permitted to leave class to watch the torch go by the school.

Joseph joined some friends on the sidewalk across from the school to watch the torch go by. Joseph had prepared a banner that read, "Bong Hits 4 Jesus," and he and his friends waited for the television cameras to display the banner. The principal confiscated the banner and suspended Joseph from school. The Juneau District argued that displaying the banner compromised the school's ability to send a consistent message against the use of illegal drugs.

Chief Justice John Roberts, writing the majority decision, ruled that the principal had the right to suspend the student for advocating illegal drugs. The Court said that advocating illegal drugs at school could not be treated as protected speech.

An important distinction in this case from *Tinker v. Des Moines* is the illegal drug message. The court majority stressed that they would have come to a different conclusion if the banner had carried a political or social message. For example, if the message had read "Impeach George Bush," or "Stop the War" the Court might have concluded it was free speech and, therefore protected.

## Dariano v. Morgan Hill School District—2014

The *Tinker* case appeared to settle the question of student rights to free speech on a school campus as long as their actions do not lead to a "substantial disruption." However, in recent years, some school officials have curtailed some political or social statements, such as wearing Confederate flags or antigay slogans. Administrators argue that some limits are necessary to avoid angering other students and charges of "bullying."

In 2009, at Live Oak High, located in San Jose, California, a Mexican-American student wore a shirt with a Mexican flag on display. The next year, 2010, several students wore shirts displaying the American flag. Some Mexican-American students called them racists and complained to the assistant principal about the shirts.

Fearing violence, the assistant principal asked the students to take their shirts off or turn them inside out. The school took this action to avoid confrontation between Latino and white students, and was a successful move in avoiding confrontation between the two rival groups. The school administration had documented more than 30 fights between the two groups over the past several years.

Los Angeles lawyer William Becker sued on behalf of several parents. He filed a free-speech suit on behalf of John and Diana Dariano. A federal judge in San Francisco dismissed the claim on the grounds that administrators had acted to avoid violence or a disruption at school. The 9th Circuit Court affirmed that decision.

In 2015, the U.S. Supreme Court refused to hear the appeal and the decision made by the 9th U.S. Circuit Court allowed the decision to stand. The court's decision sets no legal precedent, but it raises questions about whether students have meaningful free-speech rights on matters that may provoke controversy.

## Student Publications

Are there limitations on what students may publish? Do they have the same freedoms as adults under the First Amendment? Some of the most hotly debated cases in the schools have dealt with student publications.

Clearly, the Constitution protects the right of adults to a free press. In fact, it was the intent of the founding fathers to enable the press to censure the government, if needed. It was also understood that the press would endeavor to be truthful and to publish material without malice or intent to malign. However, courts view private and public individuals differently. Public individuals generally have a harder time obtaining a favorable judgement in a libel action (Yudof, 1991).

Similarly, freedom of the press in public schools is governed by a different set of rules from those that pertain to newspapers for the public at large. The courts have typically ruled that a valid educational purpose must be served by student publications. On the other hand, school officials do not have *carte blanche* to censor student newspapers. Of additional concern to the courts is that rules governing student publications are uniformly enforced.

## Hazelwood School District v. Kuhlmeier—1988

Each court decision must consider a unique set of circumstances. *Hazelwood School District v. Kuhlmeier* (1988) demonstrates the court's interpretation of the First Amendment in combination with the importance of maintaining an educational purpose. We note that *Hazelwood* is unusual in that a decision of the U.S. Supreme Court is not the "last word" for California. First we examine the Supreme Court decision.

*Hazelwood* reviewed the extent of editorial control of a student newspaper by school officials. The petitioners on appeal were school officials from the Hazelwood School District in St. Louis County, Missouri. Respondents were three former Hazelwood students. The students had been staff members of the school newspaper, *Spectrum*. In the original suit, the students charged that school officials had violated their First Amendment rights by deleting two pages of articles from the May 13, 1983, issue.

*Spectrum* was written and edited by the Journalism II class at Hazelwood. During most of the 1982–83 school year, the course had been taught by Robert Stergos. The newspaper had been published every three weeks, with 4,500 copies distributed to students, school personnel, and members of the community. Stergos left Hazelwood to take a job in private industry on April 29, 1983, when the May 13 edition of *Spectrum* was nearing completion. At that time appellant Emerson took Stergos's place as newspaper adviser for the remaining weeks of the term.

Typically, the journalism teacher would submit proofs of each *Spectrum* issue to Principal Reynolds for his review prior to publication. On May 10, Emerson delivered the proofs of the May 13 edition to Reynolds, who objected to two of the articles scheduled to appear in that edition. One of the stories described three Hazelwood students' experiences with pregnancy; the other discussed the impact of divorce on students at the school. The students who wrote the articles brought suit because the articles about pregnancy and divorce were omitted from the final copy.

The U.S. Supreme Court found that the administration at Hazelwood had not violated the students' First Amendment rights. This opinion gives educators the power to exercise editorial control over the style and content of student speech in school-sponsored expressive activities, as long as their actions are reasonably related to legitimate pedagogical concerns. Moreover, school authorities can control the time, place, and manner of the distribution of a student newspaper. Publications paid for with school funds or produced as part of the curriculum (for example, in a journalism class) are subject to more controls than are student school newspapers published off campus.

Now we turn to the application of *Hazelwood* in California. According to Romero and Huguenin (1988), staff attorneys for the California Teachers' Association, the *Hazelwood* decision is more restrictive of student rights than Section 48907 in the California Education Code. That code directs public school personnel to allow student expression unless it is "obscene, libelous, or slanderous" or threatens to incite students to "commission of unlawful acts on school premises or the violation of lawful school regulations or the substantial disruption of the orderly operation of the school."

This restriction specifically includes school publications, bulletin boards, and such expressions as petitions and badges. It further requires school personnel to show that the material falls into the prohibited categories of Section 48907 before, not after, suppressing the publication or other expression. Romero and Huguenin conclude that Section 48907 "would probably survive any specific challenge to it because of current California Supreme Court precedent." It appears, then, that the role of the U.S. Supreme Court is to ensure that citizens have *at least* the freedoms guaranteed by the Constitution, specifically the Bill of Rights, but that a state may enact legislation that sets a broader definition.

## Novato School District v. Smith—2008

The U.S. Supreme Court provided additional clarification of the rights of student journalists against censorship. The 2008 Court let stand a 2007 ruling by a California Appellate Court, which held that the Novato School District had violated state law when it censored an article written by student Andrew Smith opposing illegal immigration.

In 2001, Smith wrote a commentary piece in the school paper about illegal immigration. He wrote that there should be no tolerance for illegal immigrants. His strongest criticism of the immigrants included the statement, "If you can't comply with our requirements, then stay out of the country" (Beard, 2009). The journalism teacher and the principal approved the article for publication.

However, the school backtracked when the article led to conflict and the day after it ran as many as 150 students urged other students to leave class to protest Smith's article. As a result of the protest, the high school principal ordered that the remaining issues of the paper be pulled from circulation and sent a letter to parents stating that the article should not have been published.

Smith was attacked soon after the commentary was published and threatened with murder. He was not disciplined by the school for writing the article and continued writing for the school paper.

Soon thereafter, Smith filed suit with the Marin County Superior Court charging that his free speech rights had been violated. The question was, did the Novato School District violate Education Code 48907, which guarantees students free speech in California public schools? The judge rejected Smith's claim, but was overruled by the First District Court of Appeals in San Francisco.

The Appellate Court stated that a school cannot prohibit student speech for presenting controversial ideas. The Court relied on a 1971 California statute that states that students are entitled to freedom of speech and the press unless what they say is obscene or libelous or creates a "clear and present" danger of lawbreaking or disorder on campus. The Court also cited California's Education Code 48907, which states that a school may not prohibit student speech simply because controversial ideas are presented and opponents may cause disruption at the school.

Mike Beard (2009), who represented Smith stated that the U.S. Supreme Court's decision not to hear the appeal was a conclusive victory for Smith and all student journalists as the case establishes once and for all that students can't be censored for not conforming to some ideological agenda.

## Protection for Journalism Advisors

Journalism teachers walk a fine line in instructing and guiding their students. They are charged with teaching the concepts of journalism, good writing, investigative reporting, and the concepts of a free press. They also must be loyal to their school. For example, is it appropriate to report in the school newspaper that the cafeteria food is bad, that bathrooms are dirty, and that some teachers are not doing a good job? A California high school journalism teacher lost her job when these topics appeared in the school newspaper.

Robert Lopez (Los Angeles Times, January 4, 2009) quotes Jim Ewert, legal counsel for the California Newspaper Publishers Association, that in the last three years, at least 15 high school journalism advisors lost their jobs or were reassigned as a result of articles written by students. That situation is less likely to happen in California with the approval of the Journalism Teacher Protection Act, which became law in 2009.

Senate Bill 1370 amends Education Code 48907 that for years has given free speech rights to students but failed to protect advisors. Senate Bill 1370 prohibits school administrators from retaliation against the advisor for articles printed by students. Lopez again quotes Ewert that only one other state, Kansas, has similar protection for advisors.

## Search, Seizure, and Drug Testing

School administrators are frequently confronted with the decision whether or not to search a student's desk, locker, pockets, purse, book bag, coat, shoes and socks, or automobile. On the one hand, an administrator is charged to maintain order and discipline on campus and to protect the health and welfare of all students. On the other hand, this necessity must be balanced against the protected privacy rights of students. The Fourth Amendment and several court cases provide guidance in answering this question.

The Fourth Amendment of the United States Constitution, quoted earlier, guarantees citizens the right "to be secure in their persons, houses, papers and effects, against unreasonable searches and seizures." To support this right, "no warrants shall issue, but upon probable cause."

The Fourth Amendment includes five important components. First an individual's control over his or her person and property is emphasized: "persons, houses, papers, and effects." Second, "unreasonable searches and seizures" are forbidden. Third, a search cannot be instituted without probable cause or evidence that a search is necessary. Fourth, a warrant must be specific, describing the place to be searched and the articles to be seized. Last, a magistrate or judge is interposed between the individual and the government, requiring that the government justify the necessity of the search.

Three of these five components are applicable to a student search. Students have a right to privacy in their person and property, they are protected from unreasonable seizures and searches, and a search must be specific as to what is sought and where. Although school officials need not provide evidence of probable cause or obtain a search warrant from a judge, they must have "reasonable suspicion" as a basis for a search.

## New Jersey v. T.L.O.—1985

The prevailing case regarding school searches and seizures is *New Jersey v. T.L.O.* (1985). This case clearly upheld the principle of *in loco parentis*.

On March 7, 1980, a teacher at Piscataway High School in Middlesex County, New Jersey, discovered two girls smoking in a lavatory. One of the girls was T.L.O., who at the time was a 14-year-old high school freshman. Because smoking in the lavatory violated a school rule, the two girls were taken to the principal's office. T.L.O. denied that she had been smoking at all. A subsequent search of her purse revealed a pack of cigarettes, cigarette rolling papers, a small amount of marijuana, a pipe, an index card of names of students who appeared to owe money to T.L.O., and a quantity of one dollar bills.

T.L.O. was then turned over to her mother, who took her to a police station, where she ultimately confessed to selling marijuana. On the basis of the confession and the evidence, the state brought delinquency charges against T.L.O. in the Juvenile and Domestic Relations Court of Middlesex County. T. L.O., contending that the administrator's search of her purse violated the Fourth Amendment, and moved to suppress the evidence found in her purse.

The Supreme Court upheld the right of the school to conduct the search, holding that as long as a school official "has reasonable grounds to believe that the student possesses evidence of illegal activity or activity that would interfere with school discipline and order," the search was legal. The court upheld the *in loco parentis* doctrine by considering the Fourth Amendment search and seizure restrictions while also recognizing the necessity of reasonable action to promote student learning and safety.

The court indicated that the Fourth Amendment is applicable in school situations, but that reasonableness must prevail if a search is to be constitutionally valid. A major consideration of the court was whether a teacher or administrator gives consideration to "reasonableness" when a search is initiated. To be judged reasonable, a search must have been pointed to by the factors leading up to it. For example, prior to the search, had a school administrator observed that the student appeared to be under the influence of drugs? Or had the administrator been informed that drugs were in the student's locker? The more intensive the search, the stronger must be the basis for suspicion. However, individual privacy is still observed in most cases, even intrusive drug searches.

## Strip Searches—Safford Unified School District v. Savanna Redding—2009

The Supreme Court's decision in *New Jersey v. T.L.O.* clarified the right of school administrators to conduct student searches, but the U.S. Supreme Court did not resolve the issue of "strip searches" until 2009. In an eight to one decision, The U.S. Supreme Court heard the case of *Safford Unified School District v. Savanna Redding* on April 22, 2009 and made its ruling on June 25, 2009.

The case took six years to wind its way to the Supreme Court. It started in 2003 in Safford, Arizona. Savanna Redding was an eighth grade honors student at Safford Middle School. She knew she was in trouble when the vice principal, Kerry Wilson, came to her math class and told her to come to the office. That morning another eighth grade student, Marissa Glines, was found with several 400-milligram Ibuprofen pills tucked into a folded school planner.

Redding had loaned Marissa the folder and when Marissa was asked where she got the pills, she named Redding. Wilson asked Redding if he could search her backpack and Redding agreed. When it was found that the backpack did not contain pills, Wilson sent Redding to the nurse's office, where the nurse and an office assistant had her remove her T-shirt and stretch pants. She was asked to pull her underwear to the side and to shake out any possible pills. No pills were found.

Redding's mother sued the school district for damages. The Civil Liberties Union represented the Reddings and argued that the strip-search went beyond the bounds of reasonableness and argued there was no imminent danger to students. A federal magistrate in Tucson held that the search was reasonable because the vice principal was relying on the tip from another student.

In a 2-1 decision, the U.S. 9th Circuit Court of Appeals agreed. However, in 2008, the full 9th Circuit Court took up the case and ruled 6 to 5 for the Reddings. In the fall of 2008, the school district appealed the Circuit Court's decision.

In an 8-1 decision, the U.S. Supreme Court called the search degrading, unreasonable, and unconstitutional. Justice Souter, writing for the majority, stated that a strip-search is different from other searches to find drugs or weapons as it is embarrassing and humiliating to the student who is targeted. The Court stated that such a search would be justified only if a school official had strong reason to believe a student was hiding a dangerous drug or a weapon in his or her underwear.

Educators cannot force students to remove their clothing unless student safety is a risk. Adam Wolf of the American Civil Liberties Union said that the court's decision sends a clear signal to school officials that they can strip search only in the most extraordinary situations (Holland, 2009).

California and six other states including Washington, Iowa, New Jersey, Oklahoma, South Carolina, and Wisconsin have approved legislation defining or prohibiting strip searches. California's Education Code 49050 states that no school employee shall conduct a search of a body cavity. School officials are prohibited from removing or arranging any or all clothing of a student to permit a visual inspection of the underclothing, breast, buttocks, or genitalia of the student. School administrators are strongly encouraged to research the laws of their state and school policies prior to conducting a strip search.

## Canine Searches

Drug-sniffing dogs have been on campus since the 1980s. Interquest Group, a major company that trains drug-sniffing dogs and contracts with school districts started sending dogs to Texas schools in 1987. That company now contracts with over 1200 districts in 19 states (Robinson, B. 2009). Trained dogs and handlers work in school systems to detect and, even more importantly, deter the presence of drugs, alcohol, weapons, and explosives. Law enforcement and private companies perform this job.

It is a difficult decision by a school board to decide to use the drug dogs. They have to decide if they wish to use the local police or sheriff's departments to do the job or a private company. If the local law enforcement agency does not have trained detection dogs,

the school won't have that option. The major difference between the two choices is the presence of law enforcement on campus when the local officials complete this task. When a private company provides the service, the findings are turned over to the school to determine what action to take. The case could still be turned over to law enforcement, but the school's primary role is not to arrest kids, but to keep the school environment free of dangerous contraband and safe for students and teachers.

Drug dogs in schools can be any breed, but private companies prefer dogs that are non-threatening to students. It is desirable for the students to like the dog. The dogs usually put in a full day's work. Therefore, larger breeds with more stamina, Labrador and Golden Retrievers are often used. Other friendly breeds such as Springer Spaniels, Weimaraners, and similar mixes with the aptitude for the work are also good choices (Davis, 2006).

A major job of the school is to effectively communicate the goals of the program to parents. Students and parents need to understand that the goal of the program is to keep drugs off campus and keep students safe.

It is interesting how one California school manages the potential drug problem on campus. La Jolla High School has a canine cop on campus and her name is Bucky. Bucky is a golden retriever and is on duty to sniff out alcohol, tobacco, and other drugs. Bucky randomly scans lockers and backpacks, but not students. If Bucky alerts on drugs, the administrator will take over at that point (Weekly Reader, 2005).

Canine searches predate the *New Jersey v. T.L.O.* case (1985). The Tenth Circuit Court of Appeals in *Zamora v. Pomeroy* (1981) upheld the use of dogs in the exploratory sniffing of lockers. The court noted that since the schools gave notice at the beginning of the year that the lockers might be periodically opened, the lockers were jointly possessed by both student and school. The Seventh Circuit Court in *Doe v. Renfrow* (1980) ruled that school officials stood *in loco parentis* and had the right to use dogs to seek out drugs. The court affirmed that school officials had a duty to maintain an educational environment that was conducive to learning.

In a federal district court case, *Jones v. Latexo Independent School District* (1980), the decision did not conform with *Doe* and *Zamora*. In this case the district used dogs to sniff both students and automobiles. The court ruled that in the absence of individual suspicion, having the dogs sniff the students was unreasonable and intrusive. Moreover, since the students could not go to their cars during the school day, sniffing the vehicles was also unreasonable.

The use of drug-sniffing dogs on a school campus was challenged in a California case (*B.C. v. Plumas*) in 1999. The Plumas Unified School District, concerned with possible possession of drugs, asked the sheriff to bring a drug-sniffing dog to the campus. Students were required to walk by a deputy sheriff and his dog. The dog alerted on the same student twice; however, when the student was searched, no drugs were found.

A classmate of the student who was searched, "B.C.," sued in federal court, alleging that he had been deprived of his Fourth Amendment right to be free from unreasonable search. The Ninth Circuit Court of Appeals ruled that the school had the right to sniff students' belongings, but—except in case of reasonable suspicion of drug possession—not their person. In response, the District Attorney of Alameda County posted on the Internet the view *(District Attorney,* n.d.) that the court opinion was "logically and legally unsound" and encouraging law enforcement officers to continue use of drug-sniffing dogs "so long as [there is no] physical contact with a person for whom reasonable suspicion or probable cause does not exist." This posting further noted that "decisions of the U.S. Court of Appeals interpreting federal law are not binding on California courts."

In 2005, the U.S. Supreme Court in *Illinois v. Caballes* provided additional clarification for the use of drug-sniffing dogs. The case started with a traffic violation. In 1998, Roy Caballes was driving from Las Vegas to Chicago. He was stopped by an Illinois Police Officer for driving six miles over the speed limit. After questioning Caballes, the officer asked if he could search his car. Caballes said, "No."

When the officer was writing the speeding ticket, a second officer arrived with a drug-detection dog. The dog did an alert on the trunk of the car where a quarter of a million dollars' worth of marijuana was found. Caballes argued that the evidence should have been suppressed and that the officer did not have probable cause to search his car as canine searches were unreliable. An Illinois lower court convicted Caballes of cannabis trafficking and sentenced him to 12 years in prison.

Upon appeal, the Illinois Supreme Court reversed the lower court's decision and concluded that the use of a drug-detection dog during a traffic stop violated the defendant's Fourth Amendment rights. The U.S. Supreme Court reversed the Illinois decision by a vote of 6-2. The Court concluded that a dog sniff conducted during a lawful traffic stop does not violate the Fourth Amendment. This decision by the highest court gives the police greater latitude for the use of drug-detection dogs.

Turning from law to policy, many high schools have eliminated student lockers for fear that drugs or weapons might be kept there. While this action may protect students from drugs or weapons, the downside is that many secondary students carry 40 to 60 pounds of books around with them all day.

## *Vernonia School District v. Acton*—1995

A 1995 decision of the Supreme Court illustrates how a seeming precedent may fail to establish a foundation for later decisions. In *Vernonia v. Acton* (1995), the court chose to part with precedent by validating Vernonia School District's policy of "suspicionless" drug testing of student athletes. Few cases regarding drug searches have had such an effect as *Vernonia v. Acton*. The Supreme Court found for the district and its right to conduct random drug searches of student athletes with*out* suspicion. The court "balanced away" the Fourth Amendment protection of students when it classified the district's search as reasonable under the circumstances.

In 1991 James Acton tried out for the football team in Vernonia School District, Oregon. James was twelve years old and in the seventh grade. At practice, all of the students were given a drug testing consent form by the coach. James took the form home and discussed it with his parents. They decided that James would not sign the form. As a result, James was declared ineligible for school sports until he would sign.

James's parents filed suit on his behalf in the United States District Court for the District of Oregon (Samay, 1997). The Actons requested declaratory judgement and injunctive relief based upon their belief that the district's policy interfered with their son's rights under the Fourth Amendment and Article I, Section 9, of the Oregon Constitution. The U.S. District Court denied their petition for relief, and the Actons appealed. Reversing the District Court decision, the United States Court of Appeals for the Ninth Circuit held that the district's need to randomly search its students did not outweigh the privacy interests of student athletes.

However, recognizing the importance of the issue, the United States Supreme Court granted a petition (writ of certiorari) to determine whether random urinalysis drug testing of students who participated in Vernonia's athletic programs violated the Fourth and Fourteenth Amendments to the United States Constitution. In 1995 the U.S. Supreme Court, by a 6-3 decision, reversed the lower courts and found that the district's policy conformed with the Fourth and Fourteenth Amendments. The urine test was legitimate on the ground that governmental interest outweighs a student's privacy rights. The court found that athletes are subject to reduced privacy rights in that they have special grade and citizenship requirements as well as required medical examinations. It was also noted that athletes participate in communal undressing and showering. All these conditions reduce the claim of physical privacy.

Why did this case cause such a "stir" among students? In this decision, the Supreme Court determined that random urinalysis tests of student athletes, without reasonable suspicion, could be characterized as reasonable. Clearly, this important case would continue to serve as a precedent, as it did in Pottawatomie County, Oklahoma.

## Pottawatomie School District v. Earls —2002

The U.S. Supreme Court extended the *Vernonia* decision in 2002, when it reviewed the case of *Board of Education of Independent School District No. 92 of Pottawatomie County et al. v. Earls et al.* The school collected urine samples for drug testing not only from athletes, but from all students engaged in competitive extracurricular activities. The U.S. District court had found for the district, the Tenth Circuit court reversed that decision, and the U.S. Supreme Court again found for the district. Based on *Vernonia,* the Supreme Court allowed suspicionless drug testing.

Because the students were voluntary participants, they were seen as having a "limited expectation of privacy." The procedure, which involved a monitor waiting outside a closed restroom stall to receive the urine sample, coupled with confidentiality of the records, was regarded as meeting the requirement for negligible intrusion. Finally, there was evidence of drug use by students at the school. Taken together, these circumstances, in the opinion of the court, justified taking the urine samples as a "reasonable means" for "preventing and deterring drug use" among students in the school.

## Student Dress Codes and Uniforms

As students have sought to express their individuality in clothing, hairstyles, and ornamentation, school administrators have become concerned over possible distraction from, even disruption of, the learning environment. At times such actions have led to suspension from school.

Requiring students to wear uniforms or conform to dress codes is a practice that private schools have used for many years to help maintain order. As gang activity has increased on many campuses, strict dress codes have become commonplace. Amy Cox (2005) reports that 47 percent of public schools have established student dress codes. Twenty-one states have approved legislation authorizing districts to establish dress codes.

In California, state law specifically allows adoption of dress codes (E.C. 35183, 35294). Schoolwide uniforms are also mentioned (E.C. 35183). Such issues have elicited highly emotional responses and have given rise to a number of lawsuits.

Many public school students and parents are opposed to any student dress code. They believe that a student should maintain his or her individuality by wearing whatever is desired. The courts, on the other hand, have generally supported a district's authority to regulate student dress and personal appearance—if the dress or appearance becomes so extreme as to interfere with a school's learning atmosphere. The *Tinker* decision established the precedent for students' right to wear passive symbols to convey a message that is constitutionally protected. However, the *Tinker* decision noted that even passive symbols can become disruptive in some circumstances (Valente, 1998).

Beyond the question of a school dress code is the growing popularity of school uniforms. In 1994, Long Beach School District in California started the uniform trend in public schools. The trend of requiring school uniforms quickly became a national phenomenon and by 1997, three percent of the nation's public schools required school uniforms and by 2005 had increased to 19 percent (Cox, 2005). The most common uniforms are white polo-type shirts with khaki or navy blue pants or skirts.

David Brunsma (2005) reports that uniforms are twice as common in elementary schools as secondary schools. Uniforms are more common in schools with a high percentage of poor and minority students. Districts that require uniforms typically find a way to provide the uniforms for children of parents who cannot afford to pay.

## Cyberbullying

Webster's Dictionary defines a bully as "one who hurts, frightens, or tyrannizes those who are smaller or weaker." The term *cyber-bullying* was not included in the dictionary until the year 2000. It is defined as "bullying that takes place using electronic technology." The devices may include cell phones, computers, text messages, chats, and websites.

While bullying has always been of concern to parents, teachers, and students, it has taken on a new dimension with the cyber age where one can post a mean, threatening insult anonymously. The National Center for Education Statistics found that 9 percent of students in grades 6 through 12 had experienced cyberbullying (NCES, 2012).

The suicide of 13-year-old Megan Meier in 2006 brought the nation's attention to the seriousness of cyberbullying. Megan was under the care of a psychiatrist for depression and self-esteem issues related to her weight problems. She had a MySpace account. Here she met a 16-year-old boy named Josh. Although Megan never met Josh in person, she fell for him. Josh was nice to Megan and she loved hearing from him. However, over time, Josh's messages become cruel, and he told Megan he didn't want to be friends anymore. He wrote, "You are a bad person and everybody hates you." After receiving the message, Megan went to her mom's closet and hanged herself (Hauck, 2014).

Among the many problems in this story, Josh was not a teenage boy. Josh was an adult woman, Lori Drew, the mother of one of Megan's friends. Local authorities did not prosecute Drew as they found she did not violate any state laws. However, federal agents prosecuted the case, which is referred to as the first cyberbullying trial, and Drew was convicted on three misdemeanors for unauthorized computer access. By 2014, California and 48 other states passed laws that make it a criminal act to harass someone over the Internet. At this time, the federal government has not passed a similar law.

Five cases of student online statements and the authority of schools to discipline off-campus behavior have been litigated in the federal courts and reached the Supreme Court. All five cases involved cyberbullying. A brief summary of the five cases follows:

2007—*Wisniewski v. Board of Education of Weedsport Central School District.* Student Aaron Wisniewski created an icon depicting a gun pointing at a person's head with the words, "Kill Mr. VanderMolen." Mr. VanderMolen was Aaron's English teacher. Aaron was suspended for a semester and the Second Circuit Court of Appeals upheld the decision of the school district.

2007—*Doninger v. Niehoff.* Avery Doninger was class secretary at her high school. When school officials cancelled an event, she referred to administrators as "douche bags" in her personal blog. She was prohibited from running for class officer in her senior year. The Second Circuit agreed with the school's action.

2011—*Kowalski v. Berkeley County Schools.* Kara Kowalski created a website that ridiculed a classmate and encouraged others to join her. Her 5-day suspension was upheld.

2012—*J.S. v. Blue Mountain School District.* Jill Snyder was an eighth-grade student when she created a fake profile of her principal. Her comments were sexual in nature and the school gave her a 10-day suspension. The court upheld the suspension.

2012—*Layshock v. Hermitage School District.* Justin Layshock was a senior when he created his parody of the principal and was suspended for 10 days. The Third Circuit ruled in favor of Layshock and J.S. (Jill Snyder, named in the previous case).

A petition for certiorari was filed by either the student or school district in each of the five cases. The petitions were denied without comment. Therefore, with circuit courts divided on appropriate discipline for students who engage in cyberbulling, and the lack of guidance from the U.S. Supreme Court, school administrators must handle this serious problem with great discretion.

## Student Records

The Supreme Court has recognized that the Constitution protects student privacy. Students have the right to expect the school to keep confidential any personal information about themselves. However, this right has limits. School employees who, in the course of fulfilling their duties, have a legitimate need for information about a student may access confidential records.

Parents and guardians, too, have rights. The right to view educational records includes all records directly related to the student. Records, by definition, may be written, on film, on tape, in computers, or any other form. A school must respond to a request to view records within a reasonable time, 45 days being the maximum.

In *Fay v. South Colonie Central School District* (1986) the Second Circuit Court awarded damages to a parent who brought action against the district for refusal to provide records under the Family Education Rights and Privacy Act (20 U.S.C. 1232g [1982]). The plaintiff had joint legal custody of two minor children and requested to have report cards sent to him. School officials refused his request. The court felt that this refusal clearly violated the rights of the parent.

Legal challenges to school record-keeping procedures have sometimes resulted in court orders to school administrators to expunge irrelevant information from students' permanent folders. In some situations, students have successfully brought libel suits against school authorities who allegedly recorded and communicated defamatory information about them.

## Summary

School administrators can expect continuing involvement in resolving conflicts between the rights of students and the need to maintain safe settings for learning. In addition, state legislatures, the Congress, and the courts will confront issues in this arena. Some of the questions to be kept in mind include:

- What are the rights of students and employees on a school campus?
- How does one guard against violating a student's rights under the U.S. Constitution?
- What is "reasonable suspicion"?

- Under what circumstances may a student's locker, clothing, or automobile be searched?
- May districts install metal detectors at the entrances and exits of each campus?

Perhaps the single most important principle for the school official to keep in mind is that students do have rights. As a consequence, the school leader must maintain a balance between the rights of the individual and the right of all students to a safe and educationally sound school environment. Where to draw the line is an important choice about which reasonable people may differ.

Issues of free speech, student rights to publication, and student search will continue to surface and to change, in part due to the membership of the Supreme Court at any given time. Recent case law related to student expression shows growing deference to principals and other administrators. However, it is always important to keep abreast of the latest legislation and court rulings. In addition, wise school administrators develop clearly written, educationally sound policies that are communicated to students and parents on a regular basis.

## Key Terms

1. canine search
2. First Amendment rights
3. Fourth Amendment rights
4. Eighth Amendment rights
5. *in loco parentis*

6. metal detectors
7. reasonable suspicion
8. reasonableness
9. suspicionless drug testing

## Discussion/Essay Questions

1. If asked to explain why you had asked a student to empty her purse, how would you describe "reasonable suspicion"?

2. Assume you are the adviser to a school newspaper at the secondary level. What types of subject matter might you edit out of the newspaper? What not? Why do you believe that you are on sound legal grounds to delete the material you have described?

3. What recommendations do you have on whether and how to structure Internet communications among students at the secondary level?

4. What is the impact of the *Vernonia School Board v. Acton* case on the actions of school administrators? Do you feel that a urinalysis test given randomly is justified—or invasive and uncalled for? Why?

# CHAPTER 6

# Special Education and the Law

*"No Child Left Behind" requires states and school districts to ensure that all students are learning and reaching their highest potential...*

—Dianne Feinstein, California Senator

*Sometimes even the greatest joys bring challenge, and children with special needs inspire a very, very special love.*

—Sarah Palin, Past governor of Alaska and vice-presidential candidate

## Introduction

Two quotes were used to introduce the chapter on special education and the law, one a Democrat and one a Republican. Each of the elected politicians has had a major influence on the education of students with special needs.

A seventh-grade special education student, Philadelfio Armijo of New Mexico, was found by his parents in his bedroom, having shot himself to death. He killed himself after several altercations at school, in connection with which he was suspended. A counselor drove him home and dropped him off without contacting the parents, who filed suit in the U.S. District Court in March of 1996. The plaintiffs claimed that defendants—the district, its board and superintendent, the principal, counselor, and an aide to whom the boy had several times remarked that he might be better off dead—had violated the Individuals with Disabilities Education Act. They further argued that the district, board, and superintendent should have trained staff members to handle potentially violent and suicidal students. Finally, they alleged that defendant school personnel had violated their son's Fourteenth Amendment rights: first, by creating a danger for the boy, and second, by having established a special relationship with their son that created an exceptional responsibility to guard him from harm (Zirkel, 1999).

This case, *Armijo v. Wagon Mount Public Schools* (1998), illustrates the challenges involved in working

with students with disabilities, especially in case of violence or discipline problems. On the one hand, board policies of zero tolerance for violence and drugs require that the student be excluded from school. On the other hand, the pupil's misbehavior must be shown unrelated to his or her disability; otherwise, the student may not be excluded.

On appeal, the Tenth Circuit Court concluded that it lacked jurisdiction with respect to the first two issues, which the district court had found untenable. With respect to the "danger creation" theory, the Circuit Court acted to dismiss the complaint against the aide, but indicated that the administrator and counselor may have been responsible. The higher court decided that none of the school organizations or personnel had established a special relationship. However, the case was remanded to the district court for trial as to liability for the suicide on the part of the principal or counselor. As soon as the counselor, as directed by the principal, drove the student home and left him there, the district and administrator had become legally at risk.

It is crucial that school leaders know the laws governing the education of students with disabilities. The issues involved in serving the needs of all students while attending to those with special needs are truly complex. In addition, the legal risks are increased by the number and power of parent advocacy groups. This chapter outlines the historical development of federal and state legislation that requires states and school districts to provide for the education of handicapped children. Special education terminology, the requirements of special education programs, and important court cases are reviewed.

## Historical Context of Special Education

In the 1800s children with special needs were dubbed "idiot" and "insane." Prior to the 1970s, it was not uncommon that children with special needs were placed in special schools or did not attend school at all (Yell, 1998). The U.S. Department of Education estimates that in 1970, U.S. schools educated only one in five students with disabilities (Department of Education, 2000). This situation was soon to change as parents of special education students became more organized and took their case to legislative bodies and the courts.

The result was a combination of federal legislation and court decisions that dramatically changed public education for students identified as disabled. The watershed U.S. Supreme Court decision was *Brown v. Board of Education* (1954). In addition to the Brown decision, other major cases that advanced or clarified the educational rights of students with disabilities were *Pennsylvania Association for Retarded Citizens v. Commonwealth of Pennsylvania* (1972), and *Mills v. Board of Education* (1972).

During this same period, the U.S. Congress approved key pieces of legislation regarding education for students with disabilities. They were:

- Public Law 93-11: Vocational Rehabilitation (1973)
- Public Law 94-142: Education for All Handicapped (1975)
- Public Law 101-476: Individuals with Disabilities Education Act (1990)
- Public Law 101-336: Americans with Disabilities Act (1990)
- and H.R. 1350: Reauthorization of IDEA (2004).

Of the major laws affecting persons with disabilities, the Vocational Rehabilitation Act of 1973, often called Section 504, and the Americans with Disabilities Act of 1990 (ADA) apply generally to all disabled classes. The third, the Individuals with Disabilities Education Act of 1990 (IDEA), deals exclusively with the education of children who attend public schools that are assisted by federal funds.

## Brown v. Board of Education of Topeka—1954

Prior to the enactment of federal laws concerning students with disabilities, only the Fourteenth Amendment and state statutes addressed the needs of these young people (McCarthy, Cambron-McCabe, & Thomas, 1998). Special education was brought to the legislative agenda as an indirect result of the equality of opportunity movement in the 1950s and 1960s, which re-

sulted in the landmark case *Brown v. Board of Education* (1954). Although the 1954 *Brown* decision dealt with racial segregation, rather than special education, the court's conclusion that education must be available to all children on equal terms was later extended to include children with disabilities.

The central theme of the *Brown* decision, and one that would provide the underpinning to the movement for inclusion, was the constitutional guarantee of equal protection under the law as stipulated under the Fourteenth Amendment. The amendment reads, in part:

No State shall make or enforce any law which shall abridge the privileges or immunities of citizens of the United States; nor shall any State deprive any person of life, liberty, or property, without due process of law; nor deny to any person within its jurisdiction the equal protection of the laws.

The *Brown* decision ultimately extended this guarantee to require that each state provide a free public education for all its citizens. This decision led the way to two hallmark decisions challenging state statutes that excluded students with disabilities from school. These two decisions were *Pennsylvania Association for Retarded Citizens v. Commonwealth of Pennsylvania* and *Mills v. Board of Education of the District of Columbia*, both rendered in 1972.

## Pennsylvania Association for Retarded Citizens v. Commonwealth of Pennsylvania—1972

This Pennsylvania (PARC) case was the first major suit brought by parents of students with disabilities. It named as defendants school districts, the Pennsylvania Board of Education, and the secretaries of Education and Public Welfare. The plaintiffs argued that children with mental retardation were not receiving a publicly supported education. The plaintiffs contended that students' rights were violated under the Fourteenth Amendment. They brought forth four important points:

- All children with mental disabilities can benefit from training and education.
- The outcomes of public education are not limited to book-learning; rather, learning to feed and clothe oneself can qualify as an academic experience.
- Since Pennsylvania offered a free public education, students with disabilities should also receive this benefit.

■ Mentally disabled children who are exposed to education at an early age show higher gains overall than those who begin education at a later age.

The advocates in the PARC case scored a major victory that set the stage for continued improvements in educational programs for students with disabilities. A consent agreement was negotiated providing that all students between the ages of 6 and 21 would receive free public education. An additional clause expedited inclusion of disabled students into the regular education program. This clause required that programs for those students with mental retardation must be very similar to programs for those without disabilities.

## Mills v. Board of Education—1972

The other half of the pair of court decisions that influenced the direction of education for students with disabilities was the *Mills* case. This case was initiated in the District of Columbia for all out-of-school students with disabilities. Guardians and parents of seven children brought the suit. These seven children represented a variety of disabilities including mental retardation, epilepsy, hyperactivity, and physical disability.

The court judgement was handed down in favor of the students. The school board was directed to provide all students with disabilities a free public education. However, the most important part of this decision was institution of procedural safeguards. These safeguards include written procedures for due process, the right to appeal decisions, and access to records. In addition, the court determined that no child with a disability could be excluded on the basis of insufficient resources in a school district and, further, that each child must be individually assessed and placed in a publicly supported program suited to the child's needs. The term "least restrictive environment" originated with this case, the court stating that a child should be placed in the least restrictive environment in which he or she can function.

After these two cases were settled, the stage was set for many more cases regarding students with disabilities. They were indeed harbingers of favorable times for parents of students with disabilities. However, laws that were enacted as a result of this trend resulted in inconsistent practices. It became increasingly clear to educators and parents that some type of federal intervention was necessary.

# Federal Legislation

Although several key pieces of legislation related to students with disabilities have been enacted by Congress from 1973 to the present, four of these have had direct impact upon educational opportunities for children with special needs. In addition, a 1982 U.S. Supreme Court decision further clarified the phrase "free and appropriate public education."

## Public Law 93-112: Vocational Rehabilitation Act—1973

As a result of the previously discussed court cases, Congress enacted federal legislation designed to eliminate discrimination against disabled students. The first instance was approved in 1973 as Public Law 93-112, the Vocational Rehabilitation Act. This law forbade discrimination on the basis of an individual's handicap in any program or activity that received federal assistance. The act also defined "handicapped" and charged schools to locate all people who might qualify for special assistance. The law further required the schools to provide these individuals with a free and appropriate public education.

## Public Law 94-142: Education for All Handicapped Children Act—1975

Public Law 93-112 was followed by Public Law 94-142, the Education for All Handicapped Children Act, approved by Congress in 1975. This law, referred to as EAHCA, required all states to establish a free and appropriate educational program for students with special educational needs. It also established procedural safeguards around the Individualized Educational Program (IEP) required for each child. While this legislation has greatly benefitted children in need of special programs, it has at the same time had some negative effects on schools. For example, it has produced as much, if not more, litigation than any other federal education statute on the books.

## Public Law 101-476: Individuals with Disabilities Education Act—1990

In 1990 Congress renamed EAHCA the "Individuals with Disabilities Education Act" (IDEA). This legislation, P.L. 101-476, replaced the term "handicapped" with "disabled," so that "handicapped children" were referred to as "children with disabilities." IDEA broadly defined disabilities to include mental retardation, visual and hearing impairments, serious emotional disturbance, autism, orthopedic impairment, traumatic brain injury, and other health impairments or specific learning disabilities. Students in late stages of AIDS fall within the above coverage, but the laws are not fully developed on the point at which an AIDS condition becomes sufficiently disabling to qualify for IDEA benefits.

The act directed states and school districts to include disabled students in regular education programs whenever possible. The main tenets of IDEA include: identification and evaluation, zero rejection of students, personal development, technology-related assistance, free and appropriate public education, least restrictive environment, and, where necessary, placement in private schools.

## Public Law 101-336: Americans with Disabilities Act—1990

The last of the four significant laws approved by Congress was P.L. 101-336, the Americans with Disabilities Act (ADA). Approved in 1990, this legislation expanded into the private sector requirements for civil rights for students with disabilities.

Beginning with *Brown v. Board of Education* (1954), parents and advocacy groups have won many battles to obtain services for their children. Two key points were used in the argument for these services. The first, as noted earlier, was that many students with disabilities were receiving no education at all. The second was that there is a difference in the education needed by students with particular disabilities (Yell, 1998). These were powerful arguments in the struggle to win a free public education for all students. The requirement that schools develop an individualized education program (IEP) for each identified special education student established specific road maps for the education of disabled children.

## H.R. 1350: Reauthorization of IDEA— 2004

In December, 2004, President George W. Bush signed the law reauthorizing the IDEA legislation. The President remarked that more than 6 million children with disabilities were being educated in America. He said, "We're raising expectations for the students. . . . We're applying the reforms of the No Child Left Be-

hind Act to the Individuals with Disabilities Education Improvement Act" (Bush, 2004).

In a 32-page document summarizing the legislation, the Council for Exceptional Children (CEC) highlighted new credential requirements and took issue with them (Council, 2004). First, in CEC's view, the standards were unreasonably demanding in requiring that special education teachers meet the "highly qualified" standards of No Child Left Behind (NCLB) in academic areas. Conversely, however, CEC saw loopholes through which states might enable teachers to meet the new IDEA standard simply by passing a paper-and-pencil test.

Other features, as summarized by the National and California School Boards Associations (both in 2004), addressed multi-year IEPs, early intervention before students have been identified, outcome measures rather than monitoring of compliance, student discipline, funding of related services, attorney fees, and funding. In addition, changes in due process and hearing procedures were intended primarily to reduce lawsuits by imposing time limitations and pushing for mediation.

## *Honig v. Doe*—1988

This Supreme Court decision was a major victory for parents of disabled children. The case involved two students: one identified as John Doe and the other, Jack Smith. Each student was identified as emotionally disturbed. Honig was California's secretary of education.

Doe and Smith were expelled from the San Francisco Unified School District for violent behavior. Doe choked another student and kicked out a window as he was being taken to the principal's office. Smith extorted money from classmates and made sexual comments to female students. Each student qualified for special education services and alleged that the expulsions violated the so-called "stay-put" provisions of EAHCA.

Upon appeal, the district court stated that the two students had a right to a free, appropriate public education, and prohibited the district from suspending a student with disabilities for more than 5 days when their misconduct was disability related. The court ordered the state to provide services directly to eligible students if the local district failed to do so.

The district court addressed the IDEA's "stay-put" provision, explaining that in enacting "stay-put," Congress intended to strip schools of the unilateral authority from excluding disabled students from school. It was noted that the IEP is the centerpiece of the education delivery. The court emphasized the necessity of parental participation in the development of the IEP and any assessments of the effectiveness of the education plan. On appeal, the Ninth Circuit Court affirmed the order with a minor change: a 10-day suspension was permitted, rather than 5 days.

The U.S. Supreme Court heard the case in 1987. The Court ruled that the Doe appeal was moot as Doe had passed the age of 21and was no longer eligible for services. However, Smith was still eligible for services. The Court noted that Congress wanted to prohibit schools from unilaterally excluding disabled students from school. The Supreme Court affirmed that the state must provide services directly to students with disabilities when local boards fail to do so. However, school officials may still expel students in the interest of maintaining a safe learning environment.

## Clarification of "Free and Appropriate Public Education"

Two perplexing special education issues have confronted parents and educators regarding the interpretation of the special education laws. What is the definition of "free and appropriate education," and who pays court costs when parents disagree with a school district about the education of their child?

The first issue was somewhat clarified by the U.S. Supreme Court in *Board of Education of the Hendrick Hudson Central School District v. Rowley* (1982). The second question of who pays was addressed by the High Court in *Schaffer v. Weast,* and additional clarification is expected in *Locke v. Davey.* The Court heard this case in 2004 and rendered a 7–2 decision that Washington State could exclude a student from a publically funded scholarship who was majoring in theology.

## Board of Education of the Hendrick Hudson Central School District v. Rowley—1982

In this case, the court held that the mandate for "free and appropriate public education" is satisfied when a state provides personalized instruction with *sufficient* support services to permit the disabled child to benefit educationally from that instruction. The instruction and services must be provided at public expense and in accord with the child's IEP. The significance of *Row-*

*ley* for school personnel is that the court rejected the argument that school districts are required to provide the best possible education to disabled children.

## Schaffer v. Weast—2005

The next case has significant implications for special education students. Public Law 94-142, approved by Congress in 1975, requires all states to establish a free and appropriate educational program for students with educational needs.

The question was does the burden of proof lie with parents who challenge a student's Individualized Education Plan (IEP)? All school districts must create an IEP for each disabled child. If parents believe their child's IEP is inappropriate, they may request an impartial due process hearing.

The Act is silent as to which party bears the burden of persuasion at such a hearing. Must the district prove that the IEP is adequate, or must the parents prove it is not?

The case began in 1998 with a student who had been in private school from pre-K to seventh grade. The child's parents contacted a public school in Maryland about the possibility of enrolling their son in special education classes.

The district developed an IEP that offered 15.3 hours of special education plus 45 minutes of speech therapy each week. The parents informed the district that they felt the IEP was not adequate and that their son would be attending the private school. The parents started due process proceedings and sought tuition reimbursement.

An administrative law judge ruled the burden of proof lay with the parents, and the parents' request for reimbursement was denied. The parents then took the case to federal court and sued the district. The federal court ruled in favor of the parents. The district then appealed to the U.S. Court of Appeals, which reversed the lower court and stated that the burden of proof rested with the parents since they were the party seeking relief.

The Supreme Court in a 6-2 decision ruled that parents who challenge the district's program for their child have the burden of proving the program is not appropriate. The decision will make it more difficult for some parents to win lawsuits that seek compensation for the cost of sending their child to a private school.

Montgomery County School Superintendent Jerry Weast was quoted as saying, "The case just seems to be an issue of common sense." Common sense suggests that if people make a complaint, they should be prepared to explain, defend, and pay for it (EdCAL, 2005.)

## Arlington Central School District v. Murphy, Pearl, et vir.—2006

The ink was barely dry on the Weast decision when the U.S. Supreme Court heard the case of *Arlington v. Murphy* (2006). This case also relates to the expense of appealing a decision made by a local school board regarding an Individualized Education Plan (IEP) for a child when the parent disagrees with the school's decision.

The Murphys, parents of a disabled child, requested that the school district pay their child's tuition at a private school that specialized in educating children with learning disabilities. The district rejected the tuition claim and the claim of $29,350 in fees for an educational expert. The Murphys had employed the expert to assist with their case. The district rejected the claim and asserted that while Public Law 94-142 authorizes the reimbursement for attorney's fees, it does not have to reimburse for "expert fees."

The Murphys won their case in district court and the decision was affirmed by the 2nd Circuit Court of Appeals. The Circuit Court ruled that expert fees were implicitly covered by the Act. However, the 7th and 8th Circuit Courts of Appeals had rejected similar claims (Wright, W. D. & Darr, P., 2006).

Lawyers for the school district appealed the decision to the U.S. Supreme Court. They asked for reconciliation of the opposing arguments of the Appellate Courts. They also argued that the fees would lead to increased litigation costs for parents and schools. They also argued that the ruling conflicted with the 1991 Supreme Court precedent in *West Virginia University Hospitals, Inc. v. Casey*.

In *Casey,* the high court did not authorize awarding fees in civil rights litigation for experts. After *Casey,* Congress considered legislation that would permit payment for expert fees, but rejected the proposal.

The U.S. Supreme Court heard the appeal in April of 2006 and rendered an opinion that same year. Justice Samuel Alito, writing for the 6-3 majority, ruled that IDEA does not authorize the payment of experts' fees. If the court had ruled in favor of the families, the decision would have had a significant financial impact on school districts. The decision also impacts the services of consultants, advocates, and other individuals who assist parents during special education due process hearings.

## Winkelman v. Parma City School District—2007

Just a year after parents of students with disabilities lost the right to have school districts pay the fees for experts in cases involving the Individuals with Disabilities Education Act (IDEA), they gained the right to represent their child in court without legal counsel. The U.S. Supreme Court ruled that parents could go to court without legal representation to fight a school district's choice of a special education program for their child. This unanimous decision opened a door that had been closed in many parts of the nation, where judges decided that parents could not go to court without a lawyer to represent them.

The Winkelmans, parents of Jacob, an autistic child, disagreed with the school district's placement of Jacob in a regular kindergarten class. Instead, the parents enrolled him in a private school where tuition was $56,000 a year. They paid for the first year, but as their income was less than $40,000 they could not pay for the second year. The parents asked the school district to pay for the private school and reimburse them for the first year's tuition.

The Parma District refused, and when the Winkelmans tried to challenge the district in court, a federal judge and the U.S. Court of Appeals, 6th Circuit, dismissed their case on the grounds that they did not have a lawyer. The parents argued that private lawyers were often too expensive for the average American. The Court ruled that a private lawyer was not required as the federal law gives children with disabilities a right to a "free appropriate public education" and parents the right to fight for them in court.

Several national education groups argued that ruling in favor of the parents would spur more costly and drawn-out lawsuits. While that may be true, the U.S. Supreme Court ruling does not mean that the Winkelmans will be reimbursed for the tuition or have the district continue to pay the tuition for Jacob's enrollment in the private school. The decision does give the parents a chance to plead their case in court.

## California Master Plan for Special Education

In response to the federal legislation, each state was required to develop a master plan to provide for the education of children with special needs. The California legislature approved Senate Bill 1870 in 1980.

This legislation was created to implement a statewide Master Plan for Special Education. The plan, begun as a pilot program in 1975–76, underwent several major changes between 1975–76 and 1979–80. It was implemented statewide in 1980.

The master plan was designed to provide flexibility in program and funding. The program side of the plan requires that, prior to placing a child in a special education program, a district must conduct an assessment to determine whether the child is most appropriately served in a special education setting or in the regular classroom. If special education services are needed, an Individualized Education Program (IEP) is written for that pupil, describing the program to be provided. The IEP matches placement and services to a student's individual needs, instead of, as occurred all too often in the former system, placing him or her in a program based solely on the label for a particular handicapping condition.

## The Individualized Education Program (IEP)

Requiring teachers to develop an Individualized Education Program for each student identified as having a disability was a major milestone in the education of special education students. All aspects of the special education program are directed and monitored by the IEP. If the IEP does not properly address the student's needs, then according to the courts, the student's special education program is not valid. The purposes of this plan include communication, accountability, compliance, monitoring, and evaluation.

Although IEP format may differ slightly by district, certain components must be included in every IEP:

- goals and objectives that are annualized and include benchmarks
- specific services and service providers to be provided to the student
- present levels of educational performance, including instruments that determined this level
- dates that show the beginning and duration of services
- statements indicating how the student's progress is to be related to the parents
- how the least restrictive environment requirement is to be met.

An IEP assessment team should include the student's special education and regular education teach-ers, a representative of the school district, the parents, and, if appropriate, the student. Particular state mandates that work in concert with the IDEA must also be adhered to. The 2004 reauthorization of IDEA included provisions to pilot a multi-year IEP (Council, 2004).

## Peter P., et al., v. Compton Unified School District—2015

It's no secret that U.S. schools have a lot to work on when it comes to offering mental and emotional support for students. Childhood trauma has been linked to a number of poor school outcomes, such as failing grades, suspensions, dropouts, and lower literacy rates. Whether due to budgetary constraints or ideological ones, it can be difficult to establish an educational standard for how to treat psychological issues that occur outside of the classroom.

In 2015, a group of students and teachers filed a class-action lawsuit in federal court against the Compton Unified School District. The complaint alleges a widespread, but often ignored, problem. It is a serious health crisis that affects learning, and must be addressed. The case marks the first time that a federal law will be used to determine if complex trauma can be considered a disability. The lawsuit argues that school districts are obligated under federal disability law to offer support for students who have experienced trauma. If the court sides with the plaintiffs in the case, Compton schools will be required to hire counselors and train employees to better understand students who have been exposed to traumatic life events.

This lawsuit focuses on trauma from the home, rather than the school. The plaintiffs note the lack of health resources in Compton, a city with a notorious reputation for violence. The city's murder rate is five times the national average (Shankar, 2015).

The attorneys who represented the students hope that this case will set a precedent across the state and nation to ensure that the trauma to which young people have experienced will be treated.

## Related Services

Under IDEA, states must ensure that all children with disabilities receive a free and appropriate education. To this end, school districts are required to provide related services to identified disabled students as specified in the IEP. Such services may include speech pathology, audiology, psychological and physical assistance, and occupational therapy. Related services may also include therapeutic recreation, social work services, counseling, and medical services for diagnostic and evaluation purposes (Wenkart, 1995).

In *Irving Independent School District v. Tatro* (1984), the U.S. Supreme Court reviewed the meaning of related services. Amber Tatro was born with spina bifida. She suffered from orthopedic and speech impairments and a neurogenic bladder, which prevented her from emptying her bladder voluntarily. Therefore, catheterization was required every three or four hours to avoid injury to her kidneys.

The Supreme Court found that catheterization was essential in that it would enable the child to attend school and benefit from instruction. The court held further that clean, intermittent catheterization was a related service, as it could be provided by a lay person and did not require the services of a physician. The court noted that Congress did not intend that school districts be required to provide medical services that might be unduly expensive or beyond their range of competence. Nevertheless, school districts must provide education for children with serious medical needs, either in their home or in a hospital.

Finally, federal regulations require transportation of disabled students to and from school, even if specialized equipment is needed. A student qualifies for transportation if such service is provided for other similarly situated children or if included in the IEP. Failure to provide service to identified disabled students has resulted in courts requiring districts to reimburse parents their costs plus interest for transportation, time, effort, and babysitting.

## Residential Placement

The IDEA and federal regulations require school districts to pay for residential placement in nonpublic facilities, if such placements are necessary for the disabled child to benefit from special education. The school district must pay the cost of the program, including non-medical care and room and board. However, where the primary reason for the child's placement is medical, not educational, the school district is not liable.

The case of *Capistrano Unified School District v. Wartenberg* (1995) illustrates the complexities of this issue. (Note that the school district is listed as plaintiff because the case was on appeal; the original plaintiffs were, of course, the student and his parents.)

Jeremy was failing in school. The district increased special education services. When these did not help, the district concluded that the student's difficulties were a result of his misbehavior, not of his learning disability, and proposed reducing special education services. The parents disagreed and, without district concurrence, placed their son in a private school certified by California to serve special education students. They then sued the district for the costs of private school and for their attorney's fees. The U.S. District Court found for the parents and required the district to reimburse Jeremy's parents for costs of tuition and transportation.

The Ninth Circuit Court of Appeals outlined the legal issues: first, whether Jeremy's failure in school was the result of his learning disability or his misbehavior; second, whether in relation to the learning disability the public school had provided an appropriate program; and third, whether the district court had used appropriate procedures in reaching its decision. The court affirmed the district court in its procedures, in its conclusion that Jeremy's difficulties resulted from his learning disability, and finally, in its finding that the proposed IEP did not allow sufficient time in special services to address Jeremy's needs. In taking this position, the court rejected an argument on the district's part citing the importance of mainstreaming. On the basis of an earlier U.S. Supreme Court decision, the appeals court awarded costs of schooling and attorney fees to the Wartenbergs.

## Disciplining Students with Disabilities

A perplexing and important topic relative to education of disabled students is that of student discipline. This topic finds administrators and advocacy groups at odds. Special education laws do not exempt children from discipline for misbehavior unless that conduct is disability-related or the disciplinary punishment will defeat the purposes of those laws. Case law suggests that punishment is permissible for conduct that is within a child's reasonable control. However, the courts appear to favor less drastic action than the normal discipline procedures of suspension or expulsion for identified special education students.

Two provisions of the Education for All Handicapped Children Act must be considered when disciplinary action is taken with disabled students: free appropriate education and least restrictive environment. Acceptable environments for placement of a disabled student range from least restrictive (a regular classroom) to highly restrictive (an institution). However, either environment may be termed "least restrictive," depending on the seriousness of a particular handicap and on the individual child's ability to cope within the environment.

A 1997 amendment to IDEA finally addressed this issue. The amendment permits many disciplinary procedures for special education students, including detention, exclusionary time-outs, reprimands, and in-school suspension. However, except in isolated cases, long-term expulsions are not allowed unless it can be shown that the disability and the behavior are unrelated.

In *Honig v. Doe* (1988), the U.S. Supreme Court prohibited a school district from unilaterally excluding a disabled student from the classroom for an indeterminate period of time when dangerous or disruptive conduct is related to the student's disability. However, the court did allow school districts to suspend a student for up to ten days to protect the safety of others and to provide a "cooling down period."

As noted in chapter 4, the IDEA reauthorization allowed immediate removal of a special education student who injures someone on school grounds or at a school event and suspension if weapons or drugs are brought to school. The length of time allowed for an interim placement was also extended from approximately six to nine weeks.

## Graduation of Special Education Students

The courts have generally upheld state laws that require disabled students to pass a minimal competency test before they may receive a high school diploma. However, districts are required to give sufficient notice to the students of this requirement. In California, the Education Code gives districts the opportunity to establish differential standards for special education students. These standards must be included in the IEP. When a student achieves satisfactory progress on the differential standards, he or she may receive a certificate or document of educational achievement. A special education student who meets the criteria for a certificate may also participate in the graduation ceremony (E.C. 56390–56391).

## Attorney Fees

The courts may award "reasonable" attorney fees to parents who prevail against a school district in a hearing or court action. The fees were permitted by a 1986 amendment entitled the Handicapped Children's Protection Act (HCPA). The amendment was approved because the Congress felt that without it, the cost of attorney fees could make parents reluctant to raise valid complaints challenging school district actions. Although this amendment has provided the resources for many parents to initiate a lawsuit, it has placed a financial drain on many school districts, since the parents' attorney fees can run into hundreds of thousands of dollars.

It should also be noted that some restrictions were placed on awarding attorney fees by the IDEA legislation of 1997 and, more recently, the 2001 decision of the U.S. Supreme Court in *Buckhannon Board & Care Home v. West Virginia Department of Health and Human Resources*. Consequently, attorney fees will be paid only if the plaintiff prevails and, more specifically, is awarded relief by the court. In addition, with the reauthorization of IDEA, signed by the President in December, 2004, state and local education agencies can recover attorney fees in the event parents or their attorneys file a frivolous lawsuit (National School Boards, 2004).

## Continuing Lawsuits

As indicated in this chapter, parents of children with disabilities continue to turn to the courts in their attempt to force school districts to provide an educational program for their children. Although lawsuits against educational institutions nationwide have been declining, litigation involving special education continues to rise. A study by Lehigh's Zirkel (1999) found that special education lawsuits rose at a dramatic rate in the 1980s and a moderate rate in the 1990s. About a third of education litigation in federal courts in recent years has involved special education (Dolan, 1999). Parents of special education students bring lawyers to school meetings, and teachers have had to learn to work with the parent who brings a tape recorder to an IEP meeting.

In one case now on appeal, a school district in Santa Barbara County was ordered to pay the educational costs of a student in juvenile detention at a residential facility for troubled boys. The school had disciplined the boy for such offenses as possession of a razor knife, choking another student, and telling a teacher's aide to perform a sexual act with him. The attorney for the student said that the 14-year-old developed problems because the school district failed to provide him with appropriate services for a learning disability, and the court agreed. This case is presented as just one example of the ongoing conflict between parents who believe that a district is not providing their child with an appropriate educational program and district personnel who disagree with the perceived need or argue that the district does not have resources to meet the need.

## Summary

This chapter has reviewed major laws and court cases that have provided a foundation for special education programs in effect today. Some of the most perplexing issues for the school administrator are those relating to the discipline of special education students. Since an IEP team has formulated the student's plan, this same team would best be involved in disciplinary procedures. The process is complex because the due process rights of these students must be observed, observational data must be written, and disciplinary actions applied in a nondiscriminatory manner.

## Key Terms

1. ADA
2. California Master Plan
3. FAPE
4. HCPA
5. IDEA
6. IDEA Improvement Act
7. IEP
8. inclusion
9. least restrictive environment
10. mainstreaming
11. P.L. 94-142
12. related services

## Discussion/Essay Questions

1. Why was *Brown v. Board of Education* considered key to later special education law?

2. What issues with respect to educational placement of a child with disabilities might lead to contention between parents and school administrators?

3. Present three arguments to show why disciplining special education students can present a legal liability issue for the school administrator.

4. Why is the IEP so important for the education of special education students? What educational theories underlie its structure?

5. Do you believe that school districts should be required to pay the legal fees for parents when there is a dispute between the district and parents? Support your answer by citing appropriate statutes and case law.

# CHAPTER 7

# Sexual Harassment in Education

*No one questions that a student suffers extraordinary harm when subjected to sexual harassment and abuse by a teacher.*

—U.S. Supreme Court Justice Sandra Day O'Connor

## Introduction

A high school auto shop teacher is accused by one of his students of asking her out for dates and refusing to take "no" for an answer. He is married, but within three months of the accusation his wife has filed for divorce, and he has been fired from his job.

A school head custodian is accused of creating a hostile sexual atmosphere in the employee lounge by bringing to work some of his old *Playboy* magazines. The district fires him because of this incident.

A student calls another student a "bitch" and is expelled from the district for his action. Are these examples of sexual harassment? Was the district within its legal rights when it dismissed the employee and expelled the student?

It is clear that sexual harassment is becoming a major concern to school districts. This chapter addresses the definition of sexual harassment, the historical evolution of its significance in the workplace, its various forms (student to student, staff member to staff member, school district employee to student), and court decisions that address the issue.

## Definition of Sexual Harassment

Sexual harassment has not been clearly defined in legislation or by the courts. In 1986 the Supreme Court, in *Meritor Savings Bank v. Vinson*, defined sexual harassment as "a form of discrimination." The court recognized for the first time that a violation of Title VII of the Civil Rights Act of 1964 can be pred-

icated on "harassment that creates a hostile or offensive working environment in addition to harassment that involves receiving employment benefits based on granting sexual favors." The court noted that conduct unreasonably interfering with an individual's work performance or creating an intimidating, hostile, or offensive working environment is actionable. Furthermore, the employer may not use as a defense the fact that the individual voluntarily engaged in sex-related conduct.

The Equal Employment Opportunity Commission (EEOC) provides guidelines regarding sexual harassment. These are set forth in the Code of Federal Regulations (see Table 2). Subsection (c), dealing with harassment by supervisors, was removed to comply with two U.S. Supreme Court decisions in 1998; a separate document on this topic is posted on the EEOC Website (Equal Employment, 1999).

There are two forms of sexual harassment: *quid pro quo* harassment and creation of a hostile sexual atmosphere. *Quid pro quo* literally means "something for something." In federal law, Title IX of the Education Amendments of 1972 prohibits unwelcome sexual behavior by any party who is in an inherently unequal position in relation to another. Because they are in a position to affect students' grades, academic attainments, and career choices, teachers hold power over students. Therefore, an example of *quid pro quo* harassment occurs if a teacher offers a student an A grade in return for sexual favors. The second category of harassment, "hostile sexual atmosphere," is more difficult to define, but occurs when a student or employee is mistreated solely due to gender.

## Federal Laws Related to Sexual Harassment

The major federal statutes prohibiting sexual harassment include:

**Table 2**   **Sexual Harassment in the Code of Federal Regulations, 29CFR1604.11, implementing the Civil Rights Act of 1964, Title VII**

(a) Harassment on the basis of sex is a violation of Sec. 703 of Title VII. Unwelcome sexual advances, requests for sexual favors, and other verbal or physical conduct of a sexual nature constitute sexual harassment when (1) submission to such conduct is made either explicitly or implicitly a term or condition of an individual's employment, (2) submission to or rejection of such conduct by an individual is used for employment decisions affecting such individual, or (3) such conduct has the purpose or effect of unreasonably interfering with an individual's work performance or creating an intimidating, hostile, or offensive working environment.

(b) In determining whether alleged conduct constitutes sexual harassment, the Commission will look at the record as a whole and at the totality of the circumstances, such as the nature of the sexual advances and the context in which the alleged incidents occurred. The determination of the legality of a particular action will be made from the facts, on a case by case basis.

(c) [Reserved]

(d) With respect to conduct between fellow employees, an employer is responsible for acts of sexual harassment in the workplace where the employer (or its agents or supervisory employees) knows or should have known of the conduct, unless it can be shown that immediate and appropriate corrective action was taken.

(e) An employer may also be responsible for the acts of non-employees, with respect to sexual harassment of employees in the workplace, where the employer (or its agents or supervisory employees) knows or should have known of the conduct and fails to take immediate and appropriate corrective action. In reviewing these cases the Commission will consider the extent of the employer's control and any other legal responsibility, which the employer may have with respect to the conduct of such non-employees.

(f) Prevention is the best tool for the elimination of sexual harassment. An employer should take all steps necessary to prevent sexual harassment from occurring, such as affirmatively raising the subject, expressing strong disapproval, developing appropriate sanctions, informing employees of their right to raise and how to raise the issue of harassment under Title VII, and developing methods to sensitize all concerned.

(g) Other related practices: Where employment opportunities or benefits are granted because of an individual's submission to the employer's sexual advances or requests for sexual favors, the employer may be held liable for unlawful sex discrimination against other persons who were qualified for but denied that employment opportunity or benefit.

- The Equal Protection Clause of the Fourteenth Amendment to the Constitution
- Title VII of the Civil Rights Act of 1964
- Title IX of the Education Amendments of 1972.

The federal administrative agencies that handle complaints are the Equal Employment Opportunity Commission (EEOC) and the Office of Civil Rights (OCR).

## The Fourteenth Amendment

Already quoted earlier in this book, the Fourteenth Amendment to the U.S. Constitution provides that

No State shall make or enforce any law which shall abridge the privileges or immunities of citizens of the United States; nor shall any State deprive any person of life, liberty, or property, without due process of law; nor deny to any person within its jurisdiction the equal protection of the laws.

This provision, known as the "Equal Protection Clause," provides the basis for federal legislation and regulations governing state and local governmental agencies, including school districts, on issues such as opportunity for employment and equal access to public services.

## Civil Rights Act of 1964

Since Title VII of the Civil Rights Act of 1964 (Section 1604.11) is the basis of sexual harassment suits, it is important to know the official text of the regulations enforcing the law, which are reproduced in Table 2. It will be noted that this legislation applies primarily to the working environment.

## Title IX Regulations of 1972

Just as Title VII of the Civil Rights Act of 1964 prohibits sexual discrimination in the workplace, Title IX of 1972, a part of the Education Amendments, prohibits sexual discrimination in educational programs that are supported with federal monies. The law addresses harassment of an employee by an employee and harassment of a student by an employee or another student. Title IX is credited with sparking a revolution in women's sports.

To achieve gender equity, high schools and colleges were forced to greatly expand and improve their athletic programs for women. More recently, women's rights lawyers have also looked to Title IX as a means of protecting students from sexual harassment. They have brought damage claims against school systems that failed to prevent sexual harassment of female students, whether by teachers or others.

## Evolution in the Workplace

The Civil Rights Acts of 1964 and its 1988 amendments were important milestones in defining sexual harassment and making it illegal. Subsequent court decisions have profoundly affected the interpretation of the law (French, 1998).

The initial cases of sexual harassment emerged from private industry. The Equal Employment Opportunity Commission issued guidelines in 1980 clarifying the illegal aspects of sex-related behaviors. As noted earlier, the U.S. Supreme Court broadened the definition of sexual harassment in the case of *Meritor Savings Bank v. Vinson* (1986). In this case, the court determined that sexual harassment occurs not only when employment or salary level is threatened, but also if an "intimidating, hostile, or offensive working environment" is created by sex-related behaviors.

Sexual harassment cases in private industry have become commonplace, especially in the last decade. An example is a suit against the law firm of Baker and McKensie of San Francisco in which the firm was ordered to pay $3.5 million for sexual harassment. Another example that received widespread media coverage was a lawsuit filed by a male employee at a hot tub manufacturing company in Los Angeles. His claim, for which he was awarded $1 million, was based on an allegation that the chief financial officer, a female, made regular sexual advances that the plaintiff found unwelcome and refused.

High profile cases have made Americans more aware of sexual harassment in the workplace. The topic again captured national attention when Justice Clarence Thomas, then a Supreme Court nominee, was accused of having sexually harassed a former employee and colleague, Anita Hill. Another event that triggered attention was the U.S. Navy's Tailhook scandal, involving sexual harassment of women attending a naval conference. In yet another case, a well-established restaurant declared bankruptcy when a waitress brought suit against a supervisor.

Such stories have rocked industry, especially in the past ten years, and have had a profound effect on the workplace. Consequently, there has been a major shift in the way supervisors think about sexual harassment (Maidment, 1998). Business managers and executives have increased their understanding of the seriousness of sexual harassment charges. Many employers have sought to reduce the chance that their business will be sued. These employers have developed a policy and made certain that all employees understand it. They have taken steps to inform employees that their jobs will not be adversely affected if they lodge a complaint.

Governmental entities were latecomers to recognizing their responsibilities when sexual harassment occurs. As awareness grew, federal, state, and municipal government officials began to develop sexual awareness seminars and to develop policies to deal with this issue. However, school districts were slow to see the need for policy development and employee awareness.

## California Laws Related to Sexual Harassment

Major California laws regarding sexual harassment are included in the following:

- California Fair Employment and Housing Act
- California Education Code
- California Civil Code, Section 51.9
- California Common Law Causes of Action

The administrative agency that handles many of these cases is the Department of Fair Employment and Housing.

## Staff Member to Staff Member Sexual Harassment

Closest to the cases in private industry are instances of harassment from staff member to staff member in a school or district. Following is a situation that involved charges of sexual harassment at the highest level—between the superintendent and the chief financial officer.

## Harden Sues Dallas School District—1998

According to the *Abilene Reporter-News,* the Dallas School Board had faced an unusual situation in 1997. The chief financial officer, Matthew Harden, Jr., alleged that the District Superintendent, Yvonne Gonzalez, had sexually harassed him and intentionally ruined the careers of several competent district employees. There were 154,985 students in the Dallas school system: 41.5% black, 45.5% Hispanic, and slightly more than 10% White. In its decision to hire Gonzalez, the school board had split along racial lines; she had not received the support of the black community in her appointment.

In his suit against the district board, board president, and superintendent, Harden, who is black, alleged that Gonzalez made "personal overtures" to him and placed a tracking device on his car because "she was jealous of other women around him." Harden also claimed that Gonzalez sent him suggestive notes, such as "How about a little one-on-one?" The suit also alleged that although Gonzalez was already married, she wanted to marry Harden.

Gonzalez responded that Harden's lawsuit was an attempt to discredit her because of an ongoing probe into district corruption and mismanagement. At the time, Harden's division was the subject of internal and FBI investigations involving allegations of overtime abuse, contract fixing, and other problems. Several of Harden's top staffers had been placed on administrative leave or fired. All thirteen employees indicted on federal charges of overtime fraud were in Harden's division.

In the case of staff versus staff charges of sexual harassment, EEOC guidelines apply, as the issues involve "unwelcome sexual advances, requests for sexual favors, and other verbal and physical conduct." In this case Gonzalez was placed on administrative leave while the charges were investigated.

In February 1998, the suit was settled out of court. Harden received $600,000 in exchange for dropping his suits against the board and the board president and resigning. In the meantime, Superintendent Gonzalez had already resigned and then pleaded guilty to a charge of using district funds to purchase personal furniture (Dallas, 1998).

## Murray v. Oceanside Unified School District—2002

Another case that ended in an out-of-court settlement was brought by a lesbian teacher, Dawn Murray. Plaintiff alleged that she had been subjected to harassment, including loss of a promotion, due to her sexual orientation. She stated that the administration failed to take action when graffiti was painted outside her classroom, threatened job consequences if she continued to bring complaints, and announced her sexual orientation to the faculty.

Plaintiff lost in trial court, based on an interpretation of the Labor Code and application of a time limitation. The Superior Court of San Diego reversed that decision in 2000. Two years later the district settled for an amount in excess of $140,000 and agreed to "provide annual sensitivity training to its employees on issues of sexual orientation discrimination" (Lambda Legal, 2002).

## Employee to Student Harassment

Perhaps the most serious cases of sexual harassment occur when a school employee sexually harasses a student. The fact that students are under the care of adults and the school district greatly contributes to the seriousness of such abuse. In addition to criminal charges filed against the employee, districts are being held liable in these cases.

## Franklin v. Gwinnett County Public Schools—1988

In 1998, in *Franklin v. Gwinnett County Public Schools,* the U.S. Supreme Court indicated that a student deserves as much protection from sexual harassment by a teacher as does an employee from harassment by a supervisor. The *Franklin* case alleged teacher-to-student harassment.

Petitioner Christine Franklin was a student at North Gwinnett High School in Gwinnett County, Georgia, between 1985 and 1989. Christine charged that Andrew Hill, a sports coach and teacher, engaged her in sexually-oriented conversations and coerced her to submit to intercourse. She also charged that the school district was aware of Hill's actions, took no action to halt it, and discouraged Franklin from pressing charges against Hill. The court ruled that monetary damages are an allowable award for a successful claim of sexual harassment.

## *Gebser et al. v. Lago Vista Independent School District*—1998

In June of 1998 an additional and significant question regarding district liability was decided by the Supreme Court in *Gebser et al. v. Lago Vista Independent School District*. This decision determined when a school district may be held liable for damages in an implied right of action under Title IX of the Education Amendments of 1972. The case involved sexual harassment of a student by a district teacher. The court ruled that damages may not be recovered in those circumstances unless an official of the school district, who at a minimum has authority to institute corrective measures on the district's behalf, has had actual notice of, and is deliberately indifferent to, the teacher's misconduct.

The case involved a student who had a relationship with a teacher over a period of time. The petitioner, Alida Gebser, was an eighth-grade student at a middle school in Lago Vista Independent School District. The district received federal funds at the time, thus falling under the requirements of Title IX. Gebser joined a high school book discussion group led by Frank Waldrop, a teacher at Lago Vista's high school. During the book discussion sessions, Waldrop made sexually suggestive comments to the students. Gebser entered high school in the fall and was enrolled in classes taught by Waldrop in both of her freshman semesters.

The suit alleged that Waldrop continued making suggestive comments to Gebser and spent much time alone with her in the classroom. He initiated sexual contact with Gebser in the spring when, while visiting her home to give her a book, he kissed and fondled her. The two had sexual relationships on a number of occasions during the remainder of the school year.

Their relationship lasted for several months and they often had intercourse during class time, although never on school property.

In January of 1993 charges were filed against Waldrop for engaging in sexual relations with Gebser. Lago Vista terminated his employment and, subsequently, the Texas Education Agency revoked his teaching license. The district during this time had not distributed a formal anti-harassment policy, nor did it have a procedure for lodging complaints. Gebser and her mother filed suit against the district and Waldrop in state court in November of 1993 citing Title IX and state negligence law. They sought compensatory and punitive damages from both defendants, primarily under state law.

Upon appeal to the U.S. Supreme Court, Justice Sandra Day O'Connor, who wrote the court's opinion, stated, "No one questions that a student suffers extraordinary harm when subjected to sexual harassment and abuse by a teacher and the teacher's conduct is reprehensible." She continued, "Teachers who prey on students can be disciplined, fired, or even jailed in the worst cases, but the school system should not be required to pay large judgements for abuse of which it was unaware." The court concluded its analysis by reaffirming that "school districts are not liable in tort for teacher-student sexual harassment under title IX unless an employee who has been invested by the school board with supervisory power over the offending employee actually knew of the abuse, had the power to end the abuse, and failed to do so."

The *Lago Vista* case further established that while compensatory damages are available in theory, they may be difficult to obtain in practice. The opinion suggested that in cases of teacher-student harassment, the school's liability may be restricted (Busa, 1999).

# Student to Student Harassment

Student to student harassment has created a challenge to school authorities. On February 14, 1996, Judge Barkett, writing for the Eleventh Circuit, held that the Monroe County Board of Education *(Davis v. Monroe)* was in violation of Title IX, having allowed a "hostile environment" form of sexual harassment.

This case was the first Court of Appeals decision to allow the possibility of damages for student to student harassment. However, the decision was further modified by other court decisions, as we shall see shortly.

## Davis v. Monroe County Board of Education—1999

The Eleventh Circuit Court, in the case of *Davis v. Monroe County Board of Education* (1999), extended the established rule in *Franklin* to include the "hostile environment" protection of Title VII as compensable under Title IX. LaShonda, a fifth-grade female, had been sexually harassed by a fellow fifth-grade boy, G.F., for a period of six months between December 1992 and May 1993. Over this period, G.F. fondled LaShonda and directed sexually offensive language toward her. In December, for example, G.F. attempted to touch LaShonda's breasts and vaginal area, telling her "I want to get in bed with you" and "I want to feel your boobs." Two similar incidents occurred in January 1993. In February, G.F. placed a doorstop in his pants and behaved in a sexually suggestive manner toward LaShonda. Other incidents occurred later in February and in March. In April, G.F. rubbed up against LaShonda in the hallway in a sexually suggestive manner. G.F.'s actions increased in severity until he finally was charged with and pled guilty to sexual battery in May 1993.

LaShonda and her mother reported the incidents to both the teacher and the school principal. Other female students reported that G.F. had sexually harassed them. Neither the principal nor the teacher took remedial action to assist LaShonda or to correct G.F. Even LaShonda's request to move her seat so as not to be next to G.F. was refused for three months. He was never removed or disciplined in any way by school authorities.

The claim for damages was based upon allegations that G.F.'s uncurbed and unrestrained conduct severely curtailed LaShonda's ability to benefit from her elementary school education, lessening her capacity to concentrate on her schoolwork and causing her grades, previously all A's and B's, to deteriorate. The harassment had a debilitating effect on her mental and emotional well-being, leading her to write a suicide note in April of 1993.

The court found liability because the board had no policy and the teacher and principal took no action. The *Davis* court noted that a "female student should not be required to run a gauntlet of sexual abuse in return for being allowed to obtain an education." The court combined the Title VII doctrine regarding a sexually hostile working environment created by co-workers and tolerated by the employer with the Title IX requirements for protection of students.

Previous rulings by the federal court system had supported a broad application of Title VII guidelines for this purpose. In reaching their conclusions, some courts had interpreted the "intentional conduct" requirement (traditionally necessary for institutional liability) to read "callous indifference" in the case of educational institutions. Thus, indifference has come to meet the "intentional" requirement when school officials do not respond to complaints and fail to take prompt action to stop harassment.

In the *Davis* case, the court reasoned that when an educational institution knowingly fails to take action to remedy a hostile environment caused by a student's sexual harassment of another, the harassed student has "been denied the benefits of, or been subjected to discrimination under" that educational program. This extension of the *Franklin* doctrine created a significant media response. For example, primarily as a result of this decision, an article in the August 1996 *Reader's Digest* by Daniel Levine named Judge Barkett one of seven of America's worst judges. Levine quotes Clint Bolick, litigation director of the Institute for Justice in Washington, D.C., as follows:

> Decisions like this could cost taxpayers untold millions. Unless the decision is overturned or Congress amends the statute, every school district in America is at risk of schoolyard bullies exposing them to federal lawsuits.

The complexity of these issues may be noted, however, in that, subsequent to its 1996 decision, the Eleventh Circuit Court agreed to rehear the matter and reversed itself, thus dismissing the case. Plaintiffs appealed to the U.S. Supreme Court, which in May 1999 determined that private action for damages may be pursued against a school board, but "only for harassment that is so severe, pervasive, and objectively offensive that it effectively bars the victim's access to an educational opportunity" and, in addition, the federally-funded district acts with "deliberate indifference to known acts of harassment." The case was then remanded to the Circuit Court, which in March of 2000 sent it back to the original court for trial.

## Petaluma v. Jane Doe—1993

A highly publicized case of student-to-student harassment was that of *Petaluma v. Jane Doe* (1993). Jane Doe was a junior high school student in the Petaluma City School District in Sonoma County, California. Throughout seventh and eighth grade, other students allegedly harassed her sexually.

In fall of 1990, during her seventh-grade year, two boys said to her, "I hear you have a hot dog in your pants." Another student informed her that a rumor was spreading around the school about her "having a hot dog in her pants." Jane Doe reported this information to her guidance counselor, saying that she was very upset. He did nothing. She was continually harassed thereafter and informed the guidance counselor of this every other week. He stated that all he could do was warn the boys. He did not tell her that the vice-principal was the school's Title IX coordinator and was the appropriate person to handle the situation, nor did he tell her of the Title IX grievance procedure.

Toward the end of the semester, Jane's mother and father spoke to the counselor about the rumors. The parents described the behavior of several students who were calling Jane names, writing graffiti about her in the restrooms, and otherwise constantly harassing their daughter. The counselor replied that he was taking care of the problem. However, the harassment continued for several months, until the district's Title IX coordinator finally heard the case.

Eventually, Jane was transferred to another junior high school. She continued to be the subject of harassment. At this point, Jane's parents felt they had no choice but to enroll her in a private school. They filed suit in federal court to be compensated by the school district for monetary damages, including Jane's private school tuition and the costs of medical and psychological treatment.

The basis of their suit was Title IX of the Educational Amendments of 1972, which prohibits sexual discrimination by school districts and other entities that receive federal funds. For this purpose they relied to a significant extent on *Franklin v. Gwinnett County Public Schools* (1992). In addition, they claimed that the school district, principal, and counselor had violated Jane's substantive due process rights under the Fourteenth Amendment. According to the National Organization of Women (NOW), the case was settled out of court in January 1997 for $250,000 (*Landmark*, 1997). Although the case did not go to trial, NOW hailed it as "the first to affirm that schools are responsible for responding to sexual harassment by students." On the other hand, it should be noted that on appeal to the Northern District of California, a requirement was established that a district must have known or should have known of the harassment in order to be held liable.

The cases discussed in this chapter underscore that responsibility, while at the same time setting stringent requirements for interference with the harassed student's educational opportunities. Regardless of variations in interpretation of these conditions, recent cases have consistently emphasized that students may not be excluded from participation, denied benefits, or discriminated against because of sex.

## Appropriate School Board Actions

It is the responsibility of all school board members, school officials, teachers, and school employees to maintain an environment that is free of sexual harassment. A number of steps can be taken to ensure a work environment that is free of sexual harassment and, should such behavior occur, an appropriate response.

The first requirement is adoption of a sexual harassment policy that includes a definition of sexual harassment and the proper procedures to follow should it occur. The second requirement is designation of officials charged with the responsibility for immediately investigating and taking appropriate action to remedy any reported sexual harassment. A third requirement is that the district provide an ongoing series of information meetings for staff regarding sexual harassment and the proper procedures to be followed if and when investigation or action becomes necessary.

## Student Sexual Orientation

All schools have a major objective of providing a safe school environment. That assurance of a safe environment includes protecting students from anti-lesbian, gay, bisexual, and transgender harassment. The national organization, Gay, Lesbian, Straight Education Network, known as GLSEN (2005) reported that between 2000 and 2005, 15 cases were filed against school districts charging that students had not been protected from discrimination based on sexual orientation. In each of the cases, the student prevailed in court or achieved a settlement. Districts were required to pay from $40,000 to $1.1 million.

An example of this type harassment is *Theno v. Tonganoxie*. In 2005, the U.S. District Court for the District of Kansas awarded Dylan Theno $250,000. Theno claimed that the school failed to protect him from sexual harassment by other students. He stated that he was subjected to sexual-based rumors and other sexual innuendo from the 7th grade until the 11th grade when he left school.

Theno, who is not gay, and his parents asked teachers and administrators to protect him from the harassment to no avail. He alleged that school officials were aware of the harassment, but didn't take sufficient action to ensure that the verbal abuse stopped.

## Summary

Sexual harassment has become a very important aspect of American society. Over the past few decades this issue has received generous media attention. As a consequence, awareness of the serious nature of sexual harassment has greatly increased. Employers and employees have become aware that unwanted touching, unwanted comments, and even the display of *Playboy* magazine are unacceptable conduct in many settings, including educational institutions.

Sexual harassment can take many forms: student-to-student, employee-to-employee, and employee-to-student. All districts must take positive, proactive steps to ensure that all students and employees are provided with an environment free of sexual harassment. Proactive steps include policies, procedures, and information programs to deal with the issue. School districts have joined other government agencies and private industry in informing employees of conduct that may be sexual harassment. Supervisors have also been informed of procedures to follow when they become aware of behavior that may be a form of sexual harassment.

The Office of Civil Rights (OCR) is the federal agency that ensures that schools comply with Title IX. Students who believe they are being sexually harassed and feel the school district is not taking appropriate action should contact one of the OCR offices to receive information about filing a complaint. School administrators should also contact one of these offices for technical assistance. This agency has posted a list of some frequently asked questions (FAQs) about sexual harassment, available on the Internet (U.S. Department, n.d.).

## Key Terms

1. Equal Employment Opportunity Commission
2. hostile sexual atmosphere
3. Office of Civil Rights
4. *quid pro quo* sexual harassment
5. Title VII of the Civil Rights Act of 1964
6. Title IX of the Education Amendments of 1972

## Discussion/Essay Questions

1. What are the grievance procedures that a student in your district should follow when sexually harassed by another student?

2. A recent Supreme Court decision has clarified the issue of school district liability in sexual harassment cases. What is this Supreme Court case? How does the decision impact school district liability?

3. What is the difference between *"quid pro quo"* sexual harassment and "establishing a hostile environment" sexual harassment?

4. What is the United States Office of Civil Rights? How does this office relate to sexual harassment claims?

# CHAPTER 8

# Title IX

*Title IX had just passed, and I wanted to change the hearts and minds of people to match the legislation.*

—Billie Jean King, rated #1 tennis player in the world in the 1960s

## Introduction

This chapter is primarily about the laws and court cases that school leaders need to know regarding Title IX. Moreover, it is also about the incredible achievements of females. In 1972, "I Am Woman," co-written and sung by Helen Reddy, became an anthem for the woman's liberation movement. Reddy said that the words were her search for a song that would express her growing passion for female empowerment. "I Am Woman" quickly captured the imagination of several women's organizations that were becoming powerful during the 1970s (Wikipedia,—Helen Reddy. 2008).

The nation's attention was about to change in 1973 with a tennis match between Bobby Riggs and Billie Jean King. It was dubbed the "Battle of the Sexes," and watched by 30 million viewers on television. Bobby Riggs had been one of the world's top tennis players in the 1940s; he had won six major titles during his career. Riggs saw an opportunity in the rise of the feminist movement to make money and to elevate the popularity of a sport he loved. He stated that the female game was inferior and that even at his current age of 55 he could still beat any of the top female players.

Riggs taunted all female tennis players to a match, which was accepted by female tennis great Billie Jean King. She accepted a lucrative financial offer to play Riggs in a nationally televised match that the promoters dubbed the "Battle of the Sexes." The match, which had a winner-takes-all prize of $100,000, was held in Houston, Texas, on September 20, 1973. There were 30,000 people in attendance and another 30 million watched the match on television.

The two played in this match for different reasons. Bobby Riggs was all about the money, and Billie Jean King played because she knew this match would be one that no one would ever forget. The odds of winning favored Riggs. The odds were wrong; King defeated Riggs in straight sets: 6-4, 6-3, and 6-3.

For King, that match was more than just beating Riggs; it was about proving that women can be just as good as men. She was a women's activist and believed in equal pay for men and women. King wanted men to respect women more, which is why it was so crucial for her to win. She said, "I thought it would set us back 50 years if I didn't win that match." She knew that all of the hard work that they had done would be wiped away if she lost. It would ruin the women's tour and affect all women's self-esteem." The match she won made women feel equal to men. This went for all women's sports, not just tennis. She believed that she was born to work for gender equality in sports (Schwartz, 1973).

During the second half of the 20th century, women had achieved significant success in many facets of life. They had become a major force in the job market, achieved near-success in many occupations, including teaching and nursing, and were gradually increasing college enrollment in the sciences, medical fields, and engineering.

However, complete equality was a long way off. A noticeable example of inequality was in the nation's public schools. Female students were routinely enrolled in business courses: typing, shorthand, and home economic courses of cooking and sewing, while boys enrolled in shop classes: woodworking, metal shop, and auto mechanics. Female enrollment in higher math and science was considerably less than male enrollment.

At the vocational or college level, girls and women faced numerous barriers in education. Women trained for traditionally low-wage jobs such as health care, education aides, and cosmetologists. Very few women had broken the glass ceiling to become chief executive officers of major companies and service as university presidents. Few women represented their states in the House of Representatives or the Senate and no woman had become President of the United States. However, a nationwide awareness of societal discrimination against women was growing.

## Female Participation in Sports

Female competition and female athletics are extremely popular in the 21st century. More importantly, they are well respected. This has not always been the case. For the last century or so, female athletes have had to put in a lot of hard work and perseverance to get the respect they deserve. And in some cases, this meant women actually competing against men in the very sports that men traditionally dominated.

A clear disparity in education was enrollment in high school sports. In the early 1970s, girls' sports were but a blip on the athletic radar of high schools and colleges in the U.S. Few people paid much attention to traditional girls' sports: field hockey, fencing, archery, and gymnastics. The real attention and money went to boys' sports, particularly football and basketball. In 1972, less than 300,000 girls participated in high school athletic programs while participation by boys was more than 3.6 million (National Federation of State High School Associations, 2009).

Schools spent money on athletic programs devoted to boys while offering little opportunity for girls. High school girls who wanted to play sports were often told it was too dangerous, too unladylike, and too tomboyish. College scholarships were offered to males with few offered to females.

The previous chapter addressed the issue of sexual harassment in general. This chapter is devoted to discrimination in a more limited field: female participation in high school and college sports. The chapter contains a discussion of historic female participation in sports, the landmark Title IX legislation approved by the U.S. Congress, the effect of this legislation on female participation in sports, court and executive decisions since its passage, and the progress of girls in high school and college sports.

## History of Women in Sports

St. Lawrence University compiled a list of female participation in sports from the time of the early Greeks to the current year. It can be reviewed at http://www.Northnet.org/stlawrenceaauw/timeline.htm. A selected number of the milestones/achievements are presented to give the reader a historical perspective of the continuing struggle and achievement of girls and women for equality and full participation in sports.

776 B.C.—First Olympics were held in Greece. Women were excluded, so they competed every four years in their own games, named after Hera, the Greek Goddess who ruled over women and the earth.

1406—Dame Juliana Bernes of Great Britain wrote the first known essay on fishing. She described how to make a rod and flies, when to fish, and the fun of fishing.

1552—Mary, Queen of Scots, an avid golfer, coined the term "caddy" by calling her assistants cadets. The famous golf course, St. Andrews was built during her reign.

1866—Vassar College sponsored the first women's amateur baseball teams.

1869—The first women's croquet championship was held in England.

1872—Mills College in Oakland, California established a women's baseball team.

1890s—More than a million women owned bicycles during this decade. It was the first time in American history that an athletic activity for women became popular.

1895—Volleyball was invented in Holyoke, Massachusetts.

1900–1920—Physical education instructors opposed competition among women, arguing that participation would make them less feminine.

1908—The national anthem of baseball, "Take Me Out to the Ball Game," was written about a young girl's love of the game.

1931—The U.S. Baseball Commissioner banned women from baseball and that ban lasted until 1992.

1950—Babe Zaharias was named "woman athlete of the half century" for her outstanding performance in golf, basketball, baseball, javelin, tennis, diving, bowling, 80 meter hurdles, shot-put, high jump, and discus.

1966—Billie Jean King won her first Wimbledon singles title, and repeated that win in 1967 and 1968. An interesting aside: As the same time, she was unable to get a credit card unless it was in the name of her husband, a law student with no income.

1972—Billie Jean King was named Sports Woman of the Year in *Sports Illustrated*, the first time the award was given to a woman.

1972—Title IX was approved by Congress and went into effect in 1975.

1973—Billie Jean King won the "Battle of the Sexes" by beating tennis great Bobby Riggs. This tennis match was televised and watched by an audience of more than 50 million.

1980—Two hundred and thirty-three women competed in the Winter Olympics; just twenty-one had competed in 1932.

1990—Julie Inkster became the first woman to win the Spalding Invitational, the only professional golf tournament in the world where men and women compete head to head.

1992—Two million girls participated in high school sports.

1993—Julie Krone won the Belmont Stakes and became the first woman jockey to win a Triple Crown race.

1996—Female participation in high school sports had increased to 2.4 million.

2007—The Wimbledon tennis tournament announced it would pay men and women equal prize money.

2009—Female participation increased to 3,114,091, while male participation was 4,422,662 (National Federation of State High School Associations, 2009).

2013—Serena Williams won 78 of 82 matches.

2014—Female participation increased to 3,267,664 while male participation was 4,527,994 (National Federation of State High School Associations, 2014).

## Title IX—1972

In 1972, historic legislation was approved by the U.S. Congress and signed by President Nixon. This legislation, Title IX, only contains 37 words, but has had a profound effect on females and education:

> *"No person in the United States shall, on the basis of sex, be excluded from participation in, be denied the benefits of, or be subjected to discrimination under any education program or activity receiving federal financial assistance."*

Representative Patsy Mink from Hawaii, who co-sponsored the legislation, had experienced barriers firsthand, despite her strong undergraduate preparation when she attempted to enroll in medical school. In high school, she was student body president and valedictorian. Her college record was impressive with a dual major in zoology and chemistry. This achievement was not good enough for the 20 medical schools that rejected her application (Mink, P., 2002).

Title IX requires schools and colleges that receive federal funding to provide equitable resources and opportunities for girls and women in a non-discrim-inatory way. The Department of Education's Office for Civil Rights (OCR) is responsible for the oversight of Title IX. OCR created a three-pronged test that is used to determine gender equity compliance. Schools must meet the criteria of at least one prong of the test to be in compliance. The three prongs include:

1. The school must show that the athletic participation rates by gender are within five percent of the enrollment rate for that gender.
2. The school must provide evidence that it has a history and current practice of program expansion for girls.
3. The school must demonstrate that it offers an athletic opportunity for girls if there is sufficient interest and ability in a particular sport.

Schools do not have to provide equal funding for boys' and girls' sports. Schools are in compliance with Title IX if the quality of the girls' program is equal to that of the boys. The funding may not be equitable because of large programs, but if the total funding for overall programs is equal, then the school is in compliance. Football or basketball are examples of large programs that may require additional funding.

Other program areas that must be equitable by gender include: equipment and supplies, scheduling of practices and contests, travel, access to quality coaches with equitable pay, locker rooms and facilities, access to training facilities and medical services, publicity, and sporting opportunities.

## Ups and Downs of Title IX Over Almost Four Decades

The success of women in achieving equality of many facets of American life is beyond dispute since the passage of Title IX in 1972. However, it is difficult to quantify the precise role this legislation played in that achievement. Was Title IX just part of the natural historical achievement, or did it play a major role in that achievement?

The almost four decades since Title IX was approved is a history of expansion and contraction, depending on the culture and climate of each generation. The following milestones demonstrate the executive, legislative, and judicial actions that have advanced or slowed the objectives of Title IX.

1964—Title VII of the Civil Rights Act of 1964 was enacted. Discrimination in employment was prohibited based upon religion, national origin, race, color, or sex. Title VI of this Act specifically prohibited discrimination in federally assisted programs on the above criteria.

1972—President Nixon signed Title IX of the Education Amendments of 1972. The law was so broadly worded that it needed written regulations before it could be enforced.

1974—Congress passed an amendment directing Health, Education, and Welfare (HEW) to issue Title IX regulations, including ones for athletics.

1975—President Ford signed the Title IX athletic regulations, a product of a year of research and debate.

1975— Department of Health, Education, and Welfare issued the Final Title IX regulations. Secondary schools were given three years to comply while elementary schools were given one year to comply.

1976—The National Collegiate Athletic Association (NCAA) challenged the legality of Title IX.

1979—The United States Department of Health, Education, and Welfare determined that a "three-pronged test" was necessary to test an institution's compliance.

1980—All federal education tasks were transferred from the Health, Education, and Welfare Office to a Department of Education that has just been established. The oversight of Title IX was transferred to the new department of the Office of Civil Rights.

1980—The first case challenging sex discrimination in an entire college program was filed and resulted in a 1988 court-ordered settlement in *Haffer v. Temple*. The Third Circuit Court of Appeals heard this case. Temple University argued that the school's athletic program received no direct federal funds, and therefore was not subject to Title IX. The Court stated that Title IX is not limited to the education program and activities that are specifically earmarked for a program, but if the program indirectly benefits from federal dollars, Title IX applies. It was noted that Temple received large amounts of federal funds for grants and contacts. *Haffer v. Temple University* toughened the Title IX law by insisting on new standards for budgets, scholarships, and participation rates of male and female athletes.

1980—The U. S. Supreme Court, in *Grove City College v. Bell*, limited the scope of Title IX to athletic scholarships. The Court concluded that Title IX applied only to specific programs that receive federal funds.

1988—The Civil Rights Restoration Act of 1987 became law after President Ronald Reagan vetoed it. This Act reversed *Grove City College v. Bell* and required athletic departments to again comply with Title IX.

1992—The U.S. Supreme Court ruled in *Franklin v. Gwinnett County Schools* that monetary damages may be awarded in cases against schools under Title IX. This decision opened the door to more lawsuits by female athletes. Suits were filed against Auburn, Colorado State, and Brown University.

1996—The Office for Civil Rights issued a clarification of the three-pronged test that measures an institution's compliance with Title IX.

1996—A federal appeals court upholds a lower court's ruling in *Cohen v. Brown University* that Brown had discriminated against female athletes. Brown had argued that it did not violate Title IX, as women were less interested in sports.

1999—California State University at Bakersfield argued that limiting the number of athletes on men's teams to accommodate Title IX for women was reverse discrimination. The university lost that battle.

2005—The U.S. Supreme Court decided in *Jackson v. Birmingham* that individuals, including coaches and teachers, have a right under Title IX to sue if they are retaliated against for protesting sex discrimination.

2009—President Obama hosted the first White House celebration of Title IX. The 37th anniversary of Title IX was celebrated with a gathering of athletes, scientists, policymakers, and advocates. The president pledged full support for Title IX and cited his parenthood of two daughters.

2011—The Department of Education issued a policy that made it clear that Title IX protection against sexual harassment and sexual violence applies to all students, including athletes.

## What Progress Has Been Made?

How much credit can be given Title IX for the progress made by females over the past 37 years? Was the legislation just part of social change that was occurring in the country or did the legislation spur that social change? How many more individuals are able to buy houses because of the changes to combat discrimination in housing laws? How many more are able to obtain jobs because of the changes in the law on job discrimination? Has there been a substantial increase in the number of high school girls and college females participating in sports programs? Has there been an increase in athletic scholarships for women?

There is a long-held adage in leadership that if an event happens on the leader's watch, he or she will receive credit for the accomplishment. By the same token, if failure occurs, he or she will be blamed. The numbers show that girls and women have achieved success in the almost four decades since the passage of Title IX:

- Girls' participation increased for the 25th consecutive year with an additional 44.941 participants from 2012-13 and set an all-time record of 3,267,664 (National Federation High Schools, 2014).
- The Olympic competitions have increased the spotlight on women and girls in athletics and many stars from the games have emerged to win trophies and acquire a following.
- With the success of female athletic icons such as Lorena Ochoa, Mia Hamm, Julie Inkster, Brittany Griner, the Williams sisters, and Jennie Finch, interest and excitement is growing for women's golf, tennis, basketball, and soccer.
- College scholarships for females have greatly increased and a study by the College Sports Council in 2006/07 found that in "gender symmetric" sports (teams where both male and female athletes participate), females are accorded far more opportunities than male students to compete and earn scholarships. Overall, in "gender symmetric" sports, there are more scholarships available for women (32,656) than for men (20,206). In every "gender symmetric" sport with the exception of gymnastics, men face longer odds against getting a scholarship than women (College Sports Council, July 15, 2009).
- 2014—Female college graduation rates have been generally higher than males at each level over the past several years. In 1990, the percentages of males and females who had completed a bachelor's degree or higher were not measurably different, but in 2014 the percentage of females (37 percent) attaining this level of education was six points higher than the percentage of males doing so (31 percent). Female achievement at the graduate level was also higher—in 2014, 9 percent of females had completed a master's degree or higher, compared with 6 percent of males (National Center for Education Statistic, 2014).
- 2014—There has been progress in females becoming the CEOs of Fortune 500 companies. In 1998, just one woman led a Fortune 500 company. By 2009, the number had increased to 15 and reached 24 in 2014. While this achievement is admirable, females still only represent 5 percent of CEOs who have reached the top in the business world (Swanson, 2015).
- 2015—Females have achieved substantial success in representing the United States in Congress over the past three decades. In 1972, 13 females served in the U.S. House of Representatives; this number increased to 104 in 2015. Similar progress occurred in the U.S. Senate. There was one female senator in 1972; this number increased to 20 in 2015 (Center for Women and Politics, 2015).

## Court Challenges

Thousands of school districts and colleges have quietly and without the threat of a lawsuit added teams and athletic facilities for females. However, in some cases lawsuits have been filed, which forced districts or colleges to take action. The following three court cases demonstrate that school districts and colleges are likely to spend considerable funds when challenging Title IX, and they tend to lose.

### Cruz v. Alhambra School District—2003–2013

The city of Alhambra is a middle-class community located eight miles from downtown Los Angeles. There are three comprehensive high schools in the district and each of the schools is noted for strong academic and athletic programs. Over the years, the school district had joined the city to build impressive athletic facilities and fields.

However, not everyone agreed that the facilities and fields were equal for boys and girls. While the boys' baseball program had exclusive access to a brand new field with excellent amenities, the girls' softball teams were relegated to playing on a small, nonregulation-size field with dangerous holes in the outfield. Moreover, they had to share the field with year-round physical education classes and the freshman football team.

In 2003, the softball coach at Alhambra High School complained that the girls' softball team was not able to play on the new softball field. This complaint led to a landmark case that was the first in California to challenge Title IX compliance at the high school level.

After more than 2 years of litigation, the school district agreed to settle the case. Every student at AHS received a notice outlining the terms of the settlement. The district agreed to build two new softball fields with the same amenities and maintenance as the boys' baseball diamonds. For the next 10 years the U.S. District Court maintained oversight of the district to ensure equality was achieved. This oversight ended in 2013.

## Ollier v. Sweetwater Union High School District—2012

A second California Title IX case involves the Sweetwater High School District and the girls' softball team. Members of the softball team sued the district, stating they had inferior facilities and fewer opportunities to play than male student athletes.

The district court found that Sweetwater violated Title IX for not providing equal opportunity for girl's athletics. The court also found that the district retaliated against softball Coach Martinez by firing him after two softball team members complained to the school administration. In addition, the school canceled the team's annual awards banquet and did not allow the team to participate in a Las Vegas tournament attended by college recruiters.

The 9th Circuit Court of Appeals heard the appeal in 2012, and agreed that the Sweetwater Union High School District violated federal gender-equity laws by not providing female athletes with the same amenities as the boys had. Since that ruling, the Sweetwater district has taken action to ensure that there is parity among boys' and girls' sports. The district has made $1.6 million in improvements to the softball field. It was dedicated in April 2012.

## Jackson v. Birmingham Board of Education—2005

The first Title IX case heard by the U.S. Supreme Court was in 2005. The case involved retaliation against an employee who complained of discrimination. Roderick Jackson, a high school basketball coach, claimed he was fired for complaining that the girls' basketball team he coached was denied equal treatment by the school.

Jackson sued the Birmingham Board of Education in federal court alleging his firing violated Title IX, which bans sex discrimination in federally funded schools. Jackson claimed Title IX gave him the right to sue—a "private right of action"—because he re-

ported sex discrimination against others, despite the fact that he did not personally suffer from sex discrimination.

The United States District Court for the Northern District of Alabama dismissed Jackson's claims on the grounds that Title IX's private right of action does not include claims of retaliation. The Court of Appeals for the Eleventh Circuit affirmed the district court holding that Title IX does not provide a private right of action for retaliation.

Members of the softball team and their parents held little hope that the Supreme Court would overturn the decision of the two lower courts. However, they were surprised and pleased when the U.S. Supreme Court ruled that Title IX allowed suits alleging retaliation for reporting sex discrimination, and ruled in favor of Coach Jackson. The decision was a 5-4 opinion delivered by Justice Sandra Day O'Connor. Such retaliation, the majority reasoned, constituted intentional discrimination on the basis of sex in violation of Title IX. Jackson therefore had the right under Title IX to pursue his claim in court.

The majority opinion established that not only does Title IX protect against sex discrimination in schools and colleges, but also protects those who suffer retaliation for reporting instances of sex discrimination.

In 2006, the Birmingham Board of Education reached a settlement with Coach Jackson by naming him head coach at another high school and paying damages. The board also agreed to implement measures to ensure compliance with Title IX.

## Future Challenges

It is clear that challenges still persist in ensuring that girls have the same opportunities as boys in the area of athletic opportunities. Scheduling for the sports has been a challenge, as some schools have scheduled girls' sports in nontraditional seasons. Furthermore, publicity has been skewed toward the boys' sports rather than the girls. Many parents have complained that a typical school newspaper features many more stories about boy athletes than girl athletes.

A further challenge is that women make up less of a percentage than that of men in the head coaching positions. In 1972, Acosta and Carpenter found that females coached 90% of women college teams, whereas in 2008 that percentage had dropped to 43.

# Summary

The chapter reviewed the need for a law that would assist females in achieving equality in athletic programs and the passage of Title IX. Discussion of this important milestone in achieving equality for girls and women in high school and college programs was included in the chapter. A review of the executive, legislative, and judicial actions that advanced or distracted from females achieving equality was discussed. The chapter concluded with the progress that females have made in the 37 years since the passage of Title IX.

Enforcement of Title IX is critical, as there is still a need for more equity in the number of athletic scholarships and coaching positions for women. Many scholarships are based upon athletic prowess gained in elementary and high schools. In some cases, private schools have offered special athletic programs for girls, but many families cannot afford the tuition for private school.

Moms and dads want their daughters to have the same opportunity as their sons. Title IX has wide support even if it means reducing dollars for men's programs. There is little political support for changing Title IX.

## Key Terms

1. *Cohen v. Brown*
2. *Grove City College v. Bell*
3. *Haffer v. Temple*
4. *Jackson v. Brown*
5. Billie Jean King
6. Patsy Mink
7. Helen Reddy
8. Office of Civil Rights
9. St. Lawrence University
10. Title IX

## Discussion/Essay Questions

1. In the 1970s, there was a clear disparity in participation in high school sports by gender. Discuss three major reasons for this disparity.

2. St. Lawrence University compiled a list of female participation in sports over the years. From that list, select here major events that were major accomplishments and why you selected the events.

3. Title IX was approved by Congress and signed by President Nixon in 1972. Briefly discuss the social, cultural, and political circumstances in the U.S. that resulted in the passage of this historic legislation at that time.

4. Title IX has been the law for almost four decades. Discuss one major milestone that advanced the objectives of Title IX and why you think it is particularly important.

5. What do you foresee as the future challenges of females achieving complete equality in all aspects of life in the U.S.?

# CHAPTER 9

# Progressive Discipline and Dismissal of Employees

*Districts have complained that dismissals take too long—sometimes 18 months or longer—and can be too costly, with hundreds of thousands of dollars in legal fees and continued pay to suspended teachers until cases are resolved.*

—John Fensterwald, author and editor, EdSource

## Introduction

To recruit, select, supervise, and retain highly effective certificated and classified employees is of primary importance to all school districts. However, even when these responsibilities are performed in an outstanding fashion, there comes a time in every school and every district when an employee is not performing in an acceptable manner. At that time a second mandate of every superintendent, district supervisor, and school principal falls into place. An administrator's first responsibility is to students—and the second, to staff. The second responsibility must not be allowed to override the first one.

Corrective action may take the form of employee discipline or dismissal from employment. This chapter begins with a brief description of employee supervision and evaluation. It then defines employee discipline and includes a discussion of the several categories of employment. The historical development of tenure is included, along with the arguments pro and con. The tasks of progressive discipline, non-renewal, and dismissal are discussed.

## Employee Supervision and Evaluation

Education Code Section 44664 requires evaluation and assessment of the performance of each certificated employee at least once each school year for probationary personnel, and at least every other year for tenured personnel. By mutual agreement of employee and evaluator, a teacher who meets federal standards as "highly qualified," has been with the district at least ten years, and whose previous evaluations are satisfactory, may be evaluated every five years. If areas of improvement are identified, the evaluation must include recommendations for improvement. The evaluator must be very specific in describing expectations to be met.

As one can determine from the relevant Education Code sections, evaluation has two main purposes: (a) to determine the strengths and weaknesses of the employee so that strengths can be noted and deficiencies remedied, and (b) to document in one place data with which to make management decisions regarding teacher promotion, dismissal, non-renewal, transfer, demotion, withholding of salary increments, and tenure or continuing contract. The first of these is called "formative" evaluation; the second, "summative."

Formative evaluation is a first step in improving instruction. This task is the primary function of a school principal. The objective is to help each individual teacher develop to the optimum by strengthening existing skills while discovering and correcting weaknesses. Formative evaluation is the appraisal function principals use to develop or improve teaching performance.

Summative evaluation involves many of the techniques used in formative evaluation, but it goes further. For the competent teacher, it can be a positive recognition of commitment and growth. It seeks to build evidence on which educational decisions can be made; these may include change of assignment, professional growth opportunities, or leadership options. When a teacher seems to be doing less well, summative evaluation may require corrective action.

Although this chapter focuses on teachers, it should also be noted that principles such as formative and summative evaluation and processes such as progressive discipline apply as well to other certificated personnel and to classified staff. The procedures and timelines may vary, but the overall approach is the same.

# Employee Discipline

The term "discipline" often carries a negative connotation. This negative aspect is found in the second part of Webster's definition: "punishment inflicted by way of correction and training; instruction by means of misfortune, suffering, and the like; correction; chastisement." The first part of the dictionary definition is the positive part: "training, education, instruction, and the government of conduct or practice; the training to act in accordance with rules; drill; method of regulating principles and practice."

School district employee discipline begins with the positive view. It is based on the premise and expectation that employees will conduct themselves according to the rules and regulations of the organization and in a socially accepted manner. When this does not occur, what is the appropriate supervisory response?

It is commonly accepted in business and industry that the response of management to unsatisfactory employee performance must be corrective, rather than punitive. It is also accepted that the action must be progressive if it is to withstand the test of due process under the Fourteenth Amendment. For example, if a teacher releases students from class early, the principal should give that teacher a verbal warning. If the teacher repeats the early dismissal the following week, the principal gives a written reprimand. If the teacher's behavior continues for the third week, the teacher might be suspended from work for a few days without pay. If the inappropriate behavior continues after the suspension period, the principal must continue with progressive discipline and finally recommend dismissal of the employee from the district.

The right of a school board to terminate an employee from service is clearly established in state statutes and confirmed by the courts. The U.S. Supreme Court bestowed this authority on school boards when it held that "school authorities have the right and the duty to screen the officials, teachers, and employees as to their fitness to maintain the integrity of the schools as part of ordered society" (*Adler v. Board of Education,* 1952). However, even with its authority to terminate employment, a board cannot arbitrarily discharge personnel at any time. Except in the case of an employee convicted of a criminal act or flagrant violation of board policy (in which cases action may be immediate), a district is required to document unsatisfactory performance, demonstrate efforts to improve performance, and follow a course of progressive discipline.

# Progressive Discipline

When an employee is not performing in a satisfactory fashion, the central question is: What action, or series of actions, is appropriate to bring about adequate performance? There is a plethora of books and articles on changing inappropriate behavior through rewards, behavior modification, and staff development programs designed for the purpose. It is the judgment of the authors that those leadership techniques work with the great majority of employees. However, a supervisor must be prepared to take disciplinary action, including a recommendation for employee dismissal, when attempts to change behavior do not work.

Appropriate leadership and humane treatment of personnel call for corrective action when unsatisfactory performance occurs. Supervisors have a duty to provide training, informal correction and, if needed, formal discipline when rules or duties are not performed properly.

For example, if the district requires teachers to be on campus 30 minutes prior to the start of class, and a teacher is late one time in a semester, his tardiness probably would not even receive a rebuke for violation of the employee contract. However, positive, fair, and objective measures are required when a teacher is late on a regular basis and does not respond to a verbal reminder of the importance of being in class on time. Ruud and Woodford (1992) define progressive discipline as a general pattern of escalating disciplinary penalties designed to persuade or motivate an employee to improve performance or change behavior.

Andelson (1995) defines progressive discipline as "a series of disciplinary steps, each step calling for more serious disciplinary action." He proposes the following six levels of action.

### 1. Oral warning/conference
The supervisor states clearly the rule or policy that has been violated, the expectation that the rule be followed, and the consequence if the rule is not followed in the future. The time, date, and substance of the warning are noted on a daily calendar or some other informal written record (not the employee's personnel file). An oral warning should be brief, to the point, and directly related to a specific incident.

### 2. Written warning
The written warning is similar to the oral warning and, if possible, delivered personally to the employee. One of the consequences of further violation of the rule or policy may be notice to the employee that an

additional violation will result in a letter of reprimand to be placed in the employee's personnel file.

### 3. Letter of reprimand

The first two steps in the progressive discipline model generally do not result in placing information in the personnel file. However, a letter of reprimand is ordinarily placed there. The letter contains statements similar to those in the oral and written notice. In addition, the employee must be notified that the letter will be placed in the personnel file. He or she must have opportunity to review and respond to any document containing derogatory information. If the employee responds, that document is also placed in the personnel file (E.C. 44031). Although the law does not spell out a time limit for an employee's response to a letter of reprimand, the time is often regulated by the collective bargaining agreement—typically five to ten calendar days.

### 4. Unsatisfactory evaluation

The requirements for evaluation are outlined in the Education Code. Procedures are generally included in the collective bargaining agreement between the district and the employee association.

### 5. Suspension with pay

Suspension with pay is often a nondisciplinary step that provides time for an investigation to determine whether discipline is justified. Suspension with pay may also accompany a second reprimand to emphasize the seriousness of the infraction. Suspension without pay is practical for classified employees, but more difficult to administer with credentialed employees. The reason for this difficulty is that credentialed employees work under a contract, which creates a property right. As we have seen, the Fourteenth Amendment states that one cannot be deprived of property without due process.

### 6. Dismissal

A later section of this chapter is devoted to additional discussion of dismissal.

In summary, progressive discipline is a system of documentation and file-building that is divided into stages, each successive stage resulting in more serious disciplinary measures. Obviously, it is the responsibility of the supervisor to work extensively with an employee prior to recommending dismissal from service.

## Probationary Status

District requirements for teacher dismissal differ, depending on the employee's classification as probationary or tenured. A teacher is considered to have probationary status prior to achieving tenure. During the probationary period, a teacher is issued a contract valid for a fixed period of time. California teachers are classed as "probationary" during the first two years of service within a school district (E.C. 44929.21). During this probationary period, renewal of the contract at the end of each school year is at the discretion of the school board.

Commonly, a probationary teacher is not entitled to know the reasons for which a school board has decided to terminate the employment relationship at the end of the contract period. In most cases, a probationary teacher is not given the opportunity for a hearing. Even though the school board is not compelled to inform the probationary teacher of the reasons for non-renewal, it is important to recognize that those reasons cannot violate the teacher's constitutionally or statutorily protected rights.

The school board is required to notify a probationary employee on or before March 15th of the employee's second complete consecutive school year of employment of the decision not to reelect him or her for the next school year. If the board does not give notice on or before March 15th, the employee is deemed reelected for the next succeeding school year (E.C. 44929.21).

## Tenure Status

Tenure is defined as a statutory right to continued employment. The employer must have proof of "good cause" prior to dismissal. As defined by *Black's Law Dictionary* (2004), tenure is "a status afforded to a teacher or professor as a protection against summary dismissal without sufficient cause." The 1992 *Deskbook Encyclopedia of American School Law* described tenure as a "creation of state statute designed to maintain adequate, permanent, and qualified teaching staffs."

Generally, tenure granted by the state means at least two things for a teacher: (a) continuing employment without the necessity of annual notification; and (b) if employment is to be terminated, adequate reasons for termination and an opportunity for an impartial hearing ensuring fundamental fairness. The decision of whether to recognize "tenure status" is left to the discretion of each state legislature.

## Purpose of Tenure

Tenure provides security for a teacher. The academic rationale for tenure is that it gives the teacher academic freedom in the classroom. In addition, tenured teachers cannot be fired for holding and expressing unpopular political or social views outside the classroom. Tenure gives a teacher legal protection against unwarranted dismissal. An additional purpose served by tenure is to provide equity based on seniority when staff must be reduced because of lack of enrollment or finances; length of service is the criterion for dismissal.

## History of Tenure

The concept of rewarding one's friends with jobs or positions of influence is part of early American history. During this country's colonial period, the English government retained power by distributing jobs and influence to friends and supporters. This system of handing out jobs became known as the "spoils system" or "patronage."

The country's first President, George Washington, often made support of Federalist principles a test of appointment to office. When Jefferson became President, he complained of the number of Federalists he found holding jobs in the executive department and gradually replaced Federalists with Republicans. It was not until the presidency of Andrew Jackson that wholesale removal of jobholders was accomplished so that he could appoint his followers to office. This practice continued with each President; during the Civil War, President Lincoln expressed his frustration with the countless number of job seekers who filled his appointment schedule.

The system of awarding positions greatly accelerated after the Civil War and became a topic of national concern when President Garfield was assassinated by a half-crazy office seeker. This tragic event so excited the nation against the spoils system that in 1883 the Pendleton Act was passed by Congress. This law allowed the President to place on a "classified list" certain federal offices that then could be filled only according to rules laid down by a bipartisan Civil Service Commission. The Pendleton Act began the process of changing government employment from the spoils system to a merit system (Bragdon & McCutchen, 1961; *U.S. Statutes at Large*, 22 [1883]:403).

Gradually, the concept of employees gaining and retaining their jobs on merit spread to state and local governments. It was out of this movement that the concept of tenure for teachers developed. In 1887 the proceedings of the National Education Association carried a committee report urging that the subject of teachers' tenure be given publicity in the belief that necessary legislation would result (National Education Association, 1936).

California was the first state to approve tenure for teachers in 1921. By 2005, all but three states, Georgia, Mississippi, and Texas, had some variation of tenure for teachers (NEA-Alaska, 2005).

Tenure statutes protect teachers from arbitrary actions by local boards of education. In some states and school districts, other certificated personnel also are protected by tenure statutes. The selection of positions to be covered under tenure laws is within the prerogative of the state legislature. Employee classifications that may gain tenure rights include school nurses, counselors, psychologists, and school librarians. In some states, selected administrative positions may also obtain tenure. However, tenure is rarely granted to superintendents or assistant superintendents.

The courts have sustained the constitutionality of such statutes. Certificated Tenure Act cases have concluded that tenure exists to protect competent teachers and other members of the teaching profession against unlawful and arbitrary board actions and to provide orderly procedures for the dismissal of unsatisfactory teachers and other professional personnel (*Teachers Tenure Act Cases*, 1938).

Tenure is attained by complying with specific provisions prescribed by state statutes. The nature of these provisions varies from state to state, but certain conditions are included in most legislation. Nearly all states require that teachers serve a probationary period before tenure becomes effective. Generally, the probationary period ranges from two to five years, during which time a teacher is employed on a term contract. On completion of the probationary period, personnel acquire tenure, either automatically or by school board action.

California Governor Arnold Schwarzenegger called a special election for November 8, 2005, that included Proposition 74, which would have extended the time before a teacher becomes tenured from 2 years to 5 years. The Proposition failed and California teachers gain tenure after 2 years of successful teaching.

## Arguments For and Against Tenure

Tenure continues to be a matter of debate in the United States. Advocates strongly believe tenure is positive for children and teachers, while opponents believe it is detrimental to students and teachers. Jones and Stout (1960) advanced the following arguments in favor of and opposed to tenure.

Favorable arguments:

1. Tenure is a basic principle of economic efficiency.

2. Tenure helps to protect the teacher from unwarranted attacks.
3. The teacher is freed from anxiety over being dismissed without just cause.
4. Tenure helps parents and citizens to secure better teachers because it encourages a more careful selection of faculty.
5. There is little evidence that tenure reduces interest in professional development.
6. Tenure reduces the temptation for teachers to violate professional ethics and to yield to the whims of pressure groups.

Opposing arguments:

1. Incompetent and undesirable teachers may be retained in the profession, since tenure makes it more difficult to dismiss them.
2. It may become more difficult to supervise some teachers who know they have security of position.
3. Contrary to popular opinion, tenure has, in a number of instances, increased teacher turnover.
4. Tenure of office is not protected by law in other professions.
5. The public has, in many instances, questioned the practice of permitting teachers to hold their positions despite their failure to do a competent job.
6. Competent teachers do not need to be protected by tenure legislation.

### Vergara v. California—2014

Nine California students and an advocacy group filed a major lawsuit in 2014, which argued that the state's teacher tenure rules deprive them of a good education. After two months of testimony, the Los Angeles County Superior Court Judge ruled that California teacher protections are unconstitutional. The judge found that California teacher tenure, and firing and discipline procedures, are unconstitutional because they violate children's right to an adequate education.

The judge found that California's 2-year process for evaluating new teachers—much shorter than the 3-year period in 32 states—"does not provide nearly enough time" for making tenure decisions. The court stayed the decision to allow for appeals to reach the California Supreme Court. If the decision is upheld, it would not affect the laws in other states that are similar to California that base layoffs on classroom seniority (Deutsch, 2014).

## Reduction in Force (RIF)

School districts are often faced with a variety of factors that require them to reduce staff. Declining enrollment is one example of a situation in which a district may need to layoff teachers or classified employees. The reduction may be temporary or permanent.

This practice is commonly referred to as "reduction in force" (RIF). The conditions in which a district may use RIF are contained in E.C. 44955. A district desiring to use this procedure has the burden of documenting the need to reduce staff in response to one or more of the legislated reasons, that is, declining enrollment, fiscal exigency, school district reorganization, or "other good and just cause."

Once the district has justified the RIF, the next step is determination of the order in which to release staff. For the most part, probationary employees are released prior to the dismissal of tenured employees. Seniority, defined as years of service in the school district or within a particular classification, is most frequently used to determine the order of lay-off of employees.

## Non-Renewal and Dismissal

In discussing termination of employment of teachers and other certificated personnel, the terms "non-renewal" and "dismissal" are often used interchangeably. However, non-renewal is more properly applied to probationary teachers, while dismissal generally refers to termination of employment at any time.

There is a substantial difference in the manner of termination in each case. Courts have reasoned in non-renewal cases that the contract has simply terminated and there is no "expectancy of continued employment." Non-renewal usually requires that a school board simply give a probationary employee timely notice that his or her contract is not being renewed. In most states, the school board need not give reasons for the non-renewal of a probationary teacher (Hartmeister, 1995). If not protected by tenure, a school employee's contract may be non-renewed for any reason whatsoever or for no reason, providing the action does not violate an employee's substantive constitutional rights, for example, right of free speech or protection from racial discrimination.

Dismissal, on the other hand, whether under tenure status or during an unexpired contract, is permissible only "for cause." Because an employee has a constitutionally protected property interest in remaining employed throughout the contract term, he or she is entitled to notification of reasons for the dismissal and an opportunity for a hearing in which to respond to or rebut all stated reasons. Consequently, dismissal of a tenured employee or a non-tenured professional during a contract year calls for a fair and impartial due process hearing with all statutory and constitutional safeguards.

## Grounds for Dismissal

The most common grounds for the dismissal of teachers are incompetency, immorality, insubordination, unfitness to teach, and inadequate performance of duties. Conviction of a felony or a crime involving moral turpitude, or any cause that leads the state to revoke a teaching certificate, is also grounds for dismissal. Other grounds for dismissal include reduction in force, when a teacher's services are no longer needed due to declining enrollment or financial exigency. In addition, there is normally an "elastic" clause added to this list: "other good and just cause."

Causes for dismissal are generally specified in state statutes and differ from one state to another. However, there are similarities. For example, in Kentucky tenured employees can be dismissed for insubordination; immoral character or conduct; physical or mental disability; or inefficiency, incompetency, or neglect of duty. In Illinois, cause for dismissal is specified as incompetency, cruelty, negligence, immorality or other sufficient cause and whenever in the board's opinion a teacher is not qualified to teach or the best interests of the school require it.

In Connecticut, causes enumerated are inefficiency, incompetency, insubordination, moral misconduct, disability as shown by competent medical evidence, elimination of positions, or other due and sufficient cause. The school district has the burden of proving any charges and, to do so, must show persuasive evidence that the teacher being recommended for dismissal either failed to do something that he or she should have done—or did something that he or she should not have done.

## Grounds for Dismissal of Certificated Employees in California

Education Code Sections 44932 and 44933 are very specific regarding the grounds for dismissal of certificated employees. Twelve specific reasons are stated.

### 1. Immoral or unprofessional conduct
Immoral conduct must be judged within the context of local standards, but also must be reasonable and consistent with court decisions. One of the standards used by the courts is the health of the pupil-teacher relationship. A teacher or other employee who establishes a relationship with a student that goes beyond friendship and is exhibited in some form of "dating" is unacceptable. Of course, illegal sexual acts are cause for immediate suspension. If an employee is convicted of performing such an act, his or her employment must be terminated.

Nonconventional sexual lifestyles, however, are not a cause for employee dismissal. Such practices as wife swapping, homosexuality, and cohabitation outside of matrimony may be unacceptable to the majority of people in the community, but do not inherently affect an individual's performance in the workplace. However, if an employee advocates nonconventional sexual lifestyles at work, and those lifestyles are in direct conflict with local standards, he or she has placed himself or herself in a position such that termination is possible.

### 2. Commission, aiding, or advocating the commission of acts of criminal syndicalism

### 3. Dishonesty

### 4. Unsatisfactory performance
A significant change was made in the grounds for dismissal in 1995. Assembly Bill 729 was approved by the legislature and signed by the governor on August 10, 1995. The significant change was substituting "unsatisfactory performance" for "incompetency."

### 5. Evident unfitness for service

### 6. Physical or mental condition unfitting him or her to instruct or associate with children

### 7. Persistent violation of or refusal to obey the school laws of the state or reasonable regulations prescribed for the government of the public schools by the State Board of Education or by the governing board of the school district employing him or her
Employees are insubordinate only if they refuse to comply with a directive of their supervisor that is clearly within their job expertise. Thus, if a teacher is directed to attend a faculty meeting and refuses, the teacher is insubordinate because teachers have a job-related responsibility in this area. However, if the teacher refuses to go to the principal's house to help with administrative paperwork, the teacher is not guilty of insubordination, as this task is not within the teacher's job assignment.

The manner in which the employee responds to a directive does not usually constitute insubordination if the employee performs the task. For example, if the teacher complains about grading papers, but completes the task, the teacher is not guilty of insubordination.

### 8. Conviction of a felony or of any crime involving moral turpitude

Conviction of a felony is a reason to terminate employment of an individual. In most states, a school district employee who is found guilty of a felony is considered in breach of his or her employment contract and can be dismissed from employment. The basis in breach of contract takes as its premise that teachers are expected to be positive role models for their students. Felony convictions are not congruent with this expectation and are obviously deleterious to a teacher's effectiveness. Courts have held on numerous occasions that a civil sanction, that is, loss of employment following a criminal conviction, does not violate the principle of double jeopardy set forth in the Fifth Amendment to the Constitution.

Courts have placed restrictions on the interpretation of moral turpitude. Nevertheless, conviction of prostitution, selling of drugs, or pornography do fall within the definition of moral turpitude (Rebore, 1998). District action is not as clearly defined when teachers are convicted of a misdemeanor, a crime less serious than a felony. Generally, an employee who has been arrested, but not convicted of a criminal offense, cannot be dismissed unless found guilty.

### 9. Advocacy of or inculcation into communism

E.C. 51530 reads as follows: "No teacher giving instruction in any school, or on any property belonging to any agencies included in the public school system, shall advocate or teach communism with the intent to indoctrinate or to inculcate in the mind of any pupil a preference for communism." The code section has a second paragraph stating that the legislature did not intend to prevent the teaching of the facts about communism, but to prevent the advocacy of, or inculcation and indoctrination into, communism. The third paragraph in this section defines communism: "Communism is a political theory that the presently existing form of government of the United States or of this state should be changed, by force, violence, or other unconstitutional means, to a totalitarian dictatorship which is based on the principles of communism expounded by Marx, Lenin, and Stalin."

### 10. Knowing membership by the employee in the Communist Party

With respect to this requirement, we note that in a case involving the Board of Public Works of Los Angeles (*Garner*, 1951), the U.S. Supreme Court ruled that the U.S. Constitution did not forbid a city government from requiring its employees to state whether or not they had ever been a member of the Community Party or Communist Political Association. Moreover, the city could require employees to swear or affirm an oath stating, in part, "that I do not advise, advocate or teach . . . the overthrow by force, violence, or other unlawful means, of the Government of the United States of America or of the State of California."

### 11. Alcoholism or other drug abuse that makes the employee unfit to instruct or associate with children

### 12. Unprofessional conduct

Unprofessional conduct is made grounds for suspension without pay in Section 44932(b) and for dismissal in 44933. The latter includes the statement: "A permanent employee may be dismissed or suspended on grounds of unprofessional conduct consisting of acts or omissions other than those specified in Section 44932, but any such charge shall specify instances of behavior deemed to constitute unprofessional conduct."

## Dismissal Procedures

If a school superintendent recommends dismissal of a tenured employee, the requirements of the Education Code must be followed precisely. The procedures are detailed and specific. They contain three basic elements: (a) notice by a specific date of intention to dismiss, (b) specification of charges against the employee (E.C. 44934), and (c) a hearing at which the charges are discussed (E.C. 44944).

In accordance with the same section of the Education Code, charges against a tenured teacher, Edward Zuber, proceeded to review by a Commission on Professional Competence. When the commission found for the teacher, the district turned to the Yolo County Superior Court (*Woodland Joint Unified School District v. Commission on Professional Competence*, 1992). As recorded in the opinion of the appeals court, "The charges against Zuber fell into the following categories: failure to follow proper procedures for disciplining students, writing sarcastic and belittling notes about students, insulting students in class, using profanity in class, behaving rudely and contemptuously toward parents, making sarcastic remarks about other teachers in the hearing of students, displaying insubordination and disrespect toward administrators, bullying and threatening other teachers, and disrupting the grading process by interfering with the grading policy of a substitute who took over one of his classes." When the Yolo County Court found for the district on the basis of evident unfitness for service, the teacher appealed. Among the bases for the appeal was an argument that the district had not given notice for dismissal for unprofessional conduct; the rejoinder was that other causes were included in the allegations. The court upheld the dismissal by a 2-to-1 vote; however, the dissenting judge described Zuber as a "dedicated but crusty teacher." To read this 26-page decision and minority opinion makes clear the complexity of a dismissal process.

Besides the procedures required in the Education Code, tenure rights qualify for constitutional procedural protections encompassed within the concepts of property and liberty interests under the Due Process Clause of the Fourteenth Amendment. To hold a teaching position qualifies as a property right if the employee has an unexpired contract or has acquired tenure. The protections of the Fourteenth Amendment do not normally extend to non-tenured employees. The Supreme Court has affirmed the view of the courts that non-tenured employees have no property or liberty interests in continued employment (*Roth v. Board of Regents,* 1972).

A liberty interest would be an issue in dismissal, and due process is required when a charge has been made that might place a stigma on an employee's reputation, thus foreclosing future employment opportunities or seriously damaging the individual's standing in the community (*Roth v. Board of Regents*). A liberty interest is not at issue if school board members and school administrators refrain from making public statements or releasing information derogatory to the employee. Even when statements are made, if they simply mention unsatisfactory performance in general, they do not normally violate the employee's Fourteenth Amendment rights.

Examples of charges against employees not involving stigma usually include ineffective teaching methods, inability to maintain classroom discipline, and inability to get along with administrators and colleagues. Failure to award tenure does not automatically create a stigma. Examples of stigmas that *do* qualify for constitutional due process protection include the following charges: manifest racism, immoral conduct, lack of intellectual ability, a chronic drinking or drug problem, willful neglect of duty, and responsibility for the deterioration of a school (for example, see State Personnel Board, 1993).

## Summary

It is a major responsibility of every administrator to ensure that each child is taught by a competent teacher. Administrators must have the knowledge and skills to assist teachers and classified staff to perform in a competent fashion. However, they also have an obligation to take disciplinary action when staff performance is unsatisfactory. The effective administrator must be well versed in progressive discipline, as well as the legal procedures and requirements to dismiss an employee when progressive discipline has not been effective.

## *Key Terms*

1. discipline
2. dismissal
3. letter of reprimand
4. liberty interest
5. moral turpitude
6. non-renewal
7. oral warning/conference
8. progressive discipline
9. probationary status
10. property interest
11. reduction in force
12. suspension with pay
13. tenure
14. unsatisfactory evaluation
15. written warning

## *Discussion/Essay Questions*

1. Review the steps in the Progressive Employee Discipline Model.

2. Develop a strong argument for elimination of tenure.

3. What is the major difference between "non-renewal" and "dismissal"?

4. Review the twelve legal grounds for dismissal. Discuss the three that you think are the most serious.

5. Give examples of unsatisfactory performance and the rationale for dismissal of a teacher based on your examples.

6. Define "property interest" and "liberty interest." Which of the two do you feel would be most difficult for a district to defend if challenged in a lawsuit?

7. Define "Reduction in Force." When is this method of staff dismissal justified?

# CHAPTER 10

# Religion and the Schools

*Leave the matter of religion to the family altar, the church, and the private school, supported entirely by private contributions.*

—Ulysses S. Grant, 18th President of the United States

## Introduction

From colonial days until the mid-20th century, religious observances were prevalent in many public schools (McCarthy, Cambron-McCabe, & Thomas, 1998). However, since World War II, issues concerning church-state relations have provided a steady stream of litigation. No other area in school law, with the exception of school desegregation, has received more attention in the courts than issues involving religion in the public schools (Lunenburg, 1996).

The U.S. Constitution contains a provision that establishes the separation of church and state. This provision guarantees religious freedom on the one hand, and on the other, forbids an establishment of religion by the government. The First Amendment states that "Congress shall make no law respecting the establishment of religion, or prohibiting the free exercise thereof." These two religion clauses, the Establishment Clause and the Free Exercise Clause, protect an individual's religious liberty. The two clauses prohibit religious indoctrination in the public schools or use of public funds to support religion.

While most Americans accept the principle that public schools should be free of religious indoctrination, the issue does not end there. For example, in a presidential election year, each candidate emphasizes his support of prayer and family values. However, when pushed for specifics of his or her position on the separation of religion and schools, the candidate is usually vague on details. He or she might opt for a "silent moment of meditation" before an elementary class begins or mention the need for private, silent prayer prior to taking an exam.

This chapter addresses the Establishment Clause of the First Amendment to the Constitution, the constitutionality of daily Bible readings, prayers at graduation ceremonies, celebration of religious holidays, teaching of evolution, equal access in classrooms, separate religious public schools, and distribution of religious materials. Before studying the issues, it is important to understand how the separation of church and state came about through the influence of Thomas Jefferson and James Madison.

## Influence of Jefferson and Madison on the Separation of Church and State

Jefferson was very much influenced by the 18th-century movement called Enlightenment. The dominant spirit of the century was one of skepticism toward all received truth. This spirit permeates Jefferson's work and thought. Jefferson came to prominence in 1776, when he participated in the General Assembly of the newly established Commonwealth of Virginia (Peterson, 1998).

During its early years the Church of England had been established in the Commonwealth, one of six American colonies with an Anglican establishment. The parish was responsible for collecting taxes from individuals within the territory, regardless of the church affiliation of the taxpayer. A large part of this money was used to support the Anglican Church. Not surprisingly, dissenters protested the unfairness of a system that required them to give financial support to a church whose tenets were different from their own. The number of dissenters from this religion increased during the 18th century. By Jefferson's time, as many as two-thirds of the citizens of Virginia were dissenters from the established church.

After the Declaration of Independence was signed, Presbyterians in Virginia protested to the Virginia legislature against the "church tax." The Virginia legislature then passed a bill exempting all dissenters and minority sect members from paying taxes to the Anglican Church. Thus was the stage set for the First Amendment.

Jefferson advocated absolute religious freedom within the colony. James Madison joined Jefferson in promoting toleration of religious freedom. Drawing in part on the Toleration Act adopted in England in 1689, Madison became architect and sponsor of the Bill of Rights.

## School Prayer and Bible Reading

During America's early history many public schools began each day with a prayer and Bible reading. Three significant court decisions disallowed this practice. The cases were *Engel v. Vitale* (1962), *School District of Abington Township v. Schempp* (1963), and *Lemon v. Kurtzman* (1971). The U.S. Supreme Court decided that the Establishment Clause prohibits states and the federal government from passing laws that aid a religion or prefer one to another.

### Engel v. Vitale—1962

In 1962 school prayer in public schools had its first judicial review. The New York Supreme Court struck down a state statute requiring recitation of a prayer in the public schools on the ground that it violated the Establishment Clause. The court stated, "The Establishment Clause, unlike the Free Exercise Clause, does not depend upon any showing of direct governmental compulsion and is violated by the enactment of laws which establish an official religion whether those laws operate directly to coerce non-observing individuals or not." The court further stated that "when the power, prestige and financial support of government is placed behind a particular religious belief, the indirect coercive pressure upon religious minorities to conform to the prevailing officially approved religion is plain."

### School District of Abington Township v. Schempp—1963

One year later, in 1963, the Pennsylvania Supreme Court declared unconstitutional a Pennsylvania statute requiring Bible reading and recitation of the Lord's Prayer. The statute required that ten verses be read from the Holy Bible at the opening of each school day. Children would be excused from the exercise if their parents so requested in writing.

The suit had been brought in 1956, after Ellery Schempp told his parents he objected to the required reading of the Bible in his homeroom. Ellery read passages from the Koran during the Bible-reading time. As a result, he was sent to the principal's office.

Ellery's parents, the plaintiffs, were members of the Unitarian Church. They brought action seeking to enjoin the enforcement of the statute when this exercise was part of the school curriculum and conducted under the supervision of teachers employed by the schools. A transcript by Irons and Guitton (1993) describes how the prayer system worked.

> Between 8:15 a.m. and 8:30 a.m. every school day, all the children are in their homerooms. There's a public address system in each of the rooms. At 8:15 a.m. the morning exercise starts. First, they have what's called an introduction, a "fact for the day." The teachers pull something out of the *World Almanac* to gain the attention of the children. . . . This exercise is followed by ten verses of the Bible, read without comment. The ten verses of the Bible are followed by the Lord's Prayer, which in turn is followed by the flag salute, which in turn is followed by the school announcements for the day. . . . Then there is conclusion, where the names of the students who made the announcements are given.

On June 17, 1963, the Pennsylvania Supreme Court ruled in favor of Roger and Donna Schempp. The court ruled that public schools should not use the Bible and prayer for classroom devotion. Part of the court decision read: "What our Constitution protects is the freedom of each of us, be he Jew or Agnostic, Christian or Atheist, Buddhist or Freethinker, to believe or disbelieve, to worship, to pray or keep silent, according to his own conscience, uncoerced and unrestrained by government." So it is clear that in 1962 (*Engel*) and in 1963 (*Schempp*), the two state supreme courts struck down Bible reading and prayers in the public schools as unconstitutional.

### Lemon v. Kurtzman—1971

In *Lemon v. Kurtzman* (1971), the U.S. Supreme Court made clear that the government must maintain a neutral stance toward religion, that is, it may neither advance nor hinder any religion. This case involved a state program designed to reimburse all private schools, including religious schools, for expenses of textbooks, materials, and salaries to teach nonreligious subjects. Basing its decision primarily on the two religion clauses in the First Amendment, the court devised an entanglement standard, a set of three questions now known as "the *Lemon* Test," to determine whether a particular governmental action withstands an Establishment Clause challenge. The questions are:

1. Does the action have a secular purpose?
2. Does the action have an effect that neither advances nor impedes religion?
3. Does the action avoid excessive entanglement with religion?

Chief Justice Burger authored this decision. It was decided that any issue that failed any one of the three parts of the *Lemon* Test was unconstitutional. In summary, state aid to parochial schools through salary supplements and purchase of services constitutes impermissible entanglement between church and state. This three-factor test has been applied in most Establishment Clause cases.

## Graduation Ceremonies and Public Events

Recent cases regarding school prayer have focused on the graduation ceremony and other public events. Participation on such occasions was regarded as voluntary. The schools argued that these devotional activities were traditional and ceremonial. Initially, the courts appeared less inclined to find a violation of the Establishment Clause in baccalaureate services and prayers during graduation ceremonies than as routine devotional activities during the school day. In the mid-1980s, however, lower courts began striking down graduation prayers under the Establishment Clause, and the Supreme Court followed this lead in the case of *Lee v. Weisman* (1992).

### Lee v. Weisman—1992

This case arose in a Rhode Island School District that had a policy permitting principals to invite clergy to deliver invocations and benedictions at middle and high school graduation ceremonies. In its decision, the U.S. Supreme Court declared that opening prayers at graduation ceremonies were inconsistent with the religion clauses of the First Amendment. The court followed the standard set in *Engel* and *Abington* that

the free exercise of religion does not supersede the fundamental limitations imposed by the Establishment Clause.

The court determined that elementary and secondary schools should be particularly sensitive to institutionalized prayer. In addition, telling students that they could choose not to attend would be regarded as unfair to the student. The court recognized that high school graduation is one of the most significant occasions in life and that missing the graduation ceremony would be a major loss to a student.

The court noted that the First Amendment protects freedom of religion and freedom of speech by quite different mechanisms. Speech is protected by ensuring its full expression, even when the government participates. The method for protecting freedom of worship and freedom of conscience in religious matters is quite the reverse. In religious debate or expression, the government is not a prime participant, for the framers of the Constitution deemed religious establishment antithetical to the freedom of all. The Free Exercise Clause, therefore, embraces a freedom of conscience and worship that has close parallels in the speech provisions of the First Amendment, but the Establishment Clause is a specific prohibition on forms of state intervention in religious affairs. Such a prohibition has no precise counterpart in the speech provisions.

The explanation lies in the lesson from history that inspired the Establishment Clause: "A state-created orthodoxy puts at grave risk that freedom of belief and conscience that are the sole assurance that religious faith is real, not imposed." In *Lee v. Weisman*, Justice Souter, speaking for the court majority, based his reasoning on the *Lemon* Test. He argued that public school prayers at public school graduations appear to endorse religion and are therefore unconstitutional. However, Justices Scalia, Rehnquist, White, and Thomas dissented from this opinion. Their view was that prayer at graduation ceremonies is an American tradition. The four dissenters stated in their opinions that the *Lemon* Test should be rejected in this situation and that traditional religious practices should be allowed during graduation ceremonies.

### Santa Fe Independent School District (Galveston) v. Doe—1999

In 1999 the Supreme Court agreed to revisit this issue. The case of a Galveston, Texas area high school gave the Supreme Court its first chance to rule directly on student-led prayers (*Santa Fe Independent School*

*District v. Doe*).

In 1992 the U.S. Court of Appeals in Texas had become the first to uphold student-led invocations or benedictions, but only on condition that the religious messages were "non-sectarian and non-proselytizing." Two students, known only as "Jane Does," challenged this policy in federal court as a violation of the separation of church and state. Siding with the dissenting students, the U.S. Fifth Circuit Court of Appeals ruled that the school district had gone too far. The ruling rejected student-led prayers over the public address system at football games. Furthermore, with respect to graduation ceremonies, overtly Christian prayers carry the danger of polarizing and politicizing an event intended to celebrate the students' academic achievements, wrote Judge Wiener.

The school district appealed to the U.S. Supreme Court, arguing that it should not have to censor the religious content from student speech. Then-Governor Bush, speaking for the state of Texas, filed a brief supporting the school district. This effort was joined by the states of Alabama, Colorado, Kansas, Louisiana, Mississippi, Nebraska, South Carolina, and Tennessee. Nevertheless, when the Supreme Court issued its decision in June 2000, public prayer before a sporting event was disallowed. Forbidden was a situation in which "the state affirmatively sponsors the particular religious practice of prayer."

## Silent Meditation in Public Schools

Persistent litigation regarding prayer and Bible reading in the public schools continued in the lower courts during the 1960s and 70s. However, not until 1985 did a challenge to silent meditation reach the Supreme Court in *Wallace v. Jaffree*. The question was whether a moment of silence was permissible. The U.S. Supreme Court held that an Alabama court ruling that authorized a one-minute period of silence in public schools for "meditation or voluntary prayer" was unconstitutional.

Still open is the question of the constitutionality of a "moment of silence." As of 1998, more than one-half the states had laws permitting student meditation or silent prayer. In 2001, the U.S. Supreme Court refused to hear an appeal related to a daily minute of silence. In effect, therefore, the court approved a decision of the Fourth Circuit Court of Appeals to let stand a Virginia law requiring public schools to observe a moment of silence in which stu-dents might "meditate, pray, or engage in any other silent activity" (*Brown v. Gilmore*, 2001; Simpson, 2002).

## Religious Holidays, Celebrations, and Symbols

According to Stephen L. Carter, in his text *The Culture of Disbelief* (1993), the Supreme Court's *Lemon* Test is inadequate to determine when the Establishment Clause has been violated. Carter's view is that squaring *Lemon*'s rules with the accepted usage of our society's civil religion often requires some creative thinking. For example, how can one justify the expenditure of government funds to provide armed forces chaplains? In addition, a sticky question has revolved around use of public funds during the Christmas season to build and maintain a crèche, which celebrates the birth of Jesus Christ.

The Supreme Court, in *Lynch v. Donnelly* (1984), upheld inclusion of a nativity scene in a holiday display that also included a Santa Claus, a Christmas tree, a reindeer, a clown, a teddy bear, and other holiday symbols. The court held that the scene had a legitimate secular purpose, that of celebrating the Christmas holiday and depicting its origins. The court further held that the display may have "pushed" the Christian religion, but that any such effect was indirect, remote, and incidental.

The most memorable case on this issue was *Allegheny County v. Greater Pittsburgh American Civil Liberties Union* (1989). In this case the Supreme Court ruled that a nativity scene in the county courthouse violated the Establishment Clause because it had the effect of endorsing religion. However, a similar case showed that cultural diversity might be an acceptable alternative to showing a religious celebration. An exhibit outside a city court building showing a Christmas tree, a Chanukah menorah, and a "salute to liberty" message from the mayor was constitutional because it merely acknowledged cultural diversity and the different traditions for celebrating the holiday season.

Every year at Halloween several news stories surface regarding parent protests against this holiday. Specifically, some parents object to depicting witches, goblins, devils, and other characters that are associated in their minds with witchcraft and Satanism. However, Halloween has never been outlawed as a holiday, on the argument that it has no religious significance. On the other hand, in *Fox v. City of Los Angeles* (1978), the California Supreme Court held that erection of a cross, decidedly a symbol of Christianity, was a violation of government neutrality. The court concluded that both the California Constitution and the United States Constitution prohibited this display on the part of the city as furthering an establishment of religion.

## Released Time for Religious Instruction

The practice of releasing public school students during regular school hours for religious instruction first began in Gary, Indiana, in 1914 (Alexander & Alexander, 2001). Since then, two Supreme Court cases have addressed the issue of released time for religious instruction. In *McCollum v. Board of Education* (1948) the court invalidated a program in which religion classes were taught in the public schools. The court declared that the use of tax-supported school facilities to promote religious instruction was clearly a violation of the First Amendment.

In the second case, *Zorach v. Clausen* (1952), the court upheld an arrangement in which students were permitted to leave the school premises during the school day to receive religious instruction at various religious centers. The difference between *Zorach* and *McCollum* was that the *Zorach* case did not involve use of public school buildings or the direct use of public funds, nor were the instructors employed or paid by the district. Under such circumstances, student released time for religious instruction is common in many communities.

## Teaching of Evolution/Creation Science

It has been well established by the Supreme Court that a school district must neither prohibit instruction about evolution nor require that the instruction of evolution be balanced with the instruction of "creation science." A teacher named Peloza filed a suit involving this topic against the Capistrano Unified School District in California (*Peloza v. Capistrano Unified*, 1994).

Peloza was a biology teacher who alleged that the district had violated his constitutional rights under the Free Speech, Establishment, and Equal Protection clauses. He also charged that school district administrators had conspired to violate his rights by harassment and intimidation because of a "class-based animus against practicing Christians."

The United States Court of Appeals for the Ninth Circuit concluded that if the school district required the plaintiff to teach evolution only as a scientific theory, then summary judgment in favor of the district would be appropriate. This case suggests that school districts should review their science curriculum to ensure they can document that evolution is taught as a scientific theory. Moreover, the court stated that Peloza would violate the Establishment Clause if he were to discuss his religious beliefs with students on the school grounds during contract time. This case was appealed to the U.S. Supreme Court, which declined to review it, thus letting the decision stand.

The fight over teaching evolution has continued since the famous Scopes trial in 1925. The most recent debate continues in several states, with Kansas as the focus of attention. In 2005, the Kansas State Board of Education adopted a science framework for public schools that included the teaching of "intelligent design" along with the theory of evolution. The focus of "intelligent design" is that nature cannot account for life's complexity. The Kansas debate briefly ended in 2006 when the proponents of "intelligent design" lost their majority of the state board, and the new board vowed to return to teaching the theory of evolution.

## Use of Facilities

It is common practice for school districts to permit student organizations to use school buildings during non-instructional time. A school district that allows access to its facilities for student activities may not close them to student groups desiring to use the facilities for religious discussion and worship. This requirement is included in the federal Equal Access Act, passed in 1984, which requires public secondary schools that receive federal financial assistance to allow religious clubs to meet on the same basis as other non-curriculum-related activities.

In 1990 the Supreme Court resolved some of the legal questions regarding this issue when it rendered a decision in *Board of Education of Westside Community Schools v. Mergens* (1990). The case was a result of a group of high school students having asked permission to form a club that would meet at the public school during non-instructional time to engage in Bible discussions, prayer, and fellowship. The court decided that the school could not bar the religious club from non-curriculum-related student group meetings during non-instructional time. The court reasoned that denial of a student-initiated religious club while a variety of other non-curriculum-related student groups were recognized was a violation of the Equal Access Act. The court decided that even if a school district were to allow only one non-curriculum-related group to use its facilities, and if the other requirements of the act apply (public secondary schools receiving federal assistance), then the Equal Access Act is triggered.

The U.S. Supreme Court let a case stand that provided further clarification. In *Prince v. Jacoby* (2003), the Ninth Circuit U.S. Court of Appeals determined that when the Equal Access requirements were met, a religious club could be formed and receive the same benefits as any other extracurricular club, including, in this case, meeting during the school day, participating in fund-raising activities and support from the Associated Student Body (ASB), a place in the ASB-funded yearbook, and use of the public address system and bulletin boards *(Prince v. Jacoby*, 2003; Robinson, 2003).

The Equal Access Act has been appealed to by other student organizations. An article posted by the Ontario (Canada) Consultants for Religious Tolerance points out that, "ironically," those same conservative Christian groups that sponsored the act now find causes of which they would likely not approve—gay/lesbian/bisexual, atheist, satanic, and wiccan student groups, among others—using the same legislation to gain access to school facilities (Robinson, 2003).

California Education Code Section 38134 establishes requirements for use of school property in the state. Nonprofit organizations and clubs or associations organized to promote youth and school activities must be given access to school facilities unless other facilities are available. Examples include Girl and Boy Scouts, Camp Fire Girls, parent/teacher associations, and school-community advisory councils.

School districts may charge an amount not to exceed their direct costs for use of school facilities to any group, including religious organizations that supervise sports league activities. For other uses by religious organizations, however, the district must charge at least the amount of direct costs. Where admission fees are charged or contributions are solicited and the net receipts are not expended for the welfare of the students of the district or for charitable purposes, the district is required to charge a fair rental value for use of the property.

# Establishment of a Separate Religious School

In *Board of Education of Kiryas Joel v. Grumet* (1994) the Supreme Court, in a 6:3 decision, ruled uncon-

stitutional a New York law establishing a separate school district for a group of Orthodox Hasidic Jews. A New York religious community of about 8,500 Satmar Hasidim, a sect of Orthodox Jews who came to the United States from Europe after the holocaust, settled in a part of the town of Monroe that later became the Village of Kiryas Joel. The Satmar Hasidim are a strict religious people who speak Yiddish as their primary language. They wear distinctive clothing and keep apart from the outside world. For this reason, they neither watch television, listen to the radio, nor read English-language newspapers. Their children are educated in private, sex-segregated, parochial schools, where boys are trained in the Torah and girls for a role in the home.

Since the Satmar children attended private schools, what gave rise to this lawsuit? The difficulty was that the private schools did not provide special services for handicapped students. After 1985, when court decisions in other cases forced the local school district to discontinue sending its special education teachers to an annex of one of the Satmar private schools, the parents of these children had either to send them to a public school or to keep them at home. In public schools, the treatment accorded these young people, clothed and trained differently from their peers, led the parents to seek another solution. In response, the New York legislature passed a law in 1989 to constitute the Village of Kiryas Joel as a separate school district. In signing Chapter 748 into law, Governor Cuomo said it was designed to solve the unique problems associated with providing special education for the children of the village. The New York State School Boards Association, however, challenged Chapter 748 as an unconstitutional establishment of religion.

The trial court ruled that the statute was unconstitutional, failing all three prongs of the *Lemon Test*. The case eventually reached the Supreme Court, which also ruled against the establishment of the school. Justice Souter wrote the majority opinion, citing the necessity of government neutrality with respect to religion. The written decision of the court is notable in the sarcasm of the dissenting opinion, penned by Justice Scalia. In his dissent, Scalia berated Justice Souter and those who agreed with him for having "abandoned text and history as guides" and presenting a case that "could scarcely be weaker."

## *Sedlock v. Baird*—2013

This case was regarding the teaching of yoga in the Encinitas School District. During the 2011-12 school year, the KP Jois Foundation funded a yoga program at one school in the Encinitas district. The Foundation promotes yoga in schools as an alternative to traditional physical education. The district was pleased with the yoga program and expanded it to five schools in 2012-13, and to all nine district schools in 2013.

In February 2013, appellants Stephen and Jennifer Sedlock filed this action against the Encinitas Union School District; its superintendent, Timothy Baird; and the district's five governing board members. The Sedlocks alleged that the district's implementation of the yoga program as a component of its physical education curriculum violated religious freedom.

The case was heard by a California Superior Court, which ruled in favor of the district, and granted the district the right to continue the program. The Sedlocks appealed the decision to the Fourth Appellate District. The appellate court ruled that while the practice of yoga may be religious in some contexts, yoga classes as taught in the Encinitas district are devoid of any religious, mystical, or spiritual trappings. The court concluded that the trial court properly determined that the school district's yoga program neither constitutes an establishment of religion nor advances any religious concepts or ideas.

## Johnson v. Poway Unified School District—2007

This case is regarding bulletin boards or displays in the classroom. A Poway School District math teacher, Brad Johnson, displayed large banners in his classroom. Some of the banners included "In God We Trust—One Nation Under God—God Bless America—God Sheds His Grace on Thee—All Men Are Created Equal." For approximately 25 years, Johnson continuously displayed, without a single objection or complaint, his patriotic banners. Johnson had the banners made to order by a private company, and he purchased them with his own funds.

In 2007, school officials ordered Johnson to remove the banners stating they conveyed a "Judeo-Christian" viewpoint. Johnson argued that the banners had been in his room for approximately 25 years, and he had never had a complaint. He also argued that the banners were of a patriotic nature. The district maintained its stance that the banners had to be removed.

Johnson refused to remove the banners and filed a lawsuit, alleging that the school district violated his constitutional right to free speech by requiring him to remove the displays. The Poway district argued that the display of banners in the classroom was not the teacher's private speech, and was attributable to the school district.

The district also argued that the display violated the Establishment Clause of the U.S. Constitution.

After the trial court ruled in the teacher's favor, the school district appealed to the U.S. Court of Appeals for the Ninth Circuit. In 2011, the appellate court overturned the trial court's decision and ruled in favor of the school district. The Court of Appeals explained that while at work, the teacher speaks "not as an individual, but as a public employee," and the school had a right to ensure that the teacher's displays did not violate the Establishment Clause. Johnson filed a petition with the U.S. Supreme Court for a writ of certiorari, which was denied.

## The Pledge of Allegiance

### Elk Grove Unified School District v. Newdow—2004

In classrooms throughout the U.S., school children stand and start classroom activities by reciting the 31-word pledge each day.

> "I pledge allegiance to the Flag of the United States of America, and to the Republic for which it stands: one Nation under God, indivisible, With Liberty and Justice for all."

This tradition started in 1892 and became official in 1942 when the U.S. Congress included the Pledge to the Flag in the United States Flag Code. That very next year, 1943, a challenge to the requirement of daily recitation was challenged in the courts. The U.S. Supreme Court ruled in *West Virginia v. Barnette* that school children could not be forced to recite the Pledge as part of their daily routine.

In 1954, President Dwight Eisenhower approved adding the words "under God" to the pledge. The House Report (2006, May 29) that accompanied the legislation observed that, "From the time of our earliest history our peoples and our institutions have reflected the traditional concept that our nation was founded on a fundamental belief in God." For the next 50 years, the tradition of daily Pledge of Allegiance went relatively unchallenged in the public schools.

That was about to change in 2004 when Michael Newdow challenged Oak Grove School District's practice of having children pledging allegiance to the flag. Newdow sued the Elk Grove District, claiming that the public recitation by students violated his child's religious liberty. Lower courts ruled in favor of the school district.

However, in June of 2002, the 9th Circuit Court of Appeals declared the pledge unconstitutional. The Appellate Court, in part, based its decision on a previous high court decision, *Lee v. Weisman* (1992). In that decision, the high court had prohibited an invocation at a public high school.

The Newdow case was immediately appealed to the U.S. Supreme Court, which put on hold the Appellate decision until the Supreme Court heard the case. The U.S. Supreme Court in an 8-0 ruling reversed the lower court decision. Five justices decided that Newdow did not have the legal standing to bring the case. Newdow was involved in custody dispute with the mother of their third-grade daughter. The Court ruled that he could not speak for his child.

Newdow had never married the mother and the parents were involved in a battle over parental rights. The mother, Sandra Banning, said she had no problem with her daughter reciting the full pledge and argued that Newdow had no right to initiate the case.

The Court decided that the pledge does not violate the First Amendment, which prohibits the establishment of religion. Is this the last time this issue will reach the Supreme Court? Probably not; most opponents and supporters argue that the Supreme Court should have decided the case on its merits (Lapkoff, 2005). Newdow vowed to continue the crusade, despite the high court's ruling.

The Court dodged the central and broader question of whether the presence of the words "under God" violates the Establishment Clause. Thus, the constitutional question was prolonged (Lapkoff, 2005). Chief Justice Rehnquist and Justices Day O'Connor and Thomas argued that the court should have addressed the constitutional issue.

## Religious Dress in the Classroom

Some teachers in the public school system have challenged their district's dress code by wearing religious dress in their classrooms. Court decisions in such cases, though few in number, have held for the right of the school district to impose dress codes on employees. The prohibition of religious dress was upheld to ensure religious neutrality in the public schools.

## Curricular and Religious Materials in Public Schools

If we were to categorize the numerous articles relating to church vs. school issues, we would find those involving school curricular materials the most common. Recent cases have involved textbooks that included poems or stories considered inappropriate by one group or another. Many of these stories concerned Halloween: specifically, tales about ghosts, goblins, witches, and vampires. Plaintiffs have argued that because these characters are not in keeping with the Christian faith, they should not appear in literature for the classroom.

In *Grove v. Mead School District No. 354* (1985), parents tried to force a school district to remove from its English curriculum the book *The Learning Tree*, by Gordon Parks. The central idea of the novel is racism as viewed by an adolescent boy from an African-American family. The parents of Cassie, a sophomore high school student, were concerned that the school was requiring their daughter to read a book that violated the family's religious beliefs by advocating secular humanism. As a result of this challenge to the district, the student was assigned an alternative book. By this action, the district avoided any charge of coercion. However, the court made clear that the primary effect of the book was secular, that is, not related to religion, and that it was an appropriate selection for "exposing students to different cultural attitudes and outlooks." Thus, the district was justified in retaining the book in the curriculum. On appeal, the U.S. Supreme Court declined to review this case, thus allowing the decision to stand.

The U.S. Supreme Court has not directly addressed distribution of religious literature in public schools, and lower courts have rendered a range of opinions, most often prohibiting religious sects from distributing materials to captive public school audiences. As early as 1955, California's Attorney General rendered an opinion that the distribution of free Bibles to school children was prohibited. Subsequently, in 1993, a court of appeals dealt with a situation in which members of the Gideons International talked about their organization, then offered students a Bible from a stack laid out on a table in the classroom. In *Berger v. Rensselaer Central School Corporation* the court determined that this practice was unconstitutional. The court felt that the children were a captive audience, not free to leave the classroom during the presentation—an inappropriate entanglement of religion and government.

These and other court cases might encourage abandoning of moral and religious teaching in the schools. However, some aspects of these subjects are appropriate in public education. The *History-Social Science Framework* for California (2001) discusses ethical and cultural literacy and civic values. It also includes a five-page appendix on religion and the history-social science curriculum that includes jointly sponsored statements and references to resource materials.

# Summary

Some of the most interesting litigation in the church-school controversy involves challenges to materials and curriculum in the schools; Bible reading, prayer, and meditation in the school or classroom; prayer at graduation and other school events; religious symbols and celebrations; expressions of freedom in religious dress and speech; and conflicts related to compulsory attendance and school facilities. More than two hundred years have passed since our forefathers established the concept of religious neutrality in public education. Nevertheless, issues that were wrestled with in the 1800s continue to surface.

Such controversies will continue to arise as long as we are a people of many groups and diverse religions. Even our Supreme Court justices are not of one mind on these issues. It is essential that all public school teachers and administrators demonstrate sensitivity to the beliefs and customs of religious and nonreligious groups. The effective administrator will keep well informed about court decisions and board policies that provide guidance in this important area.

## Key Terms

1. Bill of Rights
2. compulsory education
3. Equal Access Act
4. Establishment Clause
5. Free Exercise Clause
6. *Lemon* Test

## Discussion/Essay Questions

1. Is it consistent to allow prayer before sessions of Congress, yet not at school? Why or why not?

2. Search an index covering the last three years of your nearest major California newspaper. What are the three most commonly mentioned controversies involving church versus school? Why are these such a dilemma for our citizens?

3. Do we allow a moment of silent meditation for the students in our schools? How is this different from prayer spoken out loud?

4. What curricular materials are most often objected to by parents?

5. Use the Internet to find three sites (URLs) that provide information about school law related to religion.

# CHAPTER 11

# School Finance and the Law

*School funding inequality makes education separate and unequal.*

—Arne Duncan, U.S. Secretary of Education

## Introduction

For the first two centuries of the nation's history, local communities paid for public education. Today, public education is financed by a combination of state funds, local school district taxes, federal funds, and private grants. Since education is a function of state government, local school districts have limited power over their budgets. State control is particularly evident in California, where, in recent decades, the state has largely assumed responsibility for financing public education.

Education is big business—in many communities, the major source of employment. Education expenses also take a major bite out of most state budgets. In California, public education—kindergarten through community college—is guaranteed a minimum of 40.33% of the state budget. As a consequence, school finance is of extreme importance to taxpayers, the governor, and the state legislature.

In addition to legislative controls over district revenues, the legislature exerts control by establishing rules for school board expenditures. State laws govern salaries, benefits, retirement contributions, and purchasing requirements. In addition, the law is very specific regarding a district's ability to tax and to borrow money.

Over the last several years, parents, taxpayers, and individual citizens have challenged the equality of financial support of schools at both state and national levels. This chapter provides a historical background for school finance and the major court decisions affecting school finance.

## Financing Schools at the Local Level

Historically, states relied on local property taxes for the operation of school districts. However, as citizens became more aware of the disparities in per-pupil funding among districts, a movement was started to equalize funding by student.

Teachers, administrators, parents, and students have long recognized the difference in per-pupil expenditures from district to district. In two adjoining districts, one might be noted for excellent facilities, high paying salaries, and a generous supply of instructional materials, while the second district could have run-down facilities, a low salary schedule, and minimal instructional materials. Coupled with a desire to eliminate, or at least reduce, these inequalities, is a general recognition that equal resources do not ensure equal education. For example, children with exceptional needs caused by physical or mental handicaps may deserve extra funds.

The disparity in funding among districts gave rise in some states to legislation intended to mitigate such inequality. At the same time, several court cases were brought to force passage of just such laws. Plaintiffs charged that unequal spending for education was discriminatory and deprived students of their basic right to an adequate education. This argument did not succeed at the federal level and has not always fared well in the states, either.

## Federal Challenges

The landmark case of *Brown v. Board of Education of Topeka* (1954) afforded the U.S. Supreme Court opportunity to rule on whether public education is a constitutional right. The case was appealed to the Supreme Court by attorneys representing Linda Brown. Ms. Brown was an elementary school student in Topeka, Kansas, who was required to attend an all-black school when an all-white school was located much closer to her home.

*Brown v. Topeka* was a landmark case because it reversed an earlier decision of the U.S. Supreme Court in *Plessy v. Ferguson* (1896). In that decision the court had approved the separate-but-equal doctrine. In *Brown,* however, the court ruled that public education is a constitutional right and that segregated schooling is inherently unequal. The decision addressed as critically important both opportunity for students to exchange views with students of different backgrounds and the inferiority feelings generated by separate schools. It was decided that in public education, the doctrine of separate-but-equal has no place.

## State Challenges

The *Brown* recognition of education as a constitutional right did not settle the question of equality in educational finance. That cause was taken up next at the state level. The first school finance cases asked whether states should allocate more funds to poor school districts and whether states were obligated to provide additional funds to educate students with special needs. Two state decisions helped establish legal precedents regarding school finance.

The first case was *Sawyer v. Gilmore* (1912), which challenged the school finance system in Maine. The plaintiff argued that Maine's distribution of school funds, which gave wealthier towns a larger proportion of funds, was unconstitutional. The court ruled that, although taxation might be equal and uniform, it did not necessarily follow that the benefits of that taxation must be distributed to all people in equal amounts.

The second case was *Dean v. Coddington* (1964). The South Dakota Supreme Court decided this case. The plaintiffs were taxpayers in a school district that did not have an elementary or secondary school. Therefore, the district did not receive funds from a foundation formula established by the legislature (Johns & Morphet, 1975).

As in the *Sawyer* case, the court distinguished taxation from distribution, holding that the state's constitution did not require equal distribution of funds to all school districts. These two cases established the premise that the proportion of tax money collected by a state from residents of a school district need not be matched when funds are distributed back to the districts.

## Equalization of Funding

Until the early part of the 20th century, state funding for schools was meager and typically was allocated on a flat per-pupil basis (Jordan & Lyons, 1992). No adjustments were made for differences in the wealth of a district or the educational needs of its students. As early as the turn of the century, educators were advocating a system that would equalize funds to assist low-wealth districts.

The philosophical and legal arguments for equality of funding for education centered on four issues:

- Public education is a state function, not local.
- A child is a child of the state, not of the local school district.
- All school revenues are state revenues, regardless of whether they are collected at state or local levels.
- All school children are equal under the laws of the state.

Therefore, plaintiffs argued, the state could not combine state and local tax resources in such a manner as to benefit some children while ignoring needs of others (Alexander & Salmon, 1995). The plaintiffs presented the argument (later utilized in California's *Serrano* case) that a child's circumstances, that is, living in a poor district, should not determine the quality of his or her education.

Litigation proceeded in at least 23 states under the Equal Protection and Education clauses of state constitutions (Valente, 1998). Although the litigants were not very successful through the state courts in changing the system of financing local schools, they were able to promote legislation to equalize funding of education. Many states attempted to achieve this goal by utilizing other sources of revenue—state income tax, excise taxes, and fees—to support schools.

Perhaps the most successful case, *Rose v. Council for Better Education* (1989), was filed in a state court in Kentucky. The Kentucky Constitution states that the General Assembly shall, by appropriate legislation, provide for an efficient system of common schools throughout the state. The Kentucky Supreme Court examined the meaning of "an efficient system" by considering educational achievement. The court found that poorer districts were in greater need than richer districts. It concluded that Kentucky's funding system was underfunded and inadequate, as well as unequal and inequitable, and that educational funding must be increased and equitably distributed (Burrup, Brimley, & Garfield, 1993).

This case broke new ground by overturning the state's entire education system—its organization, programs, structure, and governance. In this case the state's entire elementary and secondary education system was found in violation of the state constitution. To avoid dissolution of the entire system, the Kentucky legislature was forced, by a specified date, to pass legislation to meet the standards set by the court.

Odden and Wohlstetter (1992) report that as a result of a court mandate, or the threat of a mandate, more than 35 state legislatures enacted fundamental changes in their school finance structures between 1971 and 1985. These reforms had five major characteristics.

- They revamped the school finance equalization formula so as to send more state funds to property-poor, lower-spending districts.
- They increased the overall state role in funding schools.
- They increased state funding for special needs through compensatory, special, and bilingual education programs.
- The reforms increased aid for the extraordinary needs of large urban districts.
- Many reforms called for increased education taxes coupled with spending limitations that restricted local fiscal control over tax rates and curbed annual increases in expenditures per student.

## California's *Serrano v. Priest*—1971–1988

Perhaps the best-known challenge to the method of funding local school districts occurred in California. What actually became a series of cases is referred to as *Serrano v. Priest*. This series occurred between 1971 and 1988. *Serrano I*, the first in the series, was initiated at the trial court level. The plaintiffs alleged that California's school finance system resulted in wide disparities in the revenue available to different school districts and violated the Equal Protection Clauses of the U.S. and California constitutions by making the quality of education dependent upon the wealth of a child's parents and geographical accident. They also contended that the system failed to take into account different educational needs of children in the various school districts. The defendants in the case, a group of county and state government officials, requested dismissal based on their contention that none of the stated facts were sufficient to constitute a cause of action.

The trial court ruled in favor of the defendants and granted the dismissal. The plaintiffs appealed that decision to the California Supreme Court. Since the appeal related to the dismissal order, rather than to a decision of the lower court, the court could not rule on the merits of the case. However, the California Supreme Court ruled that the plaintiffs had a basis for their claim. In this decision, the state supreme court noted that it had previously construed certain provisions of the California Constitution as equivalent to the Equal Protection Clause of the Fourteenth Amendment. The most important finding of the California court was that "education is a fundamental right." The court gave five reasons in support of this view:

- Education is essential to preserving an individual's opportunity to compete successfully in the economic marketplace
- Education is universally relevant
- Few government services have as extensive contact with each recipient as does education
- Education is unmatched in the extent to which it molds the personality of the youth of society
- Education is so important that the state has made it compulsory.

After the California Supreme Court classified education as a fundamental right and determined that the state had not demonstrated that its funding system was adequate to the attainment of this compelling state interest, the case was remanded to the trial court, which then proceeded with a trial. The state legislature responded by changing the formula for financing public schools. In an attempt to equalize funding across districts, Senate Bill 90 was approved by the legislature and signed by the governor. This legislation set a revenue limit—the maximum dollars per student in general-purpose state and local funds a district might receive. The key equalization feature was an adjustment that provided a higher dollar amount to low-revenue districts.

Next, *Serrano II* was brought to force a review of the new state school financial formula. The new procedure was found lacking. The court decreed that disparities between districts were too great and too slow in changing. However, in 1989, the California appellate court ruled that satisfactory progress had been made on equalizing expenditures between districts and closed the case.

The *Serrano* cases illustrate a major disadvantage confronted by plaintiffs who seek to use the courts as a means of changing public financing of schools. Litigation takes an inordinate amount of time. While *Serrano* did ultimately rule in the plaintiff's favor, the final decision took more than seven years.

It is interesting to note that, almost 50 years after the Serrano decision, disparities still exist among school districts in California. For example, in 2012-13 the average per pupil spending in districts across the state was $8,823. In Los Angeles County, however, the spending in unified districts ranged from $7,515 in Glendora to $10,616 in Beverly Hills. (The data are available on the Internet at http://www.ed-data. k12.ca.us.)

## San Antonio Independent School District v. Rodriguez—1973

Between the time of *Serrano I* and *Serrano II*, the U.S. Supreme Court set an important precedent in *San Antonio Independent School District v. Rodriguez* (1973). This was the first case at the federal level relative to the disparities caused by utilizing local property taxes to finance education.

The plaintiffs in this case challenged the process for funding education in Texas, citing as their basis the Equal Protection Clause of the U.S. Constitution. Because the Texas system was similar to those in many other states, *Rodriguez* offered the Supreme Court an opportunity to force major restructuring of school funding systems across the country. An indication of the importance of this case is that 28 state attorney generals filed friend-of-the-court briefs, urging the court to uphold the existing Texas funding system, which had been declared unconstitutional by a lower court.

The court indicated that its test for determining whether a right is fundamental requires an assessment as to whether the right is explicitly or implicitly guaranteed by the Constitution. Contrary to the California decision in *Serrano*, the court decided that since education is not mentioned in the Constitution, it is not among the rights afforded explicit protection. Consequently, the court ruled in favor of the district and rejected the claim that the Texas form of taxation violated the Fourteenth Amendment's Equal Protection Clause.

Nevertheless, although dismissing the argument that public education is a fundamental right, the court acknowledged its historic dedication to public education and its abiding respect for the vital role of education in a free society. The court declared that the state's system of taxation need only be rational to withstand Fourteenth Amendment challenges. This case, in effect, closed the federal court system as a route by which to challenge inequities in school finance.

## Robinson v. Cahill—1973–1976

A series of seven separate court cases affecting education occurred in New Jersey between 1973 and 1976. The seven cases are referred to as *Robinson v. Cahill.* The first case was brought at the trial level; the court decided that the funding statutes in New Jersey violated the Equal Protection clauses of the U.S. and New Jersey constitutions. The decision was based on the fact that a high percentage of school revenue was generated from local taxation.

The trial court found that 67% of the statewide total school operating expenses came from local *ad valorem* taxation of real property, 28% from state appropriations, and 5% from federal aid (Jordan, 1992). As a result of this form of financial support for schools, a large disparity existed across districts in the amount spent per student. Therefore, the trial court held that the system unconstitutionally discriminated against students in low-wealth areas.

The New Jersey Supreme Court agreed that the system was unconstitutional, but for different reasons. The high court rejected the argument that a statewide uniformity in expenditure for education is required. The court suggested that local citizens could decide the amount of funds to be spent for education, much as they did for other services such as police and fire protection. Much like the *Rodriguez* court, New Jersey's Supreme Court rejected the argument that education is a fundamental right.

Turning to another issue, however, the court examined a clause in New Jersey's Constitution that required the legislature to provide for the maintenance and support of a thorough and efficient system of free public schools. The court decided that the state must define in some discernible way the educational obligation of school districts and compel each local district to raise the money necessary to provide that educational opportunity.

The Robinson case is important for educational finance in that a decision was made that the funding system was inconsistent with the state constitution on the basis of its Thorough and Efficient Clause, rather than under an equal protection clause. In addition, the details of the decision were more prescriptive than the previous court decisions had been in calling for remedies.

## Abbott v. Burke—1985

It is interesting to note that the state of New Jersey, while near the top of all states in expenditures per student, again found itself in court in 1985. In this case, the New Jersey Public School Education Act was challenged as unconstitutional. The argument in *Abbott* was similar to that in *Robinson* in that the plaintiffs were students in schools located in poor districts. Attorneys for the students argued that the funding formula had not resulted in a thorough and efficient education for all New Jersey students. With the state contributing only 40% of all school operating costs, the majority of school funding was derived from local property taxes—an arrangement that still resulted in a sizeable funding disparity between high-wealth and low-wealth districts.

Like *Serrano*, *Abbott v. Burke* involved a long series of decisions. In the first case (1985), the New Jersey Supreme Court determined that the funding system under the Public School Education Act should be reviewed through administrative channels before the judicial system could rule on alleged constitutional problems.

After the administrative review was completed, the court issued its decision in *Abbott v. Burke II* (1990). The court declared the funding formula unconstitutional. The decision was again based on the Thorough and Efficient Clause of the state constitution. The court's ruling indicated that many decisions made in the field of education are based on the premise that the things money can buy affect the quality of education (Jordan, 1992). *Abbott V,* decided in May 1998, specified both funding and program requirements, the latter including full-day kindergarten and half-day preschool, technology, and renovation of deficient facilities.

In 2008, New Jersey approved a new school-funding plan. Under this plan, the State allocated 7.8 billion dollars to schools in 2009, a 7% increase over 2008. All New Jersey school districts received additional funding ranging from 2 to 20%. The formula follows the principle that children with greater needs deserve greater resources. Under the plan, aid is distributed through a foundation formula that determines the amount of money each district needs to ensure every student attains New Jersey's educational standards.

On May 28, 2009, the New Jersey Supreme Court issued its 20th decision in the two decades old *Abbott v. Burke* litigation. The Court ruled unanimously that the state's new education funding system meets the constitutional requirement to provide all students a thorough and efficient education.

## Edgewood Independent School District v. Kirby—1989

Another state supreme court case, referred to as *Edgewood Independent School District v. Kirby* (1989), involved interpretation of the Texas State Constitution. This constitution contained a clause providing that since a general diffusion of knowledge is essential to the preservation of the liberties and rights of the people, it shall be the duty of the legislature of the state to establish and make suitable provision for the support and maintenance of an efficient system of public free schools.

When the court reviewed the funding formulas across school districts, it found that the difference in property values was so great that the wealthiest district had more than $14 million of property wealth per student while the poorest had only $20,000, reflecting a 700 to 1 ratio. The court decided that general diffusion of knowledge meant knowledge spread statewide. It was decided that the funding formula was unconstitutional because it resulted in education that was limited and unbalanced, rather than a diffusion of education in general.

## DeRolph v. The State of Ohio—1997

In March, 1997, the Supreme Court of Ohio, by a four-to-three ruling, declared the state's system of funding education unconstitutional. The ruling was based on the concept of equalization of spending across districts. Ohio generated about half the money for public education from local taxes and about half from state revenues. As a result, because of differences in property values and wealth in each district, annual per-pupil spending ranged from $4,000 to $12,000 per student.

The original DeRolph suit was brought in 1991. The KnowledgeWorks Foundation (2003) lists nine court actions since that time. Following on the 1997 decision that school funding in Ohio did not accord with the state constitution, the court attempted in 2001 to turn the issue over to the legislature. Lack of legislative response led to further litigation, which led the court to appoint a mediator, who ultimately reported failure to resolve the issue. That failure led to further court actions in December, 2002, and May, 2003. The court still finds the state funding system unconstitutional and still expects the legislature to solve the problem, so the issue is far from settled.

## Jane Doe and Jason Roe v. State of California—2010

California schools charging fees have been challenged many times, and were challenged again in 2010. The ACLU filed a class action lawsuit in Los Angeles County against the State of California, charging that school districts across the state were charging illegal fees for educational programs. The case relied on an investigation by the ACLU that found at least 40 schools were charging fees for course workbooks, laboratory expenses, Advanced Placement courses and exams, physical education uniforms, fine arts classes, and a variety of other programs.

The two plaintiffs, Jane Doe and Jason Roe, argued that school fees are illegal. The complaint was filed against the governor and other state officials, asking them to enforce the constitution and laws that prohibit charging student fees. The complaint did not seek monetary damages or orders against the legislature or individual school boards.

The lawsuit was settled in December 2010. The settlement does not establish any new legal ground, since it was clear under California law that school fees do violate the right to a free public education. Moreover, it provides a framework for informing students and parents of their rights not to pay the fees.

The state agreed to send a letter and guidance document to all school superintendents informing them that whenever a public school offers a curricular or extracurricular program to students, the California Constitution requires that the school provide all materials, supplies, and equipment—whether they are necessary or supplementary to the program—to students free of charge.

## Williams et al. v. California (ACLU)—2000

On May 17, 2000, the 46th anniversary of the decision in *Brown v. Board of Education*, the American Civil Liberties Union, with other organizations and individuals, filed a suit against the state of California alleging lack of instructional materials, too few credentialed teachers, overcrowded classrooms, and unhealthy conditions in eighteen districts in California. The ACLU based its suit on a five-month study of education in California. The study included interviews with parents, students, and teachers.

In September, the ACLU followed up with a motion asking the court to order the California Depart-

ment of Education to institute a tracking system that would produce data as to the textbooks actually provided to districts in the state (*Back to School*, 2000). In December, the state of California sued the eighteen districts, arguing that if their students lacked adequate materials and facilities, the fault lay with the districts. In April 2001, the California School Boards Association was granted permission to intervene in the case; CSBA spokespersons said that the organization was not entirely on either side, and on some points disagreed with both. At the same time Superior Court Judge Busch, reversing an earlier decision, determined that the ACLU suit should be settled before the state's suit against the districts (*CSBA's motion*, 2001).

The *Los Angeles Times* reported on August 11, 2004, that Governor Schwarzenegger and the ACLU had tentatively settled the suit. The governor agreed to channel as much as a billion dollars for facilities to low-performing schools and another $139 million for textbooks. The funds were to be awarded to schools over a period of several years. The major problem then became finding the money (Helfand & DiMassa, 2004).

The California legislature approved Assembly Bill 831 in 2005 to implement the Williams Act. This Act required each local education agency (LEA) that receives instructional material funds to hold a public hearing before the end of the eighth week of each school year. The governing board must certify that each pupil, including English learners, must have a standards-aligned textbook and instructional materials to use in class and to take home (O'Connell, J. 2005).

## The National Picture

Of the 50 states, 45 have been sued with allegations that funding for K-12 education was unconstitutional. The five states that have never had an educational funding lawsuit include Delaware, Hawaii, Mississippi, Nevada, and Utah. In 2015, litigation is pending against 11 states over inadequate or inequitable school funding (Lu, 2014).

## Summary

The citizens of the United States have repeatedly ranked education as the nation's number one priority. However, agreement on public education often stops there. Opinions vary widely as to what should be taught and how schools are to be financed. Moreover, great disparity is found in the financial support of education among the 50 states and individual districts within the states. Most states have attempted in some way to equalize the funding of education between wealthier and poorer districts. These attempts have in some cases been followed by lawsuits and court decisions.

It has not been easy for courts to wrestle with the societal problem of school funding and equalization of that funding. The courts tend to reflect the values and attitudes of a majority of the people toward the issues and questions on which they are ruling—values and attitudes that, with respect to school finance, have been changing. Until the early 1970s, higher courts refused to interfere or to rule in certain types

of school finance cases. This position was based on the rationale that the methods used to collect and distribute funds to local school districts were a legislative, not a judicial, problem.

*Serrano v. Priest* (1971) brought a major change when California's Supreme Court set standards that overturned the state's system of financing schools. In the wake of *Serrano*, almost every state made efforts to improve its method of financing education. Although *San Antonio Independent School District v. Rodriguez* (1973) effectively ended appeals to the federal courts, the school finance issue continues to be brought in state courts, and litigation will undoubtedly continue well into the early decades of the 21st century.

## Key Terms

1. compelling state interest
2. education as a fundamental right
3. Equal Protection Clause
4. equalization

5. friend of the court
6. general diffusion of knowledge
7. property taxes
8. Senate Bill 90

## Discussion/Essay Questions

1. *Brown v. Board of Education of Topeka* (1954) is hailed as a landmark Supreme Court decision. Discuss the important precedent that was established in this decision and the court's rationale.

2. The majority of states have attempted to equalize funding among wealthier and poorer school districts. Discuss the steps that have been taken by state legislatures in their attempts to equalize school funding.

3. California's *Serrano v. Priest* (1988) decision had a profound effect on the financing of education in that state and many other states. How did this decision affect the financing of schools?

4. The U.S. Supreme Court in *San Antonio Independent School District v. Rodriguez* (1973) made a decision contrary to that reached in *Serrano v. Priest* (1988). Compare the two decisions. What was the rationale for each?

5. The concept of "Thorough and Efficient" was argued in *Abbott v. Burke* (1990). Where did this concept originate? How did the plaintiffs use it?

LAW, RULE, REGULATION, PRECEPT, STATUTE, ORDINANCE, CANON mean a principle governing action or procedure. LAW implies imposition by a sovereign authority and the obligation of obedience on the part of all subject to that authority. RULE applies to more restricted or specific situations. REGULATION implies prescription by authority in order to control an organization or system. PRECEPT commonly suggests something advisory and not obligatory communicated typically through teaching. STATUTE implies a law enacted by a legislative body. ORDINANCE applies to an order governing some detail of procedure or conduct enforced by a limited authority such as a municipality. CANON suggests in nonreligious use a principle or rule of behavior or procedure commonly accepted as a valid guide. EDUCATE to develop mentally, morally, or aesthetically. To persuade or condition to feel, believe, or act in a desired way. to accept something as desirable to provide schooling. LAW, RULE, REGULATION, PRECEPT, STATUTE, ORDINANCE, CANON mean a principle governing action or procedure. LAW implies imposition by a sovereign authority and the obligation of obedience on the part of all subject to that authority. RULE applies to more restricted or specific situations. REGULATION implies prescription by authority in order to control an organization or system. PRECEPT commonly suggests something advisory and not obligatory communicated typically through teaching. STATUTE implies a law enacted by a legislative body. ORDINANCE applies to an order governing some detail of procedure or conduct enforced by a limited authority such as a municipality. CANON suggests in nonreligious use a principle or rule of behavior or procedure commonly accepted as a valid guide. EDUCATE to develop mentally, morally, or aesthetically. to persuade

# CHAPTER 12

# Copyright Law and Education

*If Apple Corporation or anyone else wants to stream my music, they have to pay me for the privilege.*

—Taylor Swift, pop singer, songwriter, actor

## Introduction

Breaking copyright, patent, or trademark law in the United States can be serious business. The quote at the beginning of the chapter by Taylor Swift sends a strong message to corporate America. When the Apple Corporation announced that it was not going to pay royalties to record companies, Swift challenged the decision and won. Consider what happened a couple of years ago when the Academy Awards ceremony in Los Angeles featured a dance by a man dressed up as Snow White! No one on the production staff had thought about obtaining permission from the Walt Disney company to present this spoof. However, Walt's heirs, not finding the dancing Snow White at all funny, slapped a multimillion dollar suit on the producers of Academy Awards.

More recently, the concern for intellectual ownership has been demonstrated as writers, composers, producers, and other originators file lawsuits in an attempt to protect their creative endeavors. School districts and individual educators have been the defendants in some of these suits. This fact, combined with the contributions of technology in simplifying the copying of both print and nonprint materials, has made copyright infringement a major concern to teachers.

This chapter provides the teacher and administrator with a brief history of copyright law and information about significant court cases regarding copyright infringement. A review of permissible and prohibited use of copyrighted materials in schools is also included.

## Copyright Terms

The legal structure that governs rules of ownership has developed its own language, and it is important to differentiate among some commonly used terms. The following definitions are drawn from *Black's Law Dictionary* (2008), except as indicated.

**Copyright:** A property right in an original work of authorship (such as literary, musical, artistic, photographic, or film work) fixed in any tangible medium of expression, giving the holder the exclusive right to reproduce, adapt, distribute, perform, and display the work.

**Copyright Notice:** A necessary notice in the form required by law that is placed in each published copy of a work. All copies of a product should include the name of the owner of the copyright, the year of first publication, and either the copyright symbol (©) or the word "copyright" (Fischer, Schimmel, & Kelly, 1995).

**Fair Use Doctrine:** A reasonable and limited use of a copyrighted work without the author's permission. Factors affecting the application of the definition include the purpose and character of the use, the nature of the copyrighted work, the amount of the work used, and the economic impact of the use. The Copyright Office of the Library of Congress publishes a guide to fair use for educators and librarians (*Reproduction*, 1995).

**Patent:** The exclusive right to make, use, or sell an invention for a specified period, usually seventeen years.

**Plagiarism:** The act or an instance of copying or stealing another person's words or ideas and attributing them as one's own. *Black's Law Dictionary* (2008) cites Goldstein (1994) on the point that plagiarism is an ethical offense, applying both to copyrighted works and works in the public domain. If the material plagiarized is under copyright, then the plagiarism is also illegal.

## Table 3    When U.S. Works Pass into the Public Domain

*by Lolly Gasaway University of North Carolina*

**Definition:** A public domain work is a creative work that is not protected by copyright and which may be freely used by everyone. The reasons that the work is not protected include: (1) the term of copyright for the work has expired; (2) the author failed to satisfy statutory formalities to perfect the copyright or (3) the work is a work of the U.S. Government.

| DATE OF WORK | PROTECTED FROM | TERM |
|---|---|---|
| Created 1-1-78 or after | When work is fixed in tangible medium of expression | Life + 70 years[1] (or if work of corporate authorship, the shorter of 95 years from publication, or 120 years from creation[2]) |
| Published before 1923 | In public domain | None |
| Published from 1923–1963 | When published with notice[3] | 28 years + could be renewed for 47 years, now extended by 20 years for a total of 67 years. If not so renewed, now in public domain |
| Published from 1964–1977 | When published with notice | 28 years for first term; now automatic extension of 67 years for second term |
| Created before 1-1-78 but not published | 1-1-78, the effective date of the 1976 Act which eliminated common law copyright | Life + 70 years or 12-31-2002, whichever is greater |
| Created before 1-1-78 but published between then and 12-31-2002 | 1-1-78, the effective date of the 1976 Act which eliminated common law copyright | Life + 70 years or 12-31-2047, whichever is greater |

[1]Term of joint works is measured by life of the longest-lived author.

[2]Works for hire, anonymous and pseudonymous works also have this term. 17 U.S.C. § 302(c).

[3]Under the 1909 Act, works published without notice went into the public domain upon publication. Works published without notice between 1-1-78 and 3-1-89, effective date of the Berne Convention Implementation Act, retained copyright only if effort to correct the accidental omission of notice was made within five years, such as by placing notice on unsold copies. 17 U.S.C. § 405.

(Notes courtesy of Professor Tom Field, Franklin Pierce Law Center, and Lolly Gasaway)

Last updated 11-04-03. Used by permission of the author.

**Public Domain:** A work enters the public domain upon expiration of the copyright. This has happened for materials first published in 1923 or earlier. Some works published before January 1, 1978, also fall in the public domain. For further details, see Table 3, prepared by Lolly Gasaway of the University of North Carolina. It should be noted that whether or not works fall in the public domain, and can thus be reproduced without permission, using such material without attribution is plagiarism; see definition above.

**Trademark:** A word, phrase, logo, or other graphic symbol used by a manufacturer or seller to distinguish its product or products from those of others.

## Historical Context of Copyright Law

It was in 1476 that the printing press was introduced into England and became the tool for large-scale reproduction of books (Leaffer, 1998). The printed word caused problems for the English leadership, as it gave critics an opportunity to be heard.

Under English law at that time, companies were allowed to publish manuscripts under the "protection" of the Crown. In effect, this practice allowed the government to censor all printed materials. However, even at that time, some enterprising companies copied materials without the Crown's protection.

As printing became more common and questions about authorship continued to surface, the English Parliament responded by adopting the Statute of Anne in 1709. For the first time, the right of authors was established. Under this law, authors were given ownership of their work for two 14-year terms (Foster & Shook, 1993).

Congress first enacted copyright legislation in 1790. Like the Statute of Anne, the law allowed copyright for 14 years with the possibility of a 14-year extension. Revisions occurred twice during the 19th century. However, the first comprehensive copyright law approved in the United States was the Copyright Act of 1909. This act expanded copyrightable subject matter to all works of an author. In addition, the law created a longer term of copyright protection: two terms of 28 years each.

International copyright has also been an issue. The Berne Convention of 1886, to which the United States subscribed in 1988, established mutual copyright protection among signatory nations. In these countries, copyright registration in any member nation is recognized (Association of Research Libraries, 2002).

The balance between the rights of the creator of copyrightable material and the principle of public domain in the interest of widespread access to that material is difficult to maintain. This conflict was explored in the case of *Eldred v. Ashcroft*, decided by the U.S. Supreme Court in 2003.

## *Eldred v. Ashcroft*—2003

The *Eldred* case questioned the Sonny Bono Copyright Term Extension Act of 1998, which had added 20 years to the term of copyright protection. The challenge was brought in behalf of a retired computer programmer who had become excited about making public domain books available to the public without charge. The plaintiff's argument was that this extension, the 11th in 40 years (Openlaw, n.d.), in effect created an unlimited term, or at least set the stage for an unending series of extensions. Such a practice, it was argued, would violate Article I, Section 8, of the

U.S. Constitution, which grants Congress power "to promote the progress of science and useful arts, by securing for limited times to authors and inventors the exclusive right to their respective writings and discoveries." The plaintiff's attorneys focused on the phrase "limited times." The Supreme Court found for the respondent, thus confirming the extension. Later, the plaintiff's attorney blamed himself for the defeat, concluding in retrospect that he should have built his case on the harm caused by withholding materials from public access, rather than on the point regarding limited times (Lessig, 2004). We can expect further political action and perhaps more court challenges to address the issue.

## The Copyright Act of 1976

It was not until 1976 that Congress approved legislation that set specific guidelines for copyright protection. The Copyright Act of that year was designed to clarify the copyright legislation approved in 1909. The new law extended the length of years for copyright protection and attempted to clarify which items might be subject to copyright protection.

The real revision of the 1909 copyright law started in 1949 when Barbara Ringer, a recent graduate of Columbia University's law school, joined the Copyright Office at the Library of Congress. Twenty-four years later in 1973, she was appointed as the first woman to hold the position of Register of Copyrights.

During this twenty plus years, her passion was to protect the songwriters and performers whose work was often printed or broadcast without permission. She wrote papers and commissioned studies on how the nation's copyright laws should be revised. She devoted much of her time to drafting a comprehensive copyright act, and educating congressional representatives about why it was needed.

Finally, the results of her work resulted in the Copyright Act of 1976. Arthur Levine, a copyright lawyer who worked with Ringer at the Library of Congress gives Ringer credit for the Act by stating, "I don't believe there would have been a Copyright Act if there hadn't been a Barbara Ringer" (Nierman, J. 2009).

The act established the principle of "fair use," whereby scholars and reviewers could quote briefly from copyrighted works without having to pay fees. The act is better known for allowing authors to retain greater control over their work. Under the 1909 law, an author owned the copyright for 28 years from the date of publication. Unless the copyright was renewed, the work entered the public domain, and the author lost any right to royalties. With the 1976 Act, the author owned the copyright for his or her lifetime, plus 50 years. In 1977, Ringer received the President's Award for Distinguished Federal Civilian Service, the highest honor for a federal worker (Schudel, 2009). Under this act:

- Copyright is wholly under federal jurisdiction, rather than a dual system involving both state and federal governments.
- All works with a tangible medium of expression are protected from the moment of creation.
- Length of protection, formerly 28 years and renewable, extends to the life of the author plus 50 years.
- Copyright protection, originally granted only to books, maps, and charts, has been extended over the years to include musical compositions, graphic works, photographs and motion pictures, digital technology, and multimedia productions (*Patry*, 1994, as cited in *Black's Law Dictionary*, 1999).

The new legislation moved toward codifying the concept of "fair use," which includes flexibility for teachers to use copyrighted materials in the classroom under specified conditions.

## Ward v. Knox County Board of Education—2013

Schools all around the country engage in a fundraising activity each year by selling "coupon books." This type of fundraising is generally supported by parents, school administrators, and local merchants. Across the country, students raise millions of dollars each year by the selling of the coupon books. The books sell for $10 to $30 and contain coupons from local businesses, which give a two-for-one dinner or a 10 to 20 percent reduction on merchandise.

The Knox County Schools is the third largest district in Tennessee with a student enrollment of approximately 88,000. The district serves the city of Knoxville and surrounding communities. The district engages in a variety of fundraising activities each year and the selling of coupon books is one of the sources of funds to supplement the district budget. The district has used the coupon books since 1989 and raised more than $30 million for the schools.

The school purchases the coupon books from one of more than a dozen organizations. The company that produces the coupon books solicits ads from the local community, and students sell the books to par-

ents and citizens to support the schools. Also, many community members buy the books for the discounts. Funds from coupon book sales pay for various needs at the schools, which are identified by teachers, parents, and administrators.

The Feredonna Company won the contract to print the coupon books in 1994. The relationship between Feredonna and Knox County Schools lasted until 2009, when the district switched to another company.

In 2011, Feredonna filed a suit against Knox County Schools, alleging that the new coupon books infringed on the copyright of Feredonna's coupon books. The district court denied Feredonna's requests for a temporary restraining order. Upon appeal, the Sixth District Appellate Court upheld the decision of the lower court. This ruling brought the case to closure in favor of the Knox County Schools.

## An Author's Exclusive Rights

The 1976 law outlined the rights of authors. The owner of a copyright has the exclusive right to do and to authorize any of the following:

- reproduction of the work in copies or phonorecords
- preparation of derivative works based upon the copyrighted works
- distribution to the public of copies or phonorecords, whether by sale or other transfer of ownership, or by rental, lease, or loan
- public performance or presentation of literary, musical, dramatic, choreographic, or audiovisual works, or of pantomimes or motion pictures
- public display of literary, musical, dramatic, choreographic, graphic, pictorial, or audiovisual works, or of pantomimes, sculptures, or individual images from a motion picture or other audiovisual work (Title 17, U.S.C. Section 106).

## The Doctrine of Fair Use

The right of authors to control their work is offset by the need of society to have ready access to those same works. Guidelines to balance these conflicting interests fall within the doctrine of fair use. Of particular interest to educators are privileges allowed for scholarly work and for teaching. Helpful publications for this purpose are Copyright Circular 21, *Reproduction of Copyrighted Works by Educators and Librarians* (1995) and a publication of Phi Delta

Kappa International, *An Educator's Guide to Finding Resources in the Public Domain* (Potter, 1999).

## The Four Criteria

The most important point regarding fair use is the four criteria to be applied:

- the purpose and character of the use, including commercial use versus nonprofit, educational purposes
- the nature of the copyrighted work
- the length of the portion used in relation to the copyrighted work as a whole, and
- the effect of the use upon the potential market for or value of the copyrighted work.

In addition to the four criteria above, unofficial photocopy guidelines were prepared for educators in connection with the revision of 1976. The text of these guidelines appeared in a House of Representatives report and is available in Copyright Circular 21 (*Reproduction,* 1995).

According to these guidelines, a single copy may be made by or for a teacher for the teacher's scholarly research or use in teaching or preparation to teach a class. The limit for single copies includes:

- a single chapter from a book
- an article from a periodical or newspaper
- a short story, short essay, or short poem
- a chart, graph, diagram, drawing, cartoon or picture from a book, periodical, or newspaper.

Although the guidelines permit single copies of copyrighted material for teaching or research, they are quite restrictive as to multiple copies. Up to one copy per pupil may be made if the situation meets three tests: brevity, spontaneity, *and* cumulative effect (*Reproduction,* 1995). The guidelines for these tests are, in part, as follows:

**Brevity:** In prose, limited to a complete article, story, or essay of less than 2,500 words or an excerpt from any prose work of not more than 1,000 words or 10% of the work, whichever is less.

**Spontaneity:** Initiated at the discretion and inspiration of the individual teacher and with so short a time between the decision to use the material and the effective time of its use that it would be unreasonable to expect a timely reply to a request for permission.

**Cumulative Effect:** Copied for only one course in the school; and except for current news, limited in one class term to one short poem, article, story, essay or two excerpts from a single author; three items from the same collective work or periodical volume; for a total of nine instances of such multiple copying for one course during one class term.

## Prohibited Uses of Materials

There are several prohibitions with respect to fair use:

- Copying may not be used to create or replace anthologies.
- There may be no copying from works intended to be consumable, such as standardized answer sheets.
- Copying may not substitute for the purchase of the books.
- The same teacher may not repeat copying the same item in a subsequent term.
- Students may not be charged more than the actual cost of photocopying the material.

## Libraries

Fair use privileges also extend to libraries, which may make a single copy of a copyrighted work. The primary purpose of the copy may not involve commercial advantage. If a library allows photocopying of materials, it must do so on the premise that the copy becomes the property of the user. The library must have no knowledge that the copy would be used for any other purpose other than private study, scholarship, or research. In addition, the library must prominently display in the copy area a warning against inappropriate duplication of copyrighted material.

## Performance or Display of a Work

Performance or display of a work by instructors of pupils is not an infringement, even if pupils act out the work. However, the performance must be part of systematic instructional activities, as well as directly related and of material assistance to the teaching process. The performance may not serve as recreation or entertainment for any part of the audience. It cannot be broadcast by radio or television unless primarily for reception in the classroom by students whose disabilities prohibit their attendance at the performance or for reception by a governmental employee as part of an official duty.

## Off-Air Taping of Television Programs

Many teachers tape radio broadcasts or television programs for later showing to students. This taping may constitute copyright infringement if off-the-air-taping guidelines are not followed. In 1979 representatives of education and the producers worked with a House of Representatives committee to develop "Guidelines for Off-Air Recording of Broadcast Programming for Educational Purposes." Essential excerpts from this report are included in Circular 21 from the U.S. Copyright Office (*Reproduction*, 1995). Libraries may not keep videotapes for distribution to teachers, and educational institutions are expected to establish appropriate control procedures to ensure implementation of the off-the-air guidelines.

The U.S. Supreme Court addressed this issue in 1984 in the case *Sony Corporation v. Universal City Studios*. The court upheld "time-shifting," that is taping a program to view at a more convenient time. The taped material may be used only for relevant classroom activities and only once within the first 10 days of taping. Additional use is limited to instructional review or student testing. After 45 days the tape must be erased.

## Educational Use of Music

For academic purposes other than performance, up to one copy per pupil may be made of short excerpts from a musical work, but not enough to make up a performable section. Emergency copying for a performance is also allowed, on condition that the photocopies are subsequently replaced with purchased originals. Details are included in Copyright Circular 21 (*Reproduction*, 1995).

## Copying of Computer Software

Illegal copying of computer software by school personnel concerns programmers and publishers. Limited school budgets combined with the high cost of software create a temptation for teachers to share programs—a practice that constitutes copyright abuse. The copyright law was amended in 1980 to reflect the increasing use of educational software. It is clear from the amended law that a teacher may make only one duplicate or backup copy of the master computer program.

A fundamental principle of copyright law is that the copyright protects forms of expression, and not the ideas that are expressed (Keplinger, 1981). In keeping with this principle, a copyright does not protect the algorithm, or underlying process, upon which a computer program is based. Such protection should be obtained under the laws governing patents, in which the determining standard is novelty.

# Case Law Regarding Fair Use

Recognition of the value of creative works and concern for copyright protection has resulted in several court cases. One of the most publicized was brought against Kinko's Inc., a company that specializes in copying services.

## Basic Books v. Kinko's Graphic Corp.—1991

The *Kinko's* case (*Basic Books Inc. v. Kinko's Graphics Corp.*, 1991) resulted from that company's practice of preparing instructor course materials designed for sale to students. These packets were compiled from texts and articles. The lawsuit involved eight publishing companies that sued Kinko's copy centers, alleging infringement of the Copyright Act. The plaintiffs charged that Kinko's had copied excerpts of many copyrighted books, then turned the excerpts into packets to be sold to students at a profit (Kasunic, 1992). Kinko's countered that although the packets were a profit-making venture, the material was educational in content and served an educational purpose. Therefore, Kinko's argued, the practice fell within fair use.

The court ruled that copyright permission must be obtained if packets of materials are to be sold to students on a profit basis. After weighing the fair-use factors, the courts found for the publishing companies. Their logic was that even though the photocopied material had an educational purpose, Kinko's was a commercial enterprise making a profit on the materials. The courts applied the four criteria of fair use and found that economic benefits were accruing to Kinko's Copy, Inc.

This case has caused a great deal of confusion, since many educators and educational institutions overreacted, creating rules that went beyond the limitations suggested by the court. Many campus bookstores became reluctant to copy materials assembled by college instructors and designed for sale to students. It should be remembered that the intent of the copyright law is to provide a balance between educational and cultural progress on the one hand, and an author's incentive to create works that will yield exclusive benefit, on the other.

Although copyright clearance *is* essential in assembling student packets, a number of companies now offer a service that includes obtaining copyright clearance for such materials. In addition, many schools and libraries work with the Copyright Clearance Center for this purpose. An individual faculty may also contact the copyright holder by mail or e-mail to request permission to reproduce materials for educational purposes. The request must specify the material to be copied, the number of copies to be made, and the purpose. The copyright holder may require a fee for reproduction in books or other publications.

## Campbell v. Acuff-Rose Music—1994

A case involving musical material was *Campbell v. Acuff-Rose Music* (1994). In this case, Acuff-Rose Music Company owned the copyright to Roy Orbison's 1964 hit song, "Oh, Pretty Woman." The rap group 2 Live Crew recorded a satirical version, using the same drumbeat and bass line, repeated eight times throughout the song. They substituted words such as "two-timin' woman," "bald-headed woman," and "big, hairy woman," for the original lyrics.

The Supreme Court held that a commercial parody may qualify as fair use. It was decided that a parody's "transformative" character is more important than its commercial purpose. The test question asks whether the new effort alters the original with a new "message, meaning and expression." In the decision of the court, the parody assumed this transformative spirit.

## Wihtol v. Crow—1962

One interesting case that creates a context for fair use law is the case of *Wihtol v. Crow* (1962). In this case the defendant, a music professor, created a new arrangement of a copyrighted hymn. Since the professor directed the choir at school and church, he made 48 copies of the hymn for his choir. He then attempted to sell the new arrangement to the plaintiff's publisher. The court held that the defendant violated the concept of fair use. The copyright owner earned about $25,000 annually in royalties and licenses, and the professor's action had potential to affect the plaintiff's income.

## Marcus v. Rowley—1983

Another case involved a professor and the author of a copyrighted cake-decorating textbook (*Marcus v. Rowley*, 1983). The defendant had attended the professor's class and created another cake-decorating book, which she distributed to a class she taught. She used 11 of the plaintiff's 29 pages, but failed to attribute any of these pages to the plaintiff. The court of appeals found that the use of the copyrighted work did not meet the tests of fair use. What made an impression on this court were the facts that, first, the defendant did not credit the copyright holder at all in the new text and, second, that the copied pages were such a substantial part of the new work.

It is obvious from the changes in law during the past several years that the pendulum has swung toward giving authors more power to control their works. The United States is very much in the "information age," rather than the "industrial age." Therefore, many questions involving copyright laws are still unanswered.

## Summary

"Intellectual property" is important in a technological society such as the United States. It is important to remember that it is the "use" of the property that is significant.

Educators are interested primarily in "fair use." If they make limited numbers of copies and do so spontaneously and with scholarly or educational intent, then there should be no issue. If the original work is altered and authorship is claimed by another, then the courts have intervened to determine who should be deemed owner of the work. As the Internet assumes more significance, questions of copyright protection and infringement will certainly increase in importance and complexity.

## Key Terms

1. copyright
2. Copyright Law of 1976
3. copyright notice
4. fair use

5. patent law
6. public domain
7. trademark
8. trademark law

## Discussion/Essay Questions

1. If a teacher wants to make 30 copies for her class of a current newspaper article, should she take any precautions with regard to the copyright law?

2. Can you make a copy of a computer program for a friend? Why or why not?

3. What are the four criteria that one should apply to determine whether use of copyrighted material falls under "fair use"?

4. With respect to videotaping a television program, what is the meaning of "time-shifting"?

5. Make a list of prohibited copying practices.

# CHAPTER 13

# Tort Liability in Schools and Districts

*There are too many attorneys with too much time on their hands. There are always people looking to stick it to schools.*

—Mike Turnipseed, Executive Director
Kern County Taxpayers Association

## Introduction

Xavier Castro, a 14-year-old student at Colton High School in California, was shot to death on his way home from school on May 22, 1996. The shooting occurred at about 2:20 p.m. as Xavier and two friends were headed to Kentucky Fried Chicken. A gunman began shooting at them. A bullet caught Xavier in the leg and, as he lay wounded, the attacker moved closer and shot Xavier in the head. Xavier's mother filed a $2 million wrongful death claim against the Colton School District, charging that the district failed to exercise the proper standard of care for supervising students. Does Xavier's mother have a case?

Let's examine some additional information. The alleged attacker, Ascención Gomez, had been expelled from the Colton district for an act of violence on campus. Although Ascención had been expelled, and district policy forbids students to be on campus when expelled, Ascención had sat in a Spanish teacher's class just prior to the shooting. The teacher, Edda Osaba, said she was with Gomez immediately before and after the time of the shooting. Osaba said she offered to give Gomez books to read during the summer and offered him a ride home in her car after school, although it is against school policy to drive students in personal vehicles. Does Xavier's mother now have a stronger case?

In 2006, a federal jury awarded the parents of a ten-year-old girl $700,000. The parents alleged that an elementary school teacher "rubbed a burrito in the girl's face, kicked her, and sat on her." The child at the time of the incident was age seven and suffered from Asperger Syndrome (Whitted Cleary & Takiff, 2006).

Is the reward of $700,000 settlement to parents of the child or the shooting of Xavier just an isolated incident of violence on school campuses? The answer is a resounding "No." Are lawsuits often filed against school districts? The answer this time is an equally strong "Yes."

John Wilson (2006) the director for Schools Excess Liability Fund (SELF), which provides excess liability to more than 1,000 California public school districts reports that California school districts are paying tort and other liability claims of $80 million per year. To put this sum in perspective, California could employ 1600 teachers or purchase 25,000 textbooks with the $80 million.

Wilson also reports that California leads all other states in litigation against school districts. Wrongful termination, discrimination, and sexual harassment appear to be the leading reasons for the litigation. He reports that suits over faulty equipment, physical education, and athletic participation have declined in the last several years.

These were claims, but actual costs to school districts in California for liability insurance, attorneys, and payments to successful plaintiffs were running over $80 million per year in 1998 (Wilson, 1999). These high costs have continued. Increase in lawsuits was one of three factors blamed for anticipated increases of 20% to 200% in liability insurance premiums for school districts in 2002 (Blair, 2002).

As the number and size of claims against school districts demonstrate, to provide a safe environment for children must be a district's number one priority. Teachers, administrators, school board members, and all school district employees have a duty to provide a safe environment for students at school or when involved in school-related activities. In 1982 the California Constitution was amended to require that "all students and staff of public primary, elementary, junior high, and senior high schools have the inalienable right to attend campuses that are safe, secure, and peaceful" (Article I, Section 28 c). This amendment builds on compulsory attendance, the legal requirement that children attend school.

Administrators and teachers have good reason to be concerned about liability while students are under their care. Although a school district is not expected to guarantee that no child will ever be hurt, school employees are expected to exercise the same standard of care that a reasonably prudent parent would have exercised under the same or similar circumstances. Thus, an employee may be personally liable for monetary damages if his or her actions and conduct fail to satisfy the standard of appropriate care.

In one case, a gay student who was beaten and tormented in school was awarded $900,000 by a Wisconsin jury. The principal and two assistant principals were held personally liable for not having provided an appropriate, safe school environment for the student. This case led to the first federal trial of a school district for not protecting a gay student from harassment (School Settles, 1996).

Under state tort law, each individual is granted certain rights that other persons must respect. If an individual fails to respect these rights and, in consequence, damages another person, a tort has been committed, and the offending party may be held liable. This chapter provides a definition of torts and a discussion of the various types of torts. Included are examples of tort lawsuits against districts and employees, with suggested precautions to avoid tort liability. The chapter also outlines the damages most commonly sought by plaintiffs in a civil lawsuit for tort.

## Torts Defined

A tort is not a crime, but comes from a separate and distinct body of law known as "civil law." Civil lawsuits pertain to the private rights of citizens, whereas criminal trials are initiated by the state to identify and punish those who have committed public offenses. Criminal proceedings are also intended to protect the public from actions of a wrongdoer. In a criminal case the state prosecutes, not to compensate the injured person, but rather to protect the public from further wrongful acts. Since criminal law does not compensate an injured individual, social justice demanded another avenue through which an injured party might obtain redress. Thus, tort actions became a legal tool.

Tort cases primarily involve state law and are grounded in the fundamental premise that all individuals are liable for the consequences of conduct that results in injury to others. "Tort" is defined as a civil wrong, other than breach of contract, for which a court may provide relief in the form of monetary damages. According to *Webster's Dictionary*, the word "tort" is derived from the Latin word "tortus," meaning "twisted." *Black's Law Dictionary* (2008) defines "tort" as "a civil wrong for which a remedy may be obtained, usually in the form of damages; a breach of duty that the law imposes on everyone in the same relation to one another as those involved in a given transaction." Tort law applies to school districts, school officers, and school employees.

## Types of Torts

Tort actions are grouped into five major categories: intentional, strict liability, educational malpractice, constitutional, and negligence. Each type of action is discussed in turn.

### Intentional Torts: Assault and Battery

An intentional tort occurs when one individual deliberately interferes with another, resulting in harm. Intent to harm is not necessary to establish tort liability. An intentional tort usually involves allegations of assault and battery or false imprisonment. Cases of intentional injury by school personnel in the school setting are quite rare.

Assault and battery are the most common intentional tort actions filed against school personnel. An assault is a nonphysical act that puts another person in fear of immediate bodily harm. Essentially, an assault is an invasion of a person's peace of mind or space, not a physical attack upon an individual's body. An assault may be committed without actually touching, striking, or doing bodily harm to an individual (*Black's*, 2004). However, the individual who is assaulted has reasonable grounds to fear immediate harm and knows that the offender has the ability to carry out the harm that is threatened. Assault may involve words, actions, or both. Assault may be prosecuted under criminal statutes, as well as under civil tort law.

A battery is intentional physical contact that causes bodily injury. Battery begins where assault leaves off. Like assault, battery may be prosecuted under criminal statutes, as well as civil tort law. To threaten to injure another person is an assault; actually hitting another person is battery, which always includes an assault. As a result, the two terms are commonly combined in the phrase "assault and battery" (*Black's*, 2004).

In cases in which a teacher disciplines a student, the most common basis for assault and battery in schools, courts have typically assumed that the teacher was reasonable and within the scope of his or her duty, unless proven otherwise (Alexander & Alexander, 2001).

## Intentional Torts: Defamation

Defamation is an intentional action in the form of written or spoken communication that harms a person's reputation or exposes the individual to contempt, hatred, scorn, or ridicule. In addition, it may cause a person to be shunned or avoided, or it may result in harm to a person's employment or business. To constitute defamation, the communication must be false and communicated to a third person. Redress for injury to reputation is a cherished legal right and, contrary to common belief, children and students are not barred from asserting this right.

Teachers, by the very nature of the profession, come into possession of critical, often very personal, information about students and parents. For example, each student has a cumulative folder that contains information about a student's achievement in class, test scores, and disciplinary record. Also included in the "cum" folder may be personal information about the student and family that is gleaned from parent conferences. Some of this information could be communicated to others in such a way as to justify a tort action alleging defamation. The major defense in defamation charges is authorization of school personnel to use information accompanied by special protection against liability. A defense against defamation depends upon showing that the information is true and that malice was not present (Menacker, 1987).

## Strict Liability

Strict liability involves intentional behavior that causes harm. There is no need to prove fault. Strict liability results when an injury results from the creation of an unusual hazard. An example is an injury resulting from an unfenced construction site or storage of flammable materials in an unlocked area. In this tort action, the plaintiff need not establish that the injury was knowingly or negligently caused. Tort actions based on an allegation of strict liability are rarely brought against a school district.

## Educational Malpractice

Until recent times, almost all cases filed against school districts for inappropriate instruction and appealed to a higher court involved physical harm to the student, rather than harm to the intellect. To prevail in an action for physical harm, a plaintiff must show that a teacher failed to exercise his or her duty to provide adequate and appropriate instruction prior to commencing an activity that may pose a risk of harm.

In the last couple of decades, however, students have brought suits against teachers based on alleged malpractice that deprived the student of learning or educational achievement. The concept of educational malpractice in this sense, like the better-known charges of malpractice in the medical and legal professions, is based on negligence in the application of professional skills and knowledge. Such a claim for educational malpractice is an attempt to use tort law to seek compensation when a student who has been through an educational program has failed to attain a certain level of achievement; for example, a student may have been awarded a high school diploma, but cannot read.

The same criteria apply for a plaintiff to prevail in an educational malpractice suit as apply to other tort suits:

- The school district and/or teacher owe the student an obligation that is recognized under the law.
- The standard of care required to fulfill this obligation was breached.
- The school district's or teacher's breach of this duty was the proximate cause of injury to the student.
- The student suffered an actual injury or harm.

One of the first educational malpractice claims was *Peter W. v. San Francisco Unified School District* (1976). Peter was passed from grade to grade and graduated from high school even though his reading ability was at the fifth-grade level and his mathematics ability was also low. At the time, California law required that high school students pass a proficiency test certifying that they could function at or above the eighth grade level.

Peter, an 18-year-old graduate of the district, claimed he was not provided with the basic academic skills he should have acquired during 12 years of school attendance. He alleged that teachers and administrators had failed to diagnose his reading disabilities, placed him in classes that were beyond his capabilities, and allowed him to graduate without ability to read at the eighth-grade level, as required by state law. Peter sought damages sufficient to compensate him for permanent disability and inability to gain meaningful employment, both as a result of the district's failure to exercise its duty of care. In that situation, an appellate court dismissed the student's negligence claims based on grounds of budget restrictions and public policy principles that included:

- the difficulty of establishing a standard of care by which to measure educators' conduct
- lack of a reasonable degree of certainty the student suffered harm as defined by the meaning of negligence law
- lack of an identifiable connection between the educator's conduct and the alleged injury to establish a causal link between the two.

The court determined that three of the four negligence elements were not present in this student's educational malpractice claim. Finally, the court refused to recognize educational malpractice claims because they would expose educators to tort claims by students and parents in countless numbers.

A decade ago, one could write that plaintiffs bringing educational malpractice suits had met with little success (Hartmeister, 1995). The climate may be changing, however. For example, the Iowa Supreme Court, in 2001, ruled that a guidance counselor could be liable for giving a student inaccurate information (Kauffman, 2001).

In a California case, decided the following year, the Ninth U.S. Circuit Court may have opened the door to educational malpractice suits with specific reference to Proposition 227. This measure gave a child's parent or legal guardian the right to sue for enforcement of the requirement that "nearly all" instruction be given in English. The California Teachers' Association sued Governor Davis in hopes of having the clause authorizing such a lawsuit declared unconstitutional (*California Teachers Association v. Davis*, 2002). CTA lost. In a law review, DeMitchell and DeMitchell (2003) concluded that the combination of this decision and the move toward accountability in education "may reverse the history of court aversion to the tort."

## Constitutional Torts

A constitutional tort occurs when a person has been deprived of his or her civil rights under either the U.S. Constitution or other federal law. After the Civil War, Congress sought to provide legal redress to African-Americans who had been mistreated by the government. This concern resulted in passage of the Civil Rights Act of 1871 to protect an individual's constitutional and civil rights. This act provided an avenue for suing school boards, individual board members, school administrators, and teachers for monetary damages following denial or deprivation of protected rights such as an individual's rights to due process, equal protection under the law, or freedom of speech.

## Negligence Torts

The vast majority of tort cases against educational agencies and their employees have focused on allegations of negligence. Negligence is defined as "failure to exercise the standard of care that a reasonably prudent person would have exercised in a similar situation" (*Black's*, 2004). Negligence differs from an intentional tort in that negligent acts are neither expected nor intended. Many student injury lawsuits involve allegations of administrator or teacher negligence.

In California, Section 1714 of the Civil Code provides,

> Everyone is responsible, not only for the result of his lawful acts, but also for an injury occasioned to another by his want of ordinary care or skill in the management of his property or person, except so far as the latter has, willfully or by the want of ordinary care, brought the injury upon himself.

This statute is the key to California's negligence law. In order to find negligence on the part of a defendant, California courts have held that the following four factors must be present:

- The defendant must have a duty of care to the plaintiff.
- There must have been negligence constituting a breach of that duty.
- There must be an injury to the plaintiff.
- The injury must have occurred as a proximate, or legal, result of the defendant's negligence (*Peter W. v. San Francisco Unified School District*, 1976).

Duty, actual injury, and proximate cause are usually matters of fact and not open to subjective judgement. Should there be any question about these issues in negligence cases, the jury is called to decide upon the facts, being guided by the judge on applicable law. The major task for a plaintiff is to prove that the district or employee breached its duty by failure to exercise a reasonable standard of care.

**Duty to the Plaintiff:** An injured student usually has little difficulty in proving that the district owes a duty of care to him or her.

**Breach of Duty:** The second, and most important, issue is whether the teacher, administrator, or district failed to meet its duty of care. This issue has two facets: "standard of care" and "proper supervision."

"Standard of care" requires a plaintiff to show that the defendant failed to act as a "reasonably prudent person" would have acted, given the circumstances. In this sense, a "reasonable person" is considered to be a fictional being of normal intelligence, normal perception, and possessing the physical attributes of the defendant (Hartmeister, 1995). Courts have required, in order to establish a causal relationship between breach of duty and an injury, that an accident or injury must have been foreseeable. School employees will not be held liable when they could not have foreseen, in the reasonable exercise of their legal duty to a student, the injurious consequences of an activity or action.

"Proper supervision" is often at issue when a court weighs an allegation of breach of duty. There is no absolute rule for defining proper supervision because the facts in each case are different. In general, school administrators and teachers are under a duty to exercise only the degree of reasonable care and supervision that a parent of ordinary prudence would have exercised under similar circumstances. Two principles govern supervision:

- Do not create danger through negligent conduct.
- Avoid foreseeable hazards created by others (Hartmeister, 1995).

An example of a court's interpretation of proper supervision is found in the 1970 case of *Dailey v. Los Angeles Unified School District* (1970). In this case, Michael Dailey, a 16-year-old student, was "slap boxing" with another student in the boys' gymnasium. The event occurred during recess and lasted for five to ten minutes. About 30 students were watching the two boys fight. Suddenly, after being slapped, Michael fell backward and fractured his skull on the pavement. A short time later, he died. Michael's parents filed a wrongful death action for damages, alleging that the district had failed to supervise the students and that this failure caused their son's death.

During the trial, it was determined that the physical education department was responsible for supervising the gymnasium. The chair of that department stated that he did not know he was to assign a teacher to supervise on any particular day, and there was no formal schedule of supervision times. At the time of the incident, the chair of the department was in the office playing bridge!

The court found that the district had failed to meet the standard of care, and that this failure resulted in Michael's death. *Dailey* illustrates an increasing willingness on the part of the courts to impose upon districts a duty of care to protect students from harm.

**Proximate Cause:** For liability to be assessed, negligent conduct of school personnel must be the proximate or legal cause of a student's injury. Proximate cause means there is a substantial causal connection between the alleged misconduct and the resulting injury. Did the employee's action or failure to act cause an injury or allow it to happen? The relationship between the employee's behavior and the injury must have been close in time and foreseeable. Foreseeability implies that the employee both could and should have anticipated the potentially dangerous consequences of his or her action or inaction.

School administrators and teachers are expected to establish classroom and school standards that will result in a safe environment in which injuries to students are kept to a minimum. They are also expected to have reasonable foresight in anticipating that an injury may occur. For example, on a very warm day, in a classroom that did not have air conditioning, a teacher decided to conduct class on the school lawn. While there, a boy was playing with a knife by flipping it into the ground. The knife hit another student, injuring his eye. The court held that the teacher should have been able to predict that this dangerous practice would result in injury. His failure to stop it amounted to a breach of the duty of care owed to his students (*Lilienthal v. San Leandro Unified School District*, 1956). Today, no sharp instrument or weapon is allowed on school grounds.

A second case illustrates the necessity for school principals and teachers to foresee the possibility of an accident. At a school site in Tulare, California, a piano was kept in the high school gymnasium and moved from room to room on a dolly. The piano was not attached to the dolly; it just rested on it. One day, the piano toppled over and pinned a girl's ankle to the floor. The court said that school officials should have noticed the possibility of danger and taken steps to prevent injury to students. Consequently, the district was held liable (*Dawson v. Tulare Union District*, 1929).

## Situations Requiring Supervision of Students

As a rule of thumb, school districts are responsible for student supervision when a student is traveling to and from school, attending school, or at any school-sponsored activity. The most common supervisory situations follow.

## Classrooms and Corridors

Obviously, teachers and administrators have a paramount duty to supervise students in classrooms and school corridors. A serious question arises when a teacher leaves the classroom and students unattended. If a student is injured during the teacher's absence, the teacher and the district are at risk for a tort action. However, temporary teacher absence or distraction from the classroom or from the location of an accident does not automatically amount to negligence in supervision (Valente, 1998). When a student is injured during absence of a teacher from the classroom, the court must decide whether the absence was reasonable or negligent. Nevertheless, teachers risk being charged with negligence if they leave a class unsupervised, and a child is injured.

## Athletics, Physical Education, and Playgrounds

Approximately seven million students participate in some type of interscholastic sport during a school year (Stanitski, 1989). A 1989 article in *Education Week* (Dimensions, 1989) estimated that 36% of secondary school football players incurred at least one injury during the 1988 season. Of these, 60% occurred during practice.

The majority of playground injuries occur when children fall from playground equipment (Shoop & Dunklee, 1992). Although asphalt is commonly seen in playground areas, a fall from swings or other equipment to asphalt often results in injury. Districts would be prudent to place other materials—such as wood chips, bark, or shredded tires—under playground equipment. These materials pose another risk, as students are often tempted to throw the wood chips or bark, leading to injury. However, a fall to these resilient surfaces is less likely to result in serious injury than a fall to asphalt or cement.

California Government Code Section 831.7 provides immunity to a public entity for injuries sustained by any person while participating in a hazardous recreation activity, especially when the injury is an inherent risk of the sport. In spite of this protection for school districts and employees, coaches are favorite targets of lawsuits relating to injuries sustained by students and other members of the general public (Port, 1998). The bulk of lawsuits focus on failure or lack of supervision, but plaintiffs have also alleged inadequate or improper medical care, improper training, and improper instruction.

Such a lawsuit was filed by Denning Aaris against the Las Virgenes Unified School District (*Aaris v. Las Virgenes*, 1998). Denning, a cheerleader, was injured when practicing a gymnastic routine called a "cradle." Her case was based on the fact that the coach had insisted the girls needed to continue their practice, even though she had expressed reluctance to do so. The appeals court, after quoting from the plaintiff's documentation as to the "acrobatic gymnastic nature of modern cheerleading," nevertheless noted that cheerleading was a voluntary activity. The court verified that the plaintiff and the other girl involved in the activity had been well trained in safety and in the technique of the cradle and had been appropriately supervised. Therefore, the court found for the district.

## Equipment and Materials

An area of the educational program that frequently gives rise to allegations of improper instruction is school activities that require the use of equipment. It is not expected that every possible danger be predicted or every minor defect corrected immediately; however, all school personnel share a common responsibility to keep school equipment and facilities reasonably safe.

California Government Code Section 835 provides that a public entity is liable for injury caused by a dangerous condition of its property if the plaintiff establishes that a piece of equipment or facility was in a dangerous condition at the time of the injury. This code makes it clear that school employees are responsible to inspect the school environment regularly and to correct any known hazards.

A case in point occurred in Conejo Valley in southern California when a child was struck by a car while standing in an area next to the school parking lot that had been designated by the school. The plaintiff established that the lot was small, congested, and known by the district to be a hazard. The court upheld a jury finding, based on the dangerous condition of the property, that the district was liable. The court pointed out that a special relationship exists between a school district and its students such that, although the district cannot ensure complete safety of students, it has a heightened duty to make the school safe (*Constantinescu v. Conejo Valley Unified School District*, 1993).

## Lunch Time

The lunch period is a time when school officials are required to be particularly alert for possible injury to a student. Lunch supervision is a challenging time for the school administrator. Education Code Section 44813 provides a duty-free lunch period for teachers, who are, consequently, unavailable for supervision. However, this requirement does not free the district from responsibility for adequate supervision of students during the lunch period.

For example, a seven-year-old student was served a hot lunch at school. He was reprimanded for loud and boisterous behavior and was sitting down when he inadvertently knocked his luncheon plate over and spilled hot mashed potatoes onto his lap and down his leg. He suffered second degree burns on a large portion of his leg. The court stated that the district breached its duty of care to protect and supervise the children when it served excessively hot food (*Espinosa v. Fresno Unified School District*, 1992).

## Errands

It is common practice for teachers, counselors, and principals to send students on errands. If a student is then injured, the legal question becomes whether the school employee acted reasonably in sending the student on the errand. What constitutes reasonable action depends on the circumstances of each case. As with other examples of negligence, the teacher or principal may be held liable if, in sending a student on an errand, the child is exposed to a danger that should have been apparent to a reasonable and prudent person.

## Field Trips and Other Off-Campus Activities

Field trips are school-related activities that take place away from school grounds. Districts owe the same duty of care and supervision to students who participate in field trips, whether mandatory or voluntary, as they do to students during the normal school day on campus. As a general rule, students are subject to a greater risk of injury while on a field trip than during a normal school day. The factors that contribute to greater risk may include being transported in a bus or private vehicle, walking along a busy street, and not following usual classroom and school procedures.

Many school districts require a teacher to complete a field trip application form and obtain parent permission for students to participate in a field trip. However, as discussed at the end of this chapter, even a parent's written permission may not absolve the district from liability if a student is injured while on the trip. The best defense on a field trip is adequate supervision.

## Transportation

When a district provides student transportation, it follows that the district is obligated to provide this transportation in a safe and supervised manner. When a child is injured while being transported, the plaintiffs case usually relies on one or more of three grounds: (a) unsafe equipment, (b) negligent bus operation, or (c) negligent supervision of students at bus stops. Courts have stressed the need for special supervision at bus stops where the potential for accident is greatest.

A major risk for tort action against a school district or employee arises when arrangements are made to transport students in a private vehicle. Should an accident occur, the safety of the vehicle, the proficiency of the driver, and whether the employee was acting as an agent of the district will need to be decided.

## Before and After School

Education Code Section 44808 is very specific in stating that "no school district . . . shall be responsible or in any way liable for the conduct or safety of any pupil . . . at any time when such pupil is not on school property." There are exceptions, however. As discussed earlier, if a school district provides student transportation or sponsors school activities off campus, the district is responsible for immediate and direct supervision of students and liable for their safety.

Even with this very specific limitation on a district's responsibility for student safety, the duty to provide supervision may extend to times and locations beyond the school day and the campus. For example, although parents and students are regularly notified of the periods in which school is open and supervision is available, a principal's knowledge that students are utilizing school grounds prior to or after the school day may raise an issue as to whether a duty of supervision is created.

Courts impose reasonable limits on the scope of supervisory responsibility. A California Court of Appeals ruled that school officials did not have a duty to scout the neighborhood for gang members before releasing students at the end of the school day, even though school personnel were aware of the presence of gang members near the school during the school day (*Brownell v. Los Angeles Unified School District*, 1992).

In the *Brownell* case, a student was shot by a gang member immediately after school was dismissed. The shooting took place on a public street adjacent to school property. The student sued the school district, alleging negligent supervision because school personnel had dismissed the students after school without first ascertaining whether the street in front of the school was free of any gang members. The student claimed that the Education Code requires teachers to supervise students going to and from school. The court ruled that, under the circumstances, school personnel had exercised due care in their supervision responsibilities to protect students from gang violence by taking such general measures as prohibiting the wearing of gang colors.

Liability is limited in specified undertakings when the pupil is or should be under the immediate and direct supervision of a district employee. However, the courts have ruled in favor of students when they have determined that the district failed to exercise reasonable care under the circumstances of the case. Such a case went to trial after a ten-year-old boy left school during the middle of the day without parent or school permission. While off campus, he was struck by a motorcycle and badly injured. The California Supreme Court held the district liable because of its negligent supervision of the student. The court stated that if the student had been properly supervised, he would not have been allowed to leave school (*Hoyem v. Manhattan Beach City School District*, 1978).

# Defenses Against Negligence

In an ideal world there would be no need for a district to protect itself against charges of negligence. However, even if every employee were to exercise the utmost caution in supervising students and every piece of district equipment were in perfect order, accidents would still happen, errors would still be made, and students would sometimes misbehave. In many instances such accidents, mistakes, and misbehavior give rise to lawsuits. On what basis, then, may a district, teacher, administrator, or staff member mount a defense?

## Governmental Immunity

While the defense of governmental immunity is disappearing in most states, it once was a common practice. This type of defense is grounded in the traditional concept that "the king can do no wrong." Historically, the government could not be sued without its permission. It was immune.

The immunity rule has eroded or been abrogated in a growing number of states, although a small number of states still maintain the doctrine. Some states maintain the concept of immunity for certain classes of injury, while allowing liability claims for other classes. The erosion of the immunity rule has occurred sometimes by court decision and sometimes by legislation.

## California's Personal Liability Law

Although some states still maintain the right of governmental immunity, at least to some degree, California no longer claims this line of defense. Government Code Sections 810-996.6 give citizens the right to bring a tort action against the state or other government entity. The statute contains requirements for filing a claim and timelines that must be strictly adhered to by a party desirous of suing a public agency. For example, Government Code Section 911.2 requires a claimant to file a claim for death or injury to person or property within six months of the occurrence and any other claims within a year. The Government Code also contains claim rejection and denial procedures that must be followed to the letter.

However, in spite of the restrictions placed on the claimant, California school districts may be held liable for their tortuous acts where employees or school officials have acted in a negligent manner. California public employees, including teachers, are liable for injury caused by their acts or omissions to the same extent as private persons (Government Code Section 820). They may be personally liable if, in the performance of their school duties, their negligent or wrongful conduct causes harm to pupils or others.

The California Tort Claims Act is very specific in that, for a district to be held liable, its employee must have acted within the scope of his or her employment. Under this act, school districts have been found liable for the failure of their employees to use reasonable care to prevent foreseeable injuries resulting from school activities. Districts have also been found liable for improperly supervising students and failure to correct or warn injury victims of known dangerous conditions (Port, 1998).

Teachers face the risk of lawsuits for torts such as assault and battery, slander, libel, defamation, false arrest, and malpractice. However, Government Code Section 825 generally requires a school district to provide a defense and pay any judgment or settlement resulting from an employee's action in the course and scope of employment. In addition, school districts are required to insure against the personal liability of employees for loss or damage to property or damages for death or injury to any person as a result of any negligent act of employees within the scope of their employment (E.C. 35208). Obviously, however, school employees can be held *personally* liable for injuries resulting from negligent action or inaction outside the course and scope of employment or as a result of fraud, corruption, or malice (*Johnson v. State of California*, 1968).

## Contributory Negligence

In defending against a negligence claim, a district may be able to demonstrate that the injured student's own conduct contributed to his or her injury. Just as the court will examine what a reasonable or prudent teacher or staff member would do in a given situation, the court will consider what a reasonable or prudent student or parent would have done for his or her own protection. Whether an injured child can be contributorily negligent in a given situation usually depends on the age and maturity of the child. If a child is too young to understand the danger of his or her act, the child cannot be held to have contributed to the injury.

## Comparative Negligence

A defense of comparative negligence is viable when it can be shown that an injury was partly the fault of several persons. Under the comparative negligence doctrine, all of the parties, including the plaintiff, are liable for their respective shares of the plaintiff's loss or injury, and liability is assessed in proportion to fault.

## Assumption of Risk

Under the doctrine of assumption of risk, an injured person is not allowed to recover damages if the person sustains an injury after voluntarily participating in an activity that is known to be inherently dangerous. The legal theory is based upon an individual's ability to understand and appreciate the dangers inherent in the activity. The defense must show that the student understood the danger, knew the risk involved, and accepted the danger. Athletic activities are an example of the assumption of risk doctrine. This doctrine may protect coaches and school administrators from liability on the grounds that students who voluntarily participate in school athletic programs assume some risk.

## Notice of Claim

Most states have very specific timelines within which an injured party must file a tort claim. The timeline requires a plaintiff to file a claim within three to six months of the injury. These statutes describe how the legitimacy of tort claims is to be validated, provide for notice to the district to correct conditions that could result in additional injury, and give the district an opportunity to budget sufficient funds to employ legal defense and pay compensation, if awarded. Some states also set specific dollar ceilings for the several classes of tort claims. These ceilings range from a modest amount of several thousand dollars to several hundred thousand dollars.

## Written Waivers

Parental consent for student participation in special activities, such as field trips and athletic competition, is often required. School forms for this purpose include a declaration that the parent releases the school and its personnel from all legal responsibility for any injury the child may suffer while participating in the special event. While a release form offers a district limited protection from a civil suit, some courts hold that a parent cannot legally surrender the independent claim of a minor child.

In 1990 the Superior Court of San Diego County ruled that a Parent-Teacher-Student Association in San Diego Unified School District could be liable for damages suffered by a high school student at a hypnotist's show because the permission slip signed by the student and her father did not contain the term "negligence," even though it read that the father would "waive all liability" (*Hohe v. San Diego Unified*).

A similar case in North Dakota, decided in 2003 (*Konrad v. Bismarck Park Dist.*), led that state's supreme court to separate two sentences, one of which dealt with injuries in "activities associated with the program" (of which the student's bicycle riding was not one) from another that referred to participation in the program. Given the second clause, the court found for the park district.

Zirkel (2005) reviewed this and related cases and concluded that permission forms have both advantages and disadvantages. While they facilitate communication with parents and may discourage lawsuits, they can also discourage parents from allowing their children to participate in desirable activities and create—rather than avoid—legal problems. Principals are encouraged to give careful thought to these trade-offs.

# Compensation

To receive an award of damages or compensation, a plaintiff must have suffered an injury from the negligent conduct of the defendant. Although the defendant's conduct may be considered negligent, legal action cannot be sustained unless the conduct actually results in physical or mental injury. Compensation may cover any direct financial loss, for example, medical expenses or loss of income. Compensation for pain and suffering may also be awarded.

Several different kinds of damage may be sought by injured students as plaintiffs in a lawsuit. The most common types are:

**Compensatory Damages:** Damages that compensate an injured party for actual losses. These include medical expenses, lost salary, court costs, or compensation for physical or mental injuries to a person.

**Punitive or Exemplary Damages:** Damages awarded for the purpose of punishing the defendant for negligence. The plaintiff must prove evidence of violence, oppression, malice, fraud, or wanton or reckless disregard for the plaintiff's safety. Punitive damages are intended to prevent or deter defendants from doing the same thing again.

**Nominal Damages:** Limited monetary awards, given by a court or jury when there is technically little or no actual loss, but the plaintiff nonetheless has been mistreated.

Monetary damages are the legal system's way of making a plaintiff "whole again," and to compensate a person who has suffered loss to his person, property, or rights through unlawful acts of another.

# Summary

The school district and its personnel have a legal duty to protect students, employees, and visitors from unreasonable risks of injury. A reasonable and prudent school administrator, teacher, or school employee is expected to foresee potential dangers in the school environment, anticipate the injurious consequences of actions, and take appropriate steps to reduce risks. The law requires school leaders to meet a standard of reasonable, prudent care for the safety of students. Since school officials serve as surrogate parents, a general duty to provide adequate supervision is consistently imposed by the courts. The obligation of district personnel to provide a safe environment at all times is serious and constant.

Off-campus activities, such as athletic events and field trips, should be carefully planned and evaluated from both an educational and a safety viewpoint. To establish an appropriate level of supervision, the teacher and principal should take into account the age and maturity of students.

Courts have generally held school districts and employees liable for injury to students during the course of regular school events if there has been failure to provide a reasonably safe environment. School employees also have a moral, professional, and legal obligation to warn students of known hazards, to remove known dangers, and to instruct students properly when they participate in school activities. Educators must be knowledgeable about their potential liability and should take care to have adequate insurance protection to cover any awards that might be assessed against them.

## Key Terms

1. assault
2. assumption of risk
3. battery
4. breach of duty
5. comparative negligence
6. compensatory damages
7. constitutional tort
8. contributory negligence
9. educational malpractice
10. exemplary damages
11. governmental immunity
12. intentional tort
13. negligence
14. notice of claim
15. proximate cause
16. punitive damages
17. standard of care
18. strict liability
19. tort
20. written waiver

## Discussion/Essay Questions

1. Discuss the major differences between a criminal suit and a tort suit.

2. Tort actions can be divided into five major categories. Which is the most likely to occur in the school setting? Why is that the case?

3. School employees are responsible for observing the standard of care for students under their supervision. What does this concept mean? Give examples.

4. As a general principle, school districts are not legally responsible for accidents that occur before students arrive at school in the morning or after they have been released in the afternoon. Describe situations to which this principle does *not* apply.

5. It appears that malpractice suits against teachers will increase. Discuss several ways you believe teachers can protect themselves from this type of lawsuit.

6. Governmental immunity has protected governmental agencies, including school districts, from tort actions. California does not permit this defense. Do you agree with California's position? State reasons for your position.

# References

Acosta and Carpenter. (2008). *Women in intercollegiate sports*. Retrieved from www.women's sports foundation.org

Alexander, K., & Alexander, M. D. (1998). *American public school law* (4th ed.). St. Paul, MN: West.

Alexander, K., & Alexander, M. D. (2001). *American public school law* (5th ed.). Belmont, CA: West/Thomson Learning.

Alexander, K., & Salmon, R. (1995). *Public school finance*. Needham Heights, MA: Allyn & Bacon.

Almeida, A. (2015). Holding schools responsible for addressing childhood trauma. Retrieved from http://www.theatlantic.com/education/archive/2015/05/holding-schools-responsible-for-addressing-childhood-trauma/393695/

Andelson, S. J. (1995). *FRISK documentation model*. Torrance, CA: Four Star Printing & Graphics.

Association of Research Libraries. (2002). *Timeline: A history of copyright in the United States*. Washington, DC: Author. Retrieved from http://www.arl.org/info/frn/copy/timeline.html

*Back to school without books: Many CA students still lack textbooks, ACLU charges*. (2000, September 12). ACLU Press Release. Retrieved from http://www.aclu.org/news/2000/n091200b.htm

Ballard Spahr Andrews & Ingersoll, LLP. (2005). *The virtual chase: A research site for legal professionals*. Website at http://www.virtualchase.com/

Beard, M. (2009, February 19). *U.S. Supreme Court won't review ruling against Novato School District's censorship of student journalist*. Retrieved from http://community.pacificlegalfoundation.org

*Black's Law Dictionary* (7th ed.). (1999). Bryan A. Garner, Editor-in-Chief. St. Paul, MN: West Group.

Blair, J. (2002, February 6). Liability insurance's skyrocketing costs confound districts. *Education Week, 21*, pp. 1, 15. Retrieved from ProQuest Research database.

Boylan, E. M., & Weiser, J. (2002). *Survey of key education stakeholders on zero tolerance student discipline practices*. Newark, NJ: Education Law Center. Retrieved from http://www.edlawcenter.org/test/ELCPublic/Publications/ PDF/Survey_ZeroTolerance.pdf

Bragdon, H. W., & McCutchen, S. E. (1961). *History of a free people*. New York: Macmillan.

Browne, J. A. (2003). *Derailed: The schoolhouse to jailhouse track*. Washington, DC: Advancement Project. Retrieved from http://www.advancementproject.org/Derailerepcor.pdf

Brunsma D. (2005, February). *Do uniforms make our schools better?* American Federation of Teachers. Retrieved from http://www.aft.org/pubs-reports/american_teacher/feb05/speakout.htm

Burrup, P. E., Brimley, V., & Garfield, R. R. (1993). *Financing education in a climate of change* (5th ed.). Needham Heights, MA: Allyn & Bacon.

Busa, A. (1999). Two steps forward, one step back: The Supreme Court's treatment of teacher-student sexual harassment in *Gebser v. Lago Vista Independent School District. Harvard Civil Rights—Civil Liberties Law Review, 34*, 279–309.

Bush, G. W. (2004). *President's remarks at the signing of H.R. 1350*. Retrieved from http://www.whitehouse.gov/news/releases/2004/12/print/20041203-6.html

Bushaw, A.W., & McNee, J.A. (2014). 46th annual PDK/Gallup Poll of the public's attitudes toward the public schools. Retrieved from http://pdkiath.org/programs-resources/poll/

California School Boards Association. (2004). *Analysis: Individuals with Disabilities Education Improvement Act: H.R. 1350*. Sacramento, CA: Author. Retrieved from http://www.csba.org/csn/csnStoryTemplate.cfm?id= 179

California State Bar. (2009). *The state bar of California: annual report*. Retrieved from www.calbar.ca.gov

California State Bar Association. (2015). Retrieved from www.calbar.ca.gov

Carter, S. J. (1993). *Culture of disbelief*. New York: Doubleday.

Cauchon, D. (1999, April 13). Zero-tolerance policies lack flexibility. *USA Today*. Retrieved from http://www.usatoday.com/educate/ednews3.htm

Center for Women and Politics. (2015). Retrieved from http://www.cawp.rutgers.edu/fast_facts/levels_of_office/Congress-CurrentFacts.php

Chapman, B. (2000). *Brief introduction to using the World Wide Web to conduct legal research.* Available at http://www.personal.utulsa.edu/~benjamin-chapman/cle/weblaw.html

Collins, G. J. (1969). Constitutional and legal basis for state action. In E. Fuller & J. B. Pearson (Eds.), *Education in the states: Nationwide development since 1900.* Washington, DC: National Education Association.

Council for Exceptional Children. (2004). *The new IDEA: CEC's summary of significant issues.* Arlington, VA: Author. Retrieved from http://www.cec.sped.org/pp/idea_12020.pdf

Cox, Amy (2005, August 15.) *Custom-made fit for school.* CNN. Retrieved from www.cnn.com/2005/US

*CSBA's motion granted in school equity lawsuit.* (2001, April 12). [CSBA Legal Notice]. Retrieved from http://www.csba.org/Communications/top_stories/headline3-29.htm

Dallas Independent School District Board reaches settlement with chief financial officer. (1998, February 8). *Abilene Reporter-News.* Retrieved from http://www.reporternews.com/texas/disd0208.htm

Davis, D. (2006, February 6). *Drug dogs in schools.* Retrieved from http://www.veterinarypartner.com

DeMitchell, T. A., & DeMitchell, T. A. (2003, August). Statutes and standards: Has the door to educational malpractice been opened? *Education and Law Journal.* Retrieved from http://www.law2.byu.edu/jel/v2003_2/DeMitchell_DeMitchell.pdf

*Deskbook Encyclopedia of American School Law.* (1992). Rosemount, MN: Data Research.

Deutsch, L., & Leff, L. (2014). California tenure law unconstitutional. Retrieved from http://www.huffingtonpost.com/2014/06/10/vergara-california-decision_n_5479666.html

de Vise, D. (1996, July 18). Law urged permitting expulsion of students for fake bomb threats. *San Diego Union,* p. A3.

DeVoe, J. F., Peter, K., Kaufman, P., Ruddy, S. A., Miller, A. K., Planty, M., et al. (2003). *Indicators of school crime and safety: 2003.* Washington, DC: U.S. Departments of Education and Justice. Retrieved from http://nces.ed.gov/pubs2004/2004004.pdf

Dimensions: High school football injuries. (1989). *Education Week, 8,* 3.

*District attorney point of view online: B.C. v. Plumas Unified School District et al.* (n.d.). Alameda County, CA: District Attorney's Office. Retrieved from http://www.co.alameda.ca.us/da/pov/bc.shtml

Dolan, M. (1999, October 13). Disabled pupils get their day in court. *Los Angeles Times.*

EdCal. (2005, October 31). Supreme Court mulling special ed, IEP issue. 36, 15.

Equal Employment Opportunity Commission. (1999). *Enforcement guidance: Vicarious employer liability for unlawful harassment by supervisors.* Washington, DC: Author. Retrieved from http://www.eeoc.gov/policy/docs/harassment.html

Fensterwald, J. (2013). Effort to shorten process of firing teachers faltering again. Retrieved from http://edsource.org/2013/effort-to-shorten-process-of-firing-teachers-faltering-again/34734#.VX8nc03n_cs

Fight Crime: Invest in Kids. (2015). LCAPs show districts focusing on school climate in California schools, but still much work to be done. Retrieved from www.fightcrime.org/Lcap analysis

Fischer, L., Schimmel, D., & Kelly, C. (1995). *Teachers and the law* (4th ed.). White Plains, NY: Longman.

Foster, F. H., & Shook, R. L. (1993). *Patents, copyrights, & trademarks* (2nd ed.). New York: John Wiley.

French, W. L. (1998). *Human resources management.* Boston: Houghton Mifflin.

Frey, S. (2014). September 28. New law limits student discipline measure. Retrieved from http://edsource.org/2014/new-law-limits-student discipline-measure/67836

Gasaway, L. (2003). *When U.S. works pass into the public domain.* Retrieved from http://www.unc.edu/~unclng/public-d.htm

Giangrande, M. (2004). *Using citators.* Cincinnati, Ohio: University of Cincinnati, Law Library. Retrieved from http://www.law.uc.edu/library/

GLSEN. (2005, September 1). *Fifteen expensive reasons why safe schools legislation is in your state's best interest.* Retrieved from www.glsen.org/egi-bin/iowa/chapter/library/record/1913.html

Grabianowski, E. (2009). *How supreme court appointments work.* Retrieved from http://people.howstuffworks.com

Guaralnik, D. B., editor. (1968, 2nd edition). Webster's New World Dictionary. New York: The World Publishing Company.

Hartmeister, F. (1995). *Surviving as a teacher: The legal dimension.* Chicago, IL: Precept Press.

Hauck, A. (2014, July 1). Cyberbullying—laws by state. Retrieved from www.instantcheckmate.com/crimewire/cyberbullying-laws-by-state.

Helfand, D., & DiMassa, C. M. (2004, August 11). State, ACLU settle suit on education. *Los Angeles Times.* Retrieved from *Los Angeles Times* archives.

*History-social science framework for California public schools, kindergarten through grade twelve:*

*2001 updated edition with content standards.* (2001). Sacramento, CA: California Department of Education. Retrieved from http://www.cde.ca.gov/re/pn/fd/documents/hist-social-sci-frame.pdf

Holland, J. (2009, June 26). *Savanna Redding strip search was illegal, Supreme Court says.* Retrieved from www.huffingtonpost.com

Hunter, M. (2006, May 22). *Litigations challenging constitutionality of k–12 funding in the 50 states.* Retrieved from www.schoolfunding.info

Ingersoll, R. M. (2001). *Teacher turnover, teacher shortages, and the organization of schools.* Seattle, WA: University of Washington, Center for the Study of Teaching and Policy. Retrieved from http://depts.washington.edu/ctpmail/PDFs/Turnover-Ing-01.2001.pdf

Initiative & Referendum Institute. (2015). I & R Factsheet. Retrieved from http://www.iandrinstitute.org

Inland Empire Insurance Authority. (1996). [Annual report]. San Bernardino, CA: Author.

Irons, P., & Guitton, S. (1993). *May it please the court.* New York: University Press.

Johns, R. L., & Morphet, E. L. (1975). *The economics and financing of education: A systems approach.* Englewood Cliffs, NJ: Prentice Hall.

Jones, J. J., & Stout, I. W. (1960). *School public relations: Issues and cases.* New York: G. P. Putnam.

Jordan, K. F., & Lyons, T. S. (1992). *Financing public education in an era of change.* Bloomington, IN: Phi Delta Kappa Educational Foundation.

Judicial Council of California. (2004). *Fact sheet: California judicial branch.* San Francisco, CA: Author. Retrieved from http://www.courtinfo.ca.gov/reference/documents/cajudbranch.pdf

Kasunic, R. (1992). Fair use and the educator's right to photocopy copyrighted material for classroom use. *Journal of College and University Law, 19,* 271–273.

Kauffman, C. (2001, April 26). High school guidance counselor can be sued, Supreme Court rules. *Des Moines Register.* Retrieved from http://www.dmregister.com/news/stories/c4788993/ 14503861.html

Keim, J. (2014, March 13). Ninth circuit leading the pack for "most reversed." Retrieved from www.nationalreview.com/bencjh-memos/373273/ninth-circuit-leading-pack

Kennedy, M. J. (1995, August 19). A fashion statement with real meaning. *Los Angeles Times.*

Keplinger, M. S. (1981). Computer software—its nature and its protection. *Emory Law Journal, 30,* 483–485.

Kesler, C. G. (1998). *Direct democracy in California: The good, the bad, and the indigestible.*

Claremont, CA: Claremont Institute. Retrieved from http://www.claremont.org/projects/goldenstate/981015kesler.html

KnowledgeWorks Foundation. (2003). *DeRolph v. The State of Ohio.* Cincinnati, OH: Author. Retrieved from http://www.kwfdn.org/derolph.html

Kunzi, E. H. (1978). *The California Education Code.* St. Paul, MN: West.

Lambda Legal. (2002). *California teacher settles sexual orientation discrimination suit with school district* [Press release]. Los Angeles, CA: Author. Retrieved from http://www.youth.org/loco/PERSONProject/Alerts/States/California/settlement.html

LaMorte, M. W. (1999). *School law: Cases and concepts* (6th ed.). Boston: Allyn & Bacon.

*Landmark peer sexual harassment case settled on eve of trial.* (1997, January 6). National Organization of Women. Retrieved from http://www.nowldef.org/html/news/pr/010697e.htm

Lanham, C. (2014). Student suspension and expulsion rates drop in California. Retrieved from http://www.santamariasun.com/news/12719/student-suspension-and expulsion-rates-drop

Lapkoff, Shelley. (2005). *The amazing history of the Pledge of Allegiance.* Retrieved from www.historyofthepledge.com/news

Leaffer, M. (1995). *Understanding copyright law.* New York: Times Mirror Books.

Lee, E. C. (1991). The revision of California's Constitution. *CPS Brief. 3*(3). Retrieved from http://www.ucop.edu/cprc/caconst.pdf

Lessig, L. (2004, March–April). How I lost the big one. *Legal Affairs.* Retrieved from http://www.legalaffairs.org/issues/March-April-2004/story_lessig_marapr04.html

Libertarian Rock. (2005). *Students win $450K settlement due to strip search.* Retrieved from www.libertarianrock.com/topics/stripsearch/nyc_strip_search_ring_2005_bronx.html

Liebert, T. (2001). *GlobalCite. Is it a third citator?* Washington, DC: Law Library Resource Xchange. Retrieved from http://www.llrx.com/features/globalsite.htm

Lopez, R. (2009, January 4). *New law protects school journalism advisors.* Los Angeles Times, B4, p.6.

Losen, D. (2015, February 23). Are we closing the school discipline gap? Retrieved from http://civilrightsproject.uclas.edu/resources/projects/center-for-civil-rights-remedies/school

Lu, A. (2014). States sued over education funding. Retrieved from http://www.usatoday.com/story/news/nation/2014/02/18/stateline-states-education-funding-court/5577453

Lunenburg, F. C. (1996). *Educational administration: Concepts and practices* (2nd ed.). Belmont, CA: Wadsworth.

Maidment, F. H. (1998). *Human Resources, 1997–98.* Guilford, CT: McGraw-Hill.

Marshall, T. (1995, July 18). A world of pressures on parents, children. *Los Angeles Times.*

McCarthy, M. M., Cambron-McCabe, N. H., & Thomas, S. B. (1998). *Public school law: Teachers' and students' rights* (4th ed.). Boston: Allyn & Bacon.

McKenna, R. (1996, September 5). *New funds for reading professional development.* Sacramento, CA: California Department of Education Advisory Letter.

Menacker, J. (1987). *School law: Theoretical and case perspectives.* Englewood Cliffs, NJ: Prentice-Hall.

Mink, P. (2002). *Mink, P. T., Biography.* Retrieved from http://bioguide.congresss.gov

Moore, O. (2004, January 30). Spanking upheld by Supreme Court. *Globe and Mail.* Retrieved from http://www.canadiancrc.com/articles/Globe_and_Mail_Spanking_Upheld_30JAN04.htm

National Center for Educational Statistics. (2005). *Indicators of school crime and safety: 2005.* Retrieved from http://nces.ed.gov/pubsearch/pubsinfo.asp?pubid=2006001

National Center of Education Statistics. (2014). Fast facts. Retrieved from https://nces.ed.gov/fastfacts/display

National Education Association. (1936). *A handbook on teacher tenure* (Research Bulletin 14). Washington, DC: Author.

National Federation of State High School Associations. (2009). *Participation.* Retrieved from www.nfhs.org

National Federation of High Schools. (2014, October 30). High school participation increases for 25th consecutive year. Retrieved from http://www.nfhs.org/articles/high-school-participation-increases-for-25th-consecutive-year

National Institute on Drug Abuse. (2014, December). Drug facts: High school and youth trends. Retrieved from http://www.drugabuse.gov/publications/drugfacts/high-school-youth-trends

National School Boards Association. (2004). *Individuals with Disabilities Education Improvement Act of 2004: Expanded authority to local school boards: A quick reference guide for local school board members.* Retrieved from http://www.nsba.org/site/docs/34900/34889.pdf

National School Boards Association. (2005). *Teachers nationwide were the victims of approximately 90,000 violent crimes between 1998 and 2002.* Retrieved from http://www.nsba.org/site/doc

NEA-Alaska. (2005). *Teacher tenure frequently asked questions.* Retrieved from www.ak.nea.org/excellence/tenure%20freq%20questions.htm

Nierman, J. (2009). *Barbara Ringer, 9th Register of Copyrights.* Retrieved from www.copyright.gov/history/bios/barbaraa-ring

O'Connell, J. (2005, August 29). *Annual public hearing and resolution on sufficiency of instructional materials and Williams settlement.* Retrieved from www.cde.ca.gov

Odden, A. R. (1995). *Educational leadership for America's schools.* New York: McGraw-Hill.

Odden, A., & Wohlstetter, P. (1992). The role of agenda-setting in the politics of school finance, 1970–1990. *Educational Policy, 4,* 355–376.

*Openlaw: Eldred v. Ashcroft.* (n.d.). Retrieved from http://cyber.law.hardvard.edu/eldredvreno/

Padilla, A., California Secretary of State. (2015). California elections/ballots. Retrieved from www.sos.ca.gov/elections/ballot-measures

Palmer, W. J. (1983). *The development of law in California.* St. Paul, MN: West.

Peterson, M. D. (1998). *The Jefferson image in the American mind.* New York: University Press of Virginia.

Port, L. (1998). *Between a rock and a hard place: Law for school administrators.* Foster City, CA: School Law Publishers.

Potter, K. D. (1999). *An educator's guide to finding resources in the public domain.* Bloomington, IN: Phi Delta Kappa International.

Rebore, R. W. (1998). *Personnel administration in education* (5th ed.). Boston, MA: Allyn & Bacon.

*Reproduction of copyrighted works by educators and librarians.* (1995). Washington, DC: Copyright Office, Library of Congress. Available at http://www.loc.gov/copyright/circs/circ21.pdf

Reutter, E. E. (1994). *The law of public education* (4th ed.). Mineola, NY: Foundation Press.

Robinson, B. (2009, January 31). *Rise of drug dogs in schools.* Retrieved from http://abcnews.go.com

Robinson, B. A. (2003). *The federal Equal Access Act: Student-led clubs in public high schools.* Kingston, Ontario, Canada: Ontario Consultants on Religious Tolerance. Retrieved from http://www.religioustolerance.org/equ_acce.htm

Romero, R., & Huguenin, E., Jr. (1988, March). Respecting student First Amendment rights. *CTA Action.*

Rose, L. C. & Gallup, A. M. (2004). *The 35th annual Phi Delta Kappa/Gallup poll of the public's attitudes toward the public schools.* Retrieved from http://www.pdkintl.org/kappan/k0309pol.htm

Ruud, R. C., & Woodford, J. J. (1992). *Supervisor's guide to documentation and file building for employee discipline.* Crestline, CA: Advisory Publishing.

St. Lawrence University, (2009). *History of women in sports.* Retrieved from http://www.Northnet.org/stlawrenceaauw/timeline.htm

Samay, C. E. (1997). Judicial activism works the Constitution out of shape—*Acton* and its atrophic effect on the Fourth Amendment rights of student athletes. *Seton Hall Journal of Sport Law, 7,* 291–314.

School settles with gay man for abuse. (1996, November 21). *Los Angeles Times.*

Schudel, Mark. (2009, May 4). *Copyright law bears her imprint.* Los Angeles Times, B4. p.6.

Schwartz, L. (1973). Billie Jean won for all women. Retrieved from https://espn.go.com/sportscentury/features/00016060.html

Shandar, S. (2015). Compton Unified School District sued for allegedly ignoring concerns of traumatized students. Retrieved from www.ibtimes.com/compton-unified-school-district-sued-allegedly-ignoring-concerns-traumatized-students-1928626

Shelley, K. (2003). *2003 Initiative Update.* Retrieved from www.caag.state.ca.us/initiatives/activeindex.htm

Shoop, R., & Dunklee, D. (1992). *School law for the principal: A handbook for practitioners.* Needham Heights, MA: Allyn & Bacon.

Simpson, M. D. (2002). The courts weigh in . . . on moment of silence, seat assignments, and ESP rights [Rights Watch]. *NEA Today, 20*(4), 18. Retrieved from ProQuest Education database.

Skiba, R. (2004). Zero tolerance: The assumptions and the facts. *Education Policy Briefs, 2*(1), 1–7. Retrieved from http://ceep.indiana.edu/ChildrenLeftBehind/pdf/ZeroTolerance.pdf

Stader, D. L. (2004). Zero tolerance as public policy: The good, the bad, and the ugly. *The Clearing House, 78*(2), 62–66. Retrieved from Wilson Web database.

Stanitski, C. (1989). Common injuries in pre-adolescent and adolescent athletics. *Sports Medicine, 7*(1), 32–33.

State Personnel Board of the State of California. (1993). SPB Case No. 31638, Board Decision No. 93-31. Retrieved from http://www.spb.ca.gov/documents/preced/Warner.doc

Strauss, V. (2014). 19 states still allow corporal punishment in school. Retrieved from www.washingtonpost.com/blogs/answer-sheet/wp/2014/09-states-still-allow-corporal-punishment

Supreme Court hears case on use of drug-sniffing dogs. (2004a, November 11). *San Diego Union-Tribune.* Retrieved from http://www.signonsandiego.com/uniontrib/20041111/news_1n11scotus.html

Supreme court takes strap out of teachers' hands. (2004b, January 31). *Edmonton Journal.* Retrieved from http://www.canadiancrc.com/articles/Edmonton_Journal_Supreme_Court_Schools_strap_31JAN04.htm

Swanson, A. (2015, June 5). Fortune 500 has 24 female CEOs. An article from the Washington Post reported in the San Diego Union Tribune, C3.

The House Report. (2006, May 29). *Elk Grove School District v. Newdow.* Retrieved from www.law.umkkc.edu/faculty/projects/ftrials.con/aw/elkgrove::

Tyburski, G. (2004). *The skill of the hunt: Effect research strategies for finding information on the Web.* Philadelphia, PA: Ballard Spahr Andrews & Ingersoll. Retrieved from http://www.virtualchase.com/articles/skill.html

U.S. Department of Education (2000). "Archived: A 25 year hisory of the IDEA." Retrieved from http://www.ed.gov/policy/speced/leg/idea/history.html

U.S. Department of Education. (n.d.). *FAQs: Sexual Harassment.* Washington, DC: Author. Retrieved from http://www.ed.gov/about/offices/list/ocr/qa-sexharass.html

Valente, W. D. (1998). *Law in the schools* (4th ed.). Upper Saddle River, NJ: Prentice Hall.

Webb, L. D., Metha, A., & Jordan, K. F. (1996). *Foundations of American education* (2nd ed.). Englewood Cliffs, N.J.: Prentice Hall.

Weekly Reader. (2005). *Dog fight: drug-sniffing dogs in schools smell trouble.* Retrieved from http://findarticles.com

Wenkart, R. D. (1995). *The California educators' guide to school law* (2nd ed.). Costa Mesa, CA: Orange County Department of Education.

West Group. (2000). *Westlaw white paper: Information on your terms.* Retrieved from http://www.westlaw.com/ProductsInfo/whitepap.wl

Whitted Cleary & Takiff. (2006, February 2). *Jury awards $700K in special education abuse case.* Retrieved from www.whittedclearylaw.com

Wikipedia. (2008). *Helen Reddy-biography.* Retrieved from http://en.Wikipedia.org

Wilson, J. (2006). *Local government liability: A major cost and exposure.* Retrieved from www.cjac.org/research/0299localgovlia.cfm

Wright, W. D. & Darr, P. (2006). *Supreme Court to review Arlington v. Murphy.* Retrieved from www.wrightslaw.com/news/06/Arlington v. Murphy

Yell, M. L. (1998). *The law and special education.* Upper Saddle River, NJ: Merrill.

Yudof, M. G. (1991). *Educational policy and the law.* Belmont, CA: Wadsworth.

Zirkel, P. (2005). Politics and the principalship: It's the law. *Principal, 84*(3), 8–9. Retrieved from http://www.naesp.org/ContentLoad.do?dontendId=1446&action=print

Zirkel, P. (1999). Fatal suspension. *Phi Delta Kappan, 80,* 791–792.

# Index to Court Cases

# *Index*